PENGUIN BOOKS

562

THREE PLAYS FOR PURITANS
BY BERNARD SHAW

THREE
PLAYS FOR PURITANS

THE DEVIL'S DISCIPLE

CÆSAR AND CLEOPATRA

CAPTAIN BRASSBOUND'S CONVERSION

BY

BERNARD SHAW

PENGUIN BOOKS

HARMONDSWORTH · MIDDLESEX

"Three Plays for Puritans" first published 1901
Published in Penguin Books 1946
Reprinted 1949, 1952

"The Devil's Disciple" was first performed in New York in 1897;
in London (Kennington) in 1899. Revived in London, 1907;
at the Raimund Theatre, Vienna, 1903 (the first performance of
a Shaw play in German)

"Cæsar and Cleopatra" written in 1899, produced in Berlin and
New York, 1906; in London, 1907. The film version was first
produced in London, 1945

"Captain Brassbound's Conversion" first produced by the Stage
Society, London, 1900; London (publicly), 1906; New York,
1907

MADE AND PRINTED IN GREAT BRITAIN FOR PENGUIN BOOKS LIMITED
BY R. & R. CLARK, LIMITED, EDINBURGH

CONTENTS

THREE PLAYS FOR PURITANS

Why for Puritans?

SINCE I gave my Plays, Pleasant and Unpleasant, to the world two years ago, many things have happened to me. I had then just entered on the fourth year of my activity as a critic of the London theatres. They very nearly killed me. I had survived seven years of London's music, four or five years of London's pictures, and about as much of its current literature, wrestling critically with them with all my force and skill. After that, the criticism of the theatre came to me as a huge relief in point of bodily exertion. The difference between the leisure of a Persian cat and the labor of a cockney cab horse is not greater than the difference between the official weekly or fortnightly playgoings of the theatre critic and the restless daily rushing to and fro of the music critic, from the stroke of three in the afternoon, when the concerts begin, to the stroke of twelve at night, when the opera ends. The pictures were nearly as bad. An Alpinist once, noticing the massive soles of my boots, asked me whether I climbed mountains. No, I replied : these boots are for the hard floors of the London galleries. Yet I once dealt with music and pictures together in the spare time of an active young revolutionist, and wrote plays and books and other toilsome things into the bargain. But the theatre struck me down like the veriest weakling. I sank under it like a baby fed on starch. My very bones began to perish, so that I had to get them planed and gouged by accomplished surgeons. I fell from heights and broke my limbs in pieces. The doctors said : This man has not eaten meat for twenty years : he must eat it or die. I said : This man has been going to the London theatres for three years ; and the soul of him has become inane and is feeding unnaturally on his body. And I was right. I did not change my diet ; but I had myself carried up into a mountain where there was no theatre ; and there I began to revive. Too weak to work, I wrote books and plays : hence the second and third plays in this volume. And now I am stronger than I have been at any moment since my feet first carried me as a critic across the fatal threshold of a London play-house.

Why was this ? What is the matter with the theatre, that a strong man can die of it ? Well, the answer will make a long story ; but it must be told. And, to begin, why have I just called the theatre a playhouse ? The well-fed English-man, though he lives and dies a schoolboy, cannot play. He cannot even play cricket or football : he has to work at them : that is why he beats the foreigner who plays at them. To him playing means playing the fool. He can hunt and shoot and travel and fight : he can, when special holiday festivity is suggested to him, eat and drink, dice and drab, smoke and lounge. But play he cannot. The moment you make his theatre a place of amusement instead of a place of edification, you make it, not a real playhouse, but a place of excitement for the sportsman and the sensualist.

However, this well-fed grown-up-schoolboy Englishman counts for little in the modern metropolitan audience. In the long lines of waiting playgoers lining the pavements outside our fashionable theatres every evening, the men are only the currants in the dumpling. Women are in the majority ; and women and men alike belong to that least robust of all our social classes, the class which earns from eighteen to thirty shillings a week in sedentary employment, and lives in lonely lodgings or in drab homes with nagging relatives. These people preserve the innocence of the theatre : they have neither the philosopher's impatience to get to realities (reality being the one thing they want to escape from), nor the longing of the sportsman for violent action, nor the full-fed, experienced, disillusioned sensuality of the rich man, whether he be gentleman or sporting publican. They read a good deal, and are at home in the fool's paradise of popular romance. They love the pretty man and the pretty woman, and will have both of them fashionably dressed and exquisitely idle, posing against backgrounds of drawing room and dainty garden ; in love, but sentimentally, romantically ; always ladylike and gentlemanlike. Jejunely insipid, all this, to the stalls, which are paid for (when they *are* paid for) by people who have their own dresses and drawing rooms, and know them to be a mere masquerade behind which there is nothing romantic, and little that is interesting to most of the masqueraders except the clandestine play of natural licentiousness.

The stalls cannot be fully understood without taking into account the absence of the rich evangelical English merchant and his family, and the presence of the rich Jewish merchant and *his* family. I can see no validity whatever in the view that the influence of the rich Jews on the theatre is any worse than the influence of the rich of any other race. Other qualities being equal, men become rich in commerce in proportion to the intensity and exclusiveness of their desire for money. It may be a misfortune that the purchasing power of men who value money above art, philosophy, and the welfare of the whole community, should enable them to influence the theatre (and everything else in the market) ; but there is no reason to suppose that their influence is any nobler when they imagine themselves Christians than when they know themselves Jews. All that can fairly be said of the Jewish influence on the theatre is that it is exotic, and is not only a customer's influence but a financier's influence : so much so, that the way is smoothest for those plays and those performers that appeal specially to the Jewish taste. English influence on the theatre, as far as the stalls are concerned, does not exist, because the rich purchasing-powerful Englishman prefers politics and church-going : his soul is too stubborn to be purged by an

avowed make-believe. When he wants sensuality he prac-
tises it : he does not play with voluptuous or romantic ideas.
From the play of ideas—and the drama can never be anything more—he demands edification, and will not pay for
anything else in that arena. Consequently the box office
will never become an English influence until the theatre
turns from the drama of romance and sensuality to the
drama of edification.

Turning from the stalls to the whole auditorium, consider what is implied by the fact that the prices (all much
too high, by the way) range from half a guinea to a shilling,
the ages from eighteen to eighty, whilst every age, and nearly
every price, represents a different taste. Is it not clear that
this diversity in the audience makes it impossible to gratify
every one of its units by the same luxury, since in that
domain of infinite caprice, one man's meat is another man's
poison, one age's longing another age's loathing ? And yet
that is just what the theatres kept trying to do almost all
the time I was doomed to attend them. On the other hand,
to interest people of divers ages, classes, and temperaments
by some generally momentous subject of thought, as the
politicians and preachers do, would seem the most obvious
course in the world. And yet the theatres avoided that as a
ruinous eccentricity. Their wiseacres persisted in assuming
that all men have the same tastes, fancies, and qualities of
passion ; that no two have the same interests ; and that
most playgoers have no interests at all. This being precisely
contrary to the obvious facts, it followed that the majority
of the plays produced were failures, recognizable as such
before the end of the first act by the very wiseacres afore-
mentioned, who, quite incapable of understanding the
lesson, would thereupon set to work to obtain and produce
a play applying their theory still more strictly, with pro-
portionately more disastrous results. The sums of money
I saw thus transferred from the pockets of theatrical specu-
lators and syndicates to those of wigmakers, costumiers,

scene painters, carpenters, doorkeepers, actors, theatre
landlords, and all the other people for whose exclusive
benefit most London theatres seem to exist, would have
kept a theatre devoted exclusively to the highest drama open
all the year round. If the Browning and Shelley Societies
were fools, as the wiseacres said they were, for producing
Strafford, Colombe's Birthday, and The Cenci ; if the
Independent Theatre, the New Century Theatre, and the
Stage Society are impracticable faddists for producing the
plays of Ibsen and Maeterlinck, then what epithet is contemptuous enough for the people who produce the would-
be popular plays ?

The actor-managers were far more successful, because
they produced plays that at least pleased themselves,
whereas Commerce, with a false theory of how to please
everybody, produced plays that pleased nobody. But their
occasional personal successes in voluptuous plays, and, in
any case, their careful concealment of failure, confirmed the
prevalent error, which was exposed fully only when the
plays had to stand or fall openly by their own merits. Even
Shakespear was played with his brains cut out. In 1896,
when Sir Henry Irving was disabled by an accident at a
moment when Miss Ellen Terry was too ill to appear, the
theatre had to be closed after a brief attempt to rely on the
attraction of a Shakespearean play performed by the stock
company. This may have been Shakespear's fault : indeed
Sir Henry later on complained that he had lost a princely
sum by Shakespear. But Shakespear's reply to this, if he
were able to make it, would be that the princely sum was
spent, not on his dramatic poetry, but on a gorgeous stage
ritualism superimposed on reckless mutilations of his text,
the whole being addressed to a public as to which nothing
is certain except that its natural bias is towards reverence
for Shakespear and dislike and distrust of ritualism. No
doubt the Irving ritual appealed to a far more cultivated
sensuousness and imaginativeness than the musical farces

in which our stage Abbots of Misrule pontificated (with the same financially disastrous result) ; but in both there was the same intentional brainlessness, founded on the same theory that the public did not want brains, did not want to think, did not want anything but pleasure at the theatre. Unfortunately, this theory happens to be true of a certain section of the public. This section, being courted by the theatres, went to them and drove the other people out. It then discovered, as any expert could have foreseen, that the theatre cannot compete in mere pleasuremongering either with the other arts or with matter-of-fact gallantry. Stage pictures are the worst pictures, stage music the worst music, stage scenery the worst scenery within reach of the Londoner. The leading lady or gentleman may be as tempting to the admirer in the pit as the dishes in a cookshop window are to the penniless tramp on the pavement ; but people do not, I presume, go to the theatre to be merely tantalized.

The breakdown on the last point was conclusive. For when the managers tried to put their principle of pleasing everybody into practice, Necessity, ever ironical towards Folly, had driven them to seek a universal pleasure to appeal to. And since many have no ear for music or eye for color, the search for universality inevitably flung the managers back on the instinct of sex as the avenue to all hearts. Of course the appeal was a vapid failure. Speaking for my own sex, I can say that the leading lady was not to everybody's taste : her pretty face often became ugly when she tried to make it expressive ; her voice lost its charm (if it ever had any) when she had nothing sincere to say ; and the stalls, from racial prejudice, were apt to insist on more Rebecca and less Rowena than the pit cared for. It may seem strange, even monstrous, that a man should feel a constant attachment to the hideous witches in Macbeth, and yet yawn at the prospect of spending another evening in the contemplation of a beauteous young leading lady with voluptuous contours and longlashed eyes, painted and dressed to perfection in the latest fashions. But that is just what happened to me in the theatre.

I did not find that matters were improved by the lady pretending to be "a woman with a past," violently over-sexed, or the play being called a problem play, even when the manager, and sometimes, I suspect, the very author, firmly believed the word problem to be the latest euphemism for what Justice Shallow called a bona roba, and certainly would not either of them have staked a farthing on the interest of a genuine problem. In fact these so-called problem plays invariably depended for their dramatic interest on foregone conclusions of the most heartwearying conventionality concerning sexual morality. The authors had no problematic views : all they wanted was to capture some of the fascination of Ibsen. It seemed to them that most of Ibsen's heroines were naughty ladies. And they tried to produce Ibsen plays by making their heroines naughty. But they took great care to make them pretty and expensively dressed. Thus the pseudo-Ibsen play was nothing but the ordinary sensuous ritual of the stage become as frankly pornographic as good manners allowed.

I found that the whole business of stage sensuousness, whether as Lyceum Shakespear, musical farce, or sham Ibsen, finally disgusted me, not because I was Pharisaical, or intolerantly refined, but because I was bored ; and boredom is a condition which makes men as susceptible to disgust and irritation as headache makes them to noise and glare. Being a man, I have my share of the masculine silliness and vulgarity on the subject of sex which so astonishes women, to whom sex is a serious matter. I am not an archbishop, and do not pretend to pass my life on one plane or in one mood, and that the highest : on the contrary, I am, I protest, as accessible to the humors of The Rogue's Comedy or The Rake's Progress as to the pious decencies of The Sign of the Cross. Thus Falstaff, coarser than any of the men in our loosest plays, does not bore me :

Doll Tearsheet, more abandoned than any of the women, does not shock me. I admit that Romeo and Juliet would be a duller play if it were robbed of the solitary fragment it has preserved for us of the conversation of the husband of Juliet's nurse. No : my disgust was not mere thinskinned prudery. When my moral sense revolted, as it often did to the very fibres, it was invariably at the nauseous compliances of the theatre with conventional virtue. If I despised the musical farces, it was because they never had the courage of their vices. With all their labored efforts to keep up an understanding of furtive naughtiness between the low comedian on the stage and the drunken undergraduate in the stalls, they insisted all the time on their virtue and patriotism and loyalty as pitifully as a poor girl of the pavement will pretend to be a clergyman's daughter. True, I may have been offended when a manager, catering for me with coarse frankness as a slave dealer caters for a Pasha, invited me to forget the common bond of humanity between me and his company by demanding nothing from them but a gloatably voluptuous appearance. But this extreme is never reached at our better theatres. The shop assistants, the typists, the clerks, who, as I have said, preserve the innocence of the theatre, would not dare to let themselves be pleased by it. Even if they did, they would not get it from our reputable managers, who, when faced with the only logical conclusion from their principle of making the theatre a temple of pleasure, indignantly refuse to change the theatrical profession for Mrs Warren's. For that is what all this demand for pleasure at the theatre finally comes to ; and the answer to it is, not that people ought not to desire sensuous pleasure (they cannot help it) but that the theatre cannot give it to them, even to the extent permitted by the honor and conscience of the best managers, because a theatre is so far from being a pleasant or even a comfortable place that only by making us forget ourselves can it prevent us from realizing its inconveniences. A play that does not do this for the pleasure-seeker allows him to discover that he has chosen a disagreeable and expensive way of spending the evening. He wants to drink, to smoke, to change the spectacle, to get rid of the middle-aged actor and actress who are boring him, and to see shapely young dancing girls and acrobats doing more amusing things in a more plastic manner. In short, he wants the music hall ; and he goes there, leaving the managers astonished at this unexpected but quite inevitable result of the attempt to please him. Whereas, had he been enthralled by the play, even with horror, instead of himself enthralling with the dread of his displeasure the manager, the author and the actors, all had been well. And so we must conclude that the theatre is a place which people can endure only when they forget themselves : that is, when their attention is entirely captured, their interest thoroughly aroused, their sympathies raised to the eagerest readiness, and their selfishness utterly annihilated. Imagine, then, the result of conducting theatres on the principle of appealing exclusively to the instinct of self-gratification in people without power of attention, without interests, without sympathy : in short, without brains or heart. That is how they were conducted whilst I was writing about them ; and that is how they nearly killed me.

Yet the managers mean well. Their self-respect is in excess rather than in defect ; for they are in full reaction against the Bohemianism of past generations of actors, and so bent on compelling social recognition by a blameless respectability, that the drama, neglected in the struggle, is only just beginning to stir feebly after standing still in England from Tom Robertson's time in the sixties until the first actor was knighted in the nineties. The manager may not want good plays ; but he does not want bad plays : he wants nice ones. Nice plays, with nice dresses, nice drawing rooms and nice people, are indispensable : to be ungenteel is worse than to fail. I use the word ungenteel purposely ; for the stage presents life on thirty pounds a day, not as it is, but as it is conceived by the earners of thirty shillings a week. The real thing would shock the audience exactly as the manners of the public school and university shock a Board of Guardians. In just the same way, the plays which constitute the genuine aristocracy of modern dramatic literature shock the reverence for gentility which governs our theatres today. For instance, the objection to Ibsen is not really an objection to his philosophy : it is a protest against the fact that his characters do not behave as ladies and gentlemen are popularly supposed to behave. If you adore Hedda Gabler in real life, if you envy her and feel that nothing but your poverty prevents you from being as exquisite a creature, if you know that the accident of matrimony (say with an officer of the guards who falls in love with you across the counter whilst you are reckoning the words in his telegram) may at any moment put you in her place, Ibsen's exposure of the worthlessness and meanness of her life is cruel and blasphemous to you. This point of view is not caught by the clever ladies of Hedda's own class, who recognize the portrait, applaud its painter, and think the fuss against Ibsen means nothing more than the conventional disapproval of her discussions of a *ménage à trois* with Judge Brack. A little experience of popular plays would soon convince these clever ladies that a heroine who atones in the last act by committing suicide may do all the things that Hedda only talked about, without a word of remonstrance from the press or the public. It is not murder, not adultery, not rapine that is objected to : quite the contrary. It is an unladylike attitude towards life : in other words, a disparagement of the social ideals of the poorer middle class and of the vast reinforcements it has had from the working class during the last twenty years. Let but the attitude of the author be gentlemanlike, and his heroines may do what they please. Mrs Tanqueray was received with delight by the public : Saint Teresa would have been hissed off the same stage for her contempt for the ideal represented by a carriage, a fashionable dressmaker, and a dozen servants.

Here, then, is a pretty problem for the manager. He is convinced that plays must depend for their dramatic force on appeals to the sex instinct ; and yet he owes it to his own newly conquered social position that they shall be perfectly genteel plays, fit for churchgoers. The sex instinct must therefore proceed upon genteel assumptions. Impossible ! you will exclaim. But you are wrong : nothing is more astonishing than the extent to which, in real life, the sex instinct does so proceed, even when the consequence is its lifelong starvation. Few of us have vitality enough to make any of our instincts imperious : we can be made to live on pretences, as the masterful minority well know. But the timid majority, if it rules nowhere else, at least rules in the theatre : fitly enough too, because on the stage pretence is all that can exist. Life has its realities behind its shows : the theatre has nothing but its shows. But can the theatre make a show of lovers' endearments ? A thousand times no : perish the thought of such unladylike, ungentlemanlike exhibitions. You can have fights, rescues, conflagrations, trials-at-law, avalanches, murders and executions all directly simulated on the stage if you will. But any such realistic treatment of the incidents of sex is quite out of the question. The singer, the dramatic dancer, the exquisite declaimer of impassioned poesy, the rare artist who, bringing something of the art of all three to the ordinary work of the theatre, can enthral an audience by the expression of dramatic feeling alone, may take love for a theme on the stage ; but the prosaic walking gentleman of our fashionable theatres, realistically simulating the incidents of life, cannot touch it without indecorum.

Can any dilemma be more complete ? Love is assumed to be the only theme that touches all your audience infallibly, young and old, rich and poor. And yet love is the one subject that the drawing room drama dare not present.

Out of this dilemma, which is a very old one, has come the romantic play : that is, the play in which love is carefully kept off the stage, whilst it is alleged as the motive of all the actions presented to the audience. The result is, to me at least, an intolerable perversion of human conduct. There are two classes of stories that seem to me to be not only fundamentally false but sordidly base. One is the pseudo-religious story, in which the hero or heroine does good on strictly commercial grounds, reluctantly exercising a little virtue on earth in consideration of receiving in return an exorbitant payment in heaven : much as if an odalisque were to allow a cadi to whip her for a couple of millions in gold. The other is the romance in which the hero, also rigidly commercial, will do nothing except for the sake of the heroine. Surely this is as depressing as it is unreal. Compare with it the treatment of love, frankly indecent according to our notions, in oriental fiction. In The Arabian Nights we have a series of stories, some of them very good ones, in which no sort of decorum is observed. The result is that they are infinitely more instructive and enjoyable than our romances, because love is treated in them as naturally as any other passion. There is no cast iron convention as to its effects ; no false association of general depravity of character with its corporealities or of general elevation with its sentimentalities ; no pretence that a man or woman cannot be courageous and kind and friendly unless infatuatedly in love with somebody (is no poet manly enough to sing The Old Maids of England ?) : rather, indeed, an insistence on the blinding and narrowing power of lovesickness to make princely heroes unhappy and unfortunate. These tales expose, further, the delusion that the interest of this most capricious, most transient, most easily baffled of all instincts, is inexhaustible, and that the field of the English romancer has been cruelly narrowed by the restrictions under which he is permitted to deal with it.

The Arabian storyteller, relieved of all such restrictions, heaps character on character, adventure on adventure, marvel on marvel ; whilst the English novelist, like the starving tramp who can think of nothing but his hunger, seems to be unable to escape from the obsession of sex, and will rewrite the very gospels because the originals are not written in the sensuously ecstatic style. At the instance of Martin Luther we long ago gave up imposing celibacy on our priests ; but we still impose it on our art, with the very undesirable and unexpected result that no editor, publisher, or manager, will now accept a story or produce a play without "love interest" in it. Take, for a recent example, Mr H. G. Wells's War of The Worlds, a tale of the invasion of the earth by the inhabitants of the planet Mars : a capital story, not to be laid down until finished. Love interest is impossible on its scientific plane : nothing could be more impertinent and irritating. Yet Mr Wells has had to pretend that the hero is in love with a young lady manufactured for the purpose, and to imply that it is on her account alone that he feels concerned about the apparently inevitable destruction of the human race by the Martians. Another example. An American novelist, recently deceased, made a hit some years ago by compiling a Bostonian Utopia from the prospectuses of the little bands of devout Communists who have from time to time, since the days of Fourier and Owen, tried to establish millennial colonies outside our commercial civilization. Even in this economic Utopia we find the inevitable love affair. The hero, waking up in a distant future from a miraculous sleep, meets a Boston young lady, provided expressly for him to fall in love with. Women have by that time given up wearing skirts ; but she, to spare his delicacy, gets one out of a museum of antiquities to wear in his presence until he is hardened to the customs of the new age. When I came to that touching incident, I became as Paolo and Francesca : "in that book I read no more." I will not multiply examples : if such unendurable follies occur in the sort of story made by working out a meteorological or economic hypothesis, the extent to which it is carried in sentimental romances needs no expatiation.

The worst of it is that since man's intellectual consciousness of himself is derived from the descriptions of him in books, a persistent misrepresentation of humanity in literature gets finally accepted and acted upon. If every mirror reflected our noses twice their natural size, we should live and die in the faith that we were all Punches ; and we should scout a true mirror as the work of a fool, madman, or jester. Nay, I believe we should, by Lamarckian adaptation, enlarge our noses to the admired size; for I have noticed that when a certain type of feature appears in painting and is admired as beautiful, it presently becomes common in nature ; so that the Beatrices and Francescas in the picture galleries of one generation, to whom minor poets address verses entitled To My Lady, come to life as the parlormaids and waitresses of the next. If the conventions of romance are only insisted on long enough and uniformly enough (a condition guaranteed by the uniformity of human folly and vanity), then, for the huge compulsorily schooled masses who read romance or nothing, these conventions will become the laws of personal honor. Jealousy, which is either an egotistical meanness or a specific mania, will become obligatory ; and ruin, ostracism, breaking up of homes, duelling, murder, suicide and infanticide will be produced (often have been produced, in fact) by incidents which, if left to the operation of natural and right feeling, would produce nothing worse than an hour's soon-forgotten fuss. Men will be slain needlessly on the field of battle because officers conceive it to be their first duty to make romantic exhibitions of conspicuous gallantry. The squire who has never spared an hour from the hunting field to do a little public work on a parish council will be cheered as a patriot because he is willing to kill and get killed for the sake of conferring himself as an institution on other countries. In the courts cases will be argued, not on juridical but on romantic principles ; and vindictive damages and vindictive sentences, with the acceptance of nonsensical, and the repudiation or suppression of sensible testimony, will destroy the very sense of law. Kaisers, generals, judges, and prime ministers will set the example of playing to the gallery. Finally the people, now that their compulsory literacy enables every penman to play on their romantic illusions, will be led by the nose far more completely than they ever were by playing on their former ignorance and superstition. Nay, why should I say will be ? they *are*. Ten years of cheap reading have changed the English from the most stolid nation in Europe to the most theatrical and hysterical.

Is it clear now, why the theatre was insufferable to me ; why it left its black mark on my bones as it has left its black mark on the character of the nation ; why I call the Puritans to rescue it again as they rescued it before when its foolish pursuit of pleasure sunk it in " profaneness and immorality " ? I have, I think, always been a Puritan in my attitude towards Art. I am as fond of fine music and handsome building as Milton was, or Cromwell, or Bunyan ; but if I found that they were becoming the instruments of a systematic idolatry of sensuousness, I would hold it good statesmanship to blow every cathedral in the world to pieces with dynamite, organ and all, without the least heed to the screams of the art critics and cultured voluptuaries. And when I see that the nineteenth century has crowned the idolatry of Art with the deification of Love, so that every poet is supposed to have pierced to the holy of holies when he has announced that Love is the Supreme, or the Enough, or the All, I feel that Art was safer in the hands of the most fanatical of Cromwell's major generals than it will be if ever it gets into mine. The pleasures of the senses I can sympathize with and share ; but the substitution of sensuous ecstasy for intellectual activity and honesty is the very devil. It has already brought us to Flogging Bills in Parliament, and, by reaction, to androgynous heroes on the stage ; and if the infection spreads until the democratic attitude becomes thoroughly Romanticist, the country will become unbearable for all realists, Philistine or Platonic. When it comes to that, the brute force of the strongminded Bismarckian man of action, impatient of humbug, will combine with the subtlety and spiritual energy of the man of thought whom shams cannot illude or interest. That combination will be on one side ; and Romanticism will be on the other. In which event, so much the worse for Romanticism, which will come down even if it has to drag Democracy down with it. For all institutions have in the long run to live by the nature of things, and not by childish pretendings.

ON DIABOLONIAN ETHICS

There is a foolish opinion prevalent that an author should allow his works to speak for themselves, and that he who appends and prefixes explanations to them is likely to be as bad an artist as the painter cited by Cervantes, who wrote under his picture This is a Cock, lest there should be any mistake about it. The pat retort to this thoughtless comparison is that the painter invariably does so label his picture. What is a Royal Academy catalogue but a series of statements that This is The Vale of Rest, This The Shaving of Samson, This Chill October, This H.R.H. The Prince of Wales, and so on ? The reason most playwrights do not publish their plays with prefaces is that they cannot write them, the business of intellectually conscious philosopher and skilled critic being no necessary part of their craft. Naturally, making a virtue of their incapacity, they either repudiate prefaces as shameful, or else, with a modest air, request some popular critic to supply one, as much as to say, Were I to tell the truth about myself I must needs seem vainglorious : were I to tell less than the truth I should do myself an injustice and deceive my readers. As to the critic thus called in from the outside, what can he do but imply that his friend's transcendent ability as a dramatist is surpassed only by his beautiful nature as a man ? Now what I say is, why should I get another man to praise me when I can praise myself ? I have no disabilities to plead : produce me your best critic, and I will criticize his head off. As to philosophy, I taught my critics the little they know in my Quintessence of Ibsenism ; and now they turn their guns—the guns I loaded for them—on me, and proclaim that I write as if mankind had intellect without will, or heart, as they call it. Ingrates : who was it that directed your attention to the distinction between Will and Intellect ? Not Schopenhauer, I think, but Shaw.

Again, they tell me that So-and-So, who does not write prefaces, is no charlatan. Well, I am. I first caught the ear of the British public on a cart in Hyde Park, to the blaring of brass bands, and this not at all as a reluctant sacrifice of my instinct of privacy to political necessity, but because, like all dramatists and mimes of genuine vocation, I am a natural-born mountebank. I am well aware that the ordinary British citizen requires a profession of shame from all mountebanks by way of homage to the sanctity of the ignoble private life to which he is condemned by his incapacity for public life. Thus Shakespear, after proclaiming that Not marble nor the gilded monuments of Princes should outlive his powerful rhyme, would apologize, in the approved taste, for making himself a motley to the view ; and the British citizen has ever since quoted the apology and ignored the fanfare. When an actress writes her memoirs, she impresses on you in every chapter how cruelly it tried her feelings to exhibit her person to the public gaze ; but she does not forget to decorate the book with a dozen portraits of herself. I really cannot respond to this demand for mock-modesty. I am ashamed neither of my work nor of the way it is done. I like explaining its merits to the huge majority who dont know good work from bad. It does them good ; and it does me good, curing me of nervousness, laziness, and snobbishness. I write prefaces as Dryden did, and treatises as Wagner, because I *can* ; and I would give half a dozen of Shakespear's plays for one of the prefaces he ought to have written. I leave the delicacies of retirement to those who are gentlemen first and literary workmen afterwards. The cart and trumpet for me.

This is all very well ; but the trumpet is an instrument that grows on one ; and sometimes my blasts have been so strident that even those who are most annoyed by them have mistaken the novelty of my shamelessness for novelty in my plays and opinions. Take, for instance, the first play in this volume, entitled The Devil's Disciple. It does not contain a single even passably novel incident. Every old patron of the Adelphi pit would, were he not beglamored in a way presently to be explained, recognize the reading of the will, the oppressed orphan finding a protector, the arrest the heroic sacrifice, the court martial, the scaffold, the reprieve at the last moment, as he recognizes beefsteak pudding on the bill of fare at his restaurant. Yet when the play was produced in 1897 in New York by Mr Richard Mansfield, with a success that proves either that the melodrama was built on very safe old lines, or that the American public is composed exclusively of men of genius, the critics, though one said one thing and another another as to the play's merits, yet all agreed that it was novel—*original*, as they put it—to the verge of audacious eccentricity.

Now this, if it applies to the incidents, plot, construction, and general professional and technical qualities of the play, is nonsense ; for the truth is, I am in these matters a very old-fashioned playwright. When a good deal of the same talk, both hostile and friendly, was provoked by my last volume of plays, Mr Robert Buchanan, a dramatist who

knows what I know and remembers what I remember of
the history of the stage, pointed out that the stage tricks by
which I gave the younger generation of playgoers an
exquisite sense of quaint unexpectedness, had done duty
years ago in Cool as a Cucumber, Used Up, and many
forgotten farces and comedies of the Byron-Robertson
school, in which the imperturbably impudent comedian,
afterwards shelved by the reaction to brainless sentimentality,
was a stock figure. It is always so more or less : the
novelties of one generation are only the resuscitated fashions
of the generation before last.

But the stage tricks of The Devil's Disciple are not, like
some of those of Arms and the Man, the forgotten ones of
the sixties, but the hackneyed ones of our own time. Why,
then, were they not recognized ? Partly, no doubt, because
of my trumpet and cartwheel declamation. The critics were
the victims of the long course of hypnotic suggestion by
which G.B.S. the journalist manufactured an unconventional
reputation for Bernard Shaw the author. In England as
elsewhere the spontaneous recognition of really original
work begins with a mere handful of people, and propagates
itself so slowly that it has become a commonplace to say
that genius, demanding bread, is given a stone after its
possessor's death. The remedy for this is sedulous advertise-
ment. Accordingly, I have advertized myself so well that
I find myself, whilst still in middle life, almost as legendary
a person as the Flying Dutchman. Critics, like other people,
see what they look for, not what is actually before them.
In my plays they look for my legendary qualities, and find
originality and brilliancy in my most hackneyed claptraps.
Were I to republish Buckstone's Wreck Ashore as my latest
comedy, it would be hailed as a masterpiece of perverse
paradox and scintillating satire. Not, of course, by the
really able critics—for example, you, my friend, now reading
this sentence. The illusion that makes *you* think me so
original is far subtler than that. The Devil's Disciple has,

in truth, a genuine novelty in it. Only, that novelty is not any invention of my own, but simply the novelty of the advanced thought of my day. As such, it will assuredly lose its gloss with the lapse of time, and leave The Devil's Disciple exposed as the threadbare popular melodrama it technically is.

Let me explain (for, as Mr A. B. Walkley has pointed out in his disquisitions on Frames of Mind, I am nothing if not explanatory). Dick Dudgeon, the devil's disciple, is a Puritan of the Puritans. He is brought up in a household where the Puritan religion has died, and become, in its corruption, an excuse for his mother's master passion of hatred in all its phases of cruelty and envy. This corruption has already been dramatized for us by Charles Dickens in his picture of the Clennam household in Little Dorrit : Mrs Dudgeon being a replica of Mrs Clennam with certain circumstantial variations, and perhaps a touch of the same author's Mrs Gargery in Great Expectations. In such a home the young Puritan finds himself starved of religion, which is the most clamorous need of his nature. With all his mother's indomitable selfulness, but with Pity instead of Hatred as his master passion, he pities the devil ; takes his side ; and champions him, like a true Covenanter, against the world. He thus becomes, like all genuinely religious men, a reprobate and an outcast. Once this is understood, the play becomes straightforwardly simple.

The Diabolonian position is new to the London playgoer of today, but not to lovers of serious literature. From Prometheus to the Wagnerian Siegfried, some enemy of the gods, unterrified champion of those oppressed by them, has always towered among the heroes of the loftiest poetry. Our newest idol, the Superman, celebrating the death of godhead, may be younger than the hills ; but he is as old as the shepherds. Two and a half centuries ago our greatest English dramatizer of life, John Bunyan, ended one of his stories with the remark that there is a way to hell even from the gates of heaven, and so led us to the equally true proposition that there is a way to heaven even from the gates of hell. A century ago William Blake was, like Dick Dudgeon, an avowed Diabolonian : he called his angels devils and his devils angels. His devil is a Redeemer. Let those who have praised my originality in conceiving Dick Dudgeon's strange religion read Blake's Marriage of Heaven and Hell, and I shall be fortunate if they do not rail at me for a plagiarist. But they need not go back to Blake and Bunyan. Have they not heard the recent fuss about Nietzsche and his Good and Evil Turned Inside Out ? Mr Robert Buchanan has actually written a long poem of which the Devil is the merciful hero, which poem was in my hands before a word of The Devil's Disciple was written. There never was a play more certain to be written than The Devil's Disciple at the end of the nineteenth century. The age was visibly pregnant with it.

I grieve to have to add that my old friends and colleagues the London critics for the most part shewed no sort of connoisseurship either in Puritanism or in Diabolonianism when the play was performed for a few weeks at a suburban theatre (Kennington) in October 1899 by Mr Murray Carson. They took Mrs Dudgeon at her own valuation as a religious woman because she was detestably disagreeable. And they took Dick as a blackguard on her authority, because he was neither detestable nor disagreeable. But they presently found themselves in a dilemma. Why should a blackguard save another man's life, and that man no friend of his, at the risk of his own ? Clearly, said the critics, because he is redeemed by love. All wicked heroes are, on the stage : that is the romantic metaphysic. Unfortunately for this explanation (which I do not profess to understand) it turned out in the third act that Dick was a Puritan in this respect also : a man impassioned only for saving grace, and not to be led or turned by wife or mother, Church or State, pride of life or lust of the flesh. In the lovely home of the courageous, affectionate, practical minister who marries a pretty wife twenty years younger than himself, and turns soldier in an instant to save the man who has saved him, Dick looks round and understands the charm and the peace and the sanctity, but knows that such material comforts are not for him. When the woman nursed in that atmosphere falls in love with him and concludes (like the critics, who somehow always agree with my sentimental heroines) that he risked his life for her sake, he tells her the obvious truth that he would have done as much for any stranger—that the law of his own nature, and no interest nor lust whatsoever, forbad him to cry out that the hangman's noose should be taken off his neck only to be put on another man's.

But then, said the critics, where is the motive? *Why* did Dick save Anderson? On the stage, it appears, people do things for reasons. Off the stage they dont : that is why your penny-in-the-slot heroes, who only work when you drop a motive into them, are so oppressively automatic and uninteresting. The saving of life at the risk of the saver's own is not a common thing ; but modern populations are so vast that even the most uncommon things are recorded once a week or oftener. Not one of my critics but has seen a hundred times in his paper how some policeman or fireman or nursemaid has received a medal, or the compliments of a magistrate, or perhaps a public funeral, for risking his or her life to save another's. Has he ever seen it added that the saved was the husband of the woman the saver loved, or was that woman herself, or was even known to the saver as much as by sight ? Never. When we want to read of the deeds that are done for love, whither do we turn ? To the murder column ; and there we are rarely disappointed.

Need I repeat that the theatre critic's professional routine so discourages any association between real life and the stage, that he soon loses the natural habit of referring to the one to explain the other ? The critic who discovered a romantic motive for Dick's sacrifice was no mere literary dreamer, but a clever barrister. He pointed out that Dick Dudgeon clearly did adore Mrs Anderson ; that it was for her sake that he offered his life to save her beloved husband ; and that his explicit denial of his passion was the splendid mendacity of a gentleman whose respect for a married woman, and duty to her absent husband, sealed his passion-palpitating lips. From the moment that this fatally plausible explanation was launched, my play became my critic's play, not mine. Thenceforth Dick Dudgeon every night confirmed the critic by stealing behind Judith, and mutely attesting his passion by surreptitiously imprinting a heart-broken kiss on a stray lock of her hair whilst he uttered the barren denial. As for me, I was just then wandering about the streets of Constantinople, unaware of all these doings. When I returned all was over. My personal relations with the critic and the actor forbad me to curse them. I had not even the chance of publicly forgiving them. They meant well by me ; but if they ever write a play, may I be there to explain ! *

BETTER THAN SHAKESPEAR ?

As to the other plays in this volume, the application of my title is less obvious, since neither Julius Cæsar, Cleopatra, nor Lady Cicely Waynflete have any external political connexion with Puritanism. The very name of Cleopatra suggests at once a tragedy of Circe, with the horrible difference that whereas the ancient myth rightly represents

* As I pass these pages through the press (September 1900), the critics of Yorkshire are struggling, as against some unholy fascination, with the apparition of Dick Dudgeon on their stage in the person of Forbes Robertson. " A finished scoundrel " is the description which one of them gives of Dick. This is worth recording as an example of the extent to which the moral sense remains dormant in people who are content with the customary formulas for respectable conduct.

Circe as turning heroes into hogs, the modern romantic convention would represent her as turning hogs into heroes. Shakespear's Antony and Cleopatra must needs be as intolerable to the true Puritan as it is vaguely distressing to the ordinary healthy citizen, because, after giving a faithful picture of the soldier broken down by debauchery, and the typical wanton in whose arms such men perish, Shakespear finally strains all his huge command of rhetoric and stage pathos to give a theatrical sublimity to the wretched end of the business, and to persuade foolish spectators that the world was well lost by the twain. Such falsehood is not to be borne except by the real Cleopatras and Antonys (they are to be found in every public house) who would no doubt be glad enough to be transfigured by some poet as immortal lovers. Woe to the poet who stoops to such folly! The lot of the man who sees life truly and thinks about it romantically is Despair. How well we know the cries of that despair! Vanity of vanities, all is vanity! moans the Preacher, when life has at last taught him that Nature will not dance to his moralist-made tunes. Thackeray, scores of centuries later, was still baying the moon in the same terms. Out, out, brief candle! cries Shakespear, in his tragedy of the modern literary man as murderer and witch consulter. Surely the time is past for patience with writers who, having to choose between giving up life in despair and discarding the trumpery moral kitchen scales in which they try to weigh the universe, superstitiously stick to the scales, and spend the rest of the lives they pretend to despise in breaking men's spirits. But even in pessimism there is a choice between intellectual honesty and dishonesty. Hogarth drew the rake and the harlot without glorifying their end. Swift, accepting our system of morals and religion, delivered the inevitable verdict of that system on us through the mouth of the king of Brobdingnag, and described Man as the Yahoo, shocking his superior the horse by his every action. Strindberg, the only genuinely Shakespearean

modern dramatist, shews that the female Yahoo, measured
by romantic standards, is viler than her male dupe and slave.
I respect these resolute tragi-comedians : they are logical
and faithful : they force you to face the fact that you must
either accept their conclusions as valid (in which case it is
cowardly to continue living) or admit that their way of
judging conduct is absurd. But when your Shakespears
and Thackerays huddle up the matter at the end by killing
somebody and covering your eyes with the undertaker's
handkerchief, duly onioned with some pathetic phrase, as
The flight of angels sing thee to thy rest, or Adsum, or the
like, I have no respect for them at all : such maudlin tricks
may impose on tea-drunkards, not on me.

Besides, I have a technical objection to making sexual
infatuation a tragic theme. Experience proves that it is
only effective in the comic spirit. We can bear to see Mrs
Quickly pawning her plate for love of Falstaff, but not
Antony running away from the battle of Actium for love
of Cleopatra. Let realism have its demonstration, comedy
its criticism, or even bawdry its horselaugh at the expense
of sexual infatuation, if it must ; but to ask us to subject
our souls to its ruinous glamor, to worship it, deify it, and
imply that it alone makes our life worth living, is nothing
but folly gone mad erotically—a thing compared to which
Falstaff's unbeglamored drinking and drabbing is respectable
and rightminded. Whoever, then, expects to find Cleopatra
a Circe and Cæsar a hog in these pages, had better lay down
my book and be spared a disappointment.

In Cæsar, I have used another character with which
Shakespear has been beforehand. But Shakespear, who
knew human weakness so well, never knew human strength
of the Cæsarian type. His Cæsar is an admitted failure :
his Lear is a masterpiece. The tragedy of disillusion and
doubt, of the agonized struggle for a foothold on the quick-
sand made by an acute observation striving to verify its
vain attribution of morality and respectability to Nature,

of the faithless will and the keen eyes that the faithless will is too weak to blind : all this will give you a Hamlet or a Macbeth, and win you great applause from literary gentlemen ; but it will not give you a Julius Cæsar. Cæsar was not in Shakespear, nor in the epoch, now fast waning, which he inaugurated. It cost Shakespear no pang to write Cæsar down for the merely technical purpose of writing Brutus up. And what a Brutus ! A perfect Girondin, mirrored in Shakespear's art two hundred years before the real thing came to maturity and talked and stalked and had its head duly cut off by the coarser Antonys and Octaviuses of its time, who at least knew the difference between life and rhetoric.

It will be said that these remarks can bear no other construction than an offer of my Cæsar to the public as an improvement on Shakespear's. And in fact, that is their precise purport. But here let me give a friendly warning to those scribes who have so often exclaimed against my criticisms of Shakespear as blasphemies against a hitherto unquestioned Perfection and Infallibility. Such criticisms are no more new than the creed of my Diabolonian Puritan or my revival of the humors of Cool as a Cucumber. Too much surprise at them betrays an acquaintance with Shakespear criticism so limited as not to include even the prefaces of Dr. Johnson and the utterances of Napoleon. I have merely repeated in the dialect of my own time and in the light of its philosophy what they said in the dialect and light of theirs. Do not be misled by the Shakespear fanciers who, ever since his own time, have delighted in his plays just as they might have delighted in a particular breed of pigeons if they had never learnt to read. His genuine critics, from Ben Jonson to Mr Frank Harris, have always kept as far on this side idolatry as I.

As to our ordinary uncritical citizens, they have been slowly trudging forward these three centuries to the point which Shakespear reached at a bound in Elizabeth's time.

Today most of them have arrived there or thereabouts, with the result that his plays are at last beginning to be performed as he wrote them ; and the long line of disgraceful farces, melodramas, and stage pageants which actor-managers, from Garrick and Cibber to our own contemporaries, have hacked out of his plays as peasants have hacked huts out of the Coliseum, are beginning to vanish from the stage. It is a significant fact that the mutilators of Shakespear, who never could be persuaded that Shakespear knew his business better than they, have ever been the most fanatical of his worshippers. The late Augustin Daly thought no price too extravagant for an addition to his collection of Shakespear relics ; but in arranging Shakespear's plays for the stage, he proceeded on the assumption that Shakespear was a botcher and he an artist. I am far too good a Shakespearean ever to forgive Henry Irving for producing a version of King Lear so mutilated that the numerous critics who had never read the play could not follow the story of Gloster. Both these idolators of the Bard must have thought Forbes Robertson mad because he restored Fortinbras to the stage and played as much of Hamlet as there was time for instead of as little. And the instant success of the experiment probably altered their minds no further than to make them think the public mad. Mr Benson actually gives the play complete at two sittings, causing the aforesaid numerous critics to remark with naïve surprise that Polonius is a complete and interesting character. It was the age of gross ignorance of Shakespear and incapacity for his works that produced the indiscriminate eulogies with which we are familiar. It was the revival of serious attention to those works that coincided with the movement for giving genuine instead of spurious and silly representations of his plays. So much for Bardolatry !

It does not follow, however, that the right to criticize Shakespear involves the power of writing better plays. And

T.P.—2

in fact—do not be surprised at my modesty—I do not profess to write better plays. The writing of practicable stage plays does not present an infinite scope to human talent ; and the playwrights who magnify its difficulties are humbugs. The summit of their art has been attained again and again. No man will ever write a better tragedy than Lear, a better comedy than Le Festin de Pierre or Peer Gynt, a better opera than Don Giovanni, a better music drama than The Niblung's Ring, or, for the matter of that, better fashionable plays and melodramas than are now being turned out by writers whom nobody dreams of mocking with the word immortal. It is the philosophy, the outlook on life, that changes, not the craft of the playwright. A generation that is thoroughly moralized and patriotized, that conceives virtuous indignation as spiritually nutritious, that murders the murderer and robs the thief, that grovels before all sorts of ideals, social, military, ecclesiastical, royal and divine, may be, from my point of view, steeped in error ; but it need not want for as good plays as the hand of man can produce. Only, those plays will be neither written nor relished by men in whose philosophy guilt and innocence, and consequently revenge and idolatry, have no meaning. Such men must rewrite all the old plays in terms of their own philosophy ; and that is why, as Stuart-Glennie has pointed out, there can be no new drama without a new philosophy. To which I may add that there can be no Shakespear or Goethe without one either, nor two Shakespears in one philosophic epoch, since, as I have said, the first great comer in that epoch reaps the whole harvest and reduces those who come after to the rank of mere gleaners, or, worse than that, fools who go laboriously through all the motions of the reaper and binder in an empty field. What is the use of writing plays or painting frescoes if you have nothing more to say or shew than was said and shewn by Shakespear, Michael Angelo, and Raphael ? If these had not seen things differently, for better or worse, from the dramatic poets of the Townley mysteries, or from Giotto, they could not have produced their works : no, not though their skill of pen and hand had been double what it was. After them there was no need (and *need* alone nerves men to face the persecution in the teeth of which new art is brought to birth) to redo the already done, until in due time, when their philosophy wore itself out, a new race of nineteenth century poets and critics, from Byron to William Morris, began, first to speak coldly of Shakespear and Raphael, and then to rediscover, in the medieval art which these Renascence masters had superseded, certain forgotten elements which were germinating again for the new harvest. What is more, they began to discover that the technical skill of the masters was by no means superlative. Indeed, I defy anyone to prove that the great epoch makers in fine art have owed their position to their technical skill. It is true that when we search for examples of a prodigious command of language and of graphic line, we can think of nobody better than Shakespear and Michael Angelo. But both of them laid their arts waste for centuries by leading later artists to seek greatness in copying their technique. The technique was acquired, refined on, and elaborated over and over again ; but the supremacy of the two great exemplars remained undisputed. As a matter of easily observable fact, every generation produces men of extraordinary special faculty, artistic, mathematical and linguistic, who for lack of new ideas, or indeed of any ideas worth mentioning, achieve no distinction outside music halls and class rooms, although they can do things easily that the great epoch makers did clumsily or not at all. The contempt of the academic pedant for the original artist is often founded on a genuine superiority of technical knowledge and aptitude : he is sometimes a better anatomical draughtsman than Raphael, a better hand at triple counterpoint than Beethoven, a better versifier than Byron. Nay, this is true not merely of pedants, but of men who have produced works of art of some note. If technical facility were the secret of greatness in art, Swinburne would be greater than Browning and Byron rolled into one, Stevenson greater than Scott or Dickens, Mendelssohn than Wagner, Maclise than Madox Brown. Besides, new ideas make their technique as water makes its channel; and the technician without ideas is as useless as the canal constructor without water, though he may do very skilfully what the Mississippi does very rudely. To clinch the argument, you have only to observe that the epoch maker himself has generally begun working professionally before his new ideas have mastered him sufficiently to insist on constant expression by his art. In such cases you are compelled to admit that if he had by chance died earlier, his greatness would have remained unachieved, although his technical qualifications would have been well enough established. The early imitative works of great men are usually conspicuously inferior to the best works of their forerunners. Imagine Wagner dying after composing Rienzi, or Shelley after Zastrozzi ! Would any competent critic then have rated Wagner's technical aptitude as high as Rossini's, Spontini's, or Meyerbeer's ; or Shelley's as high as Moore's ? Turn the problem another way : does anyone suppose that if Shakespear had conceived Goethe's or Ibsen's ideas, he would have expressed them any worse than Goethe or Ibsen ? Human faculty being what it is, is it likely that in our time any advance, except in external conditions, will take place in the arts of expression sufficient to enable an author, without making himself ridiculous, to undertake to say what he has to say better than Homer or Shakespear ? But the humblest author, and much more a rather arrogant one like myself, may profess to have something to say by this time that neither Homer nor Shakespear said. And the playgoer may reasonably ask to have historical events and persons presented to him in the light of his own time, even though Homer and Shakespear have already shewn them in the light of their time. For example, Homer presented Achilles and Ajax as heroes to the world in the Iliads. In due time came Shakespear, who said, virtually : I really cannot accept this spoilt child and this brawny fool as great men merely because Homer flattered them in playing to the Greek gallery. Consequently we have, in Troilus and Cressida, the verdict of Shakespear's epoch (our own) on the pair. This did not in the least involve any pretence on Shakespear's part to be a greater poet than Homer.

When Shakespear in turn came to deal with Henry V and Julius Cæsar, he did so according to his own essentially knightly conception of a great statesman-commander. But in the XIX century comes the German historian Mommsen, who also takes Cæsar for his hero, and explains the immense difference in scope between the perfect knight Vercingetorix and his great conqueror Julius Cæsar. In this country, Carlyle, with his vein of peasant inspiration, apprehended the sort of greatness that places the true hero of history so far beyond the mere *preux chevalier*, whose fanatical personal honor, gallantry, and self-sacrifice, are founded on a passion for death born of inability to bear the weight of a life that will not grant ideal conditions to the liver. This one ray of perception became Carlyle's whole stock-in-trade ; and it sufficed to make a literary master of him. In due time, when Mommsen is an old man, and Carlyle dead, come I, and dramatize the by-this-time familiar distinction in Arms and the Man, with its comedic conflict between the knightly Bulgarian and the Mommsenite Swiss captain. Whereupon a great many playgoers who have not yet read Cervantes, much less Mommsen and Carlyle, raise a shriek of concern for their knightly ideal as if nobody had ever questioned its sufficiency since the middle ages. Let them thank me for educating them so far. And let them allow me to set forth Cæsar in the same modern light, taking the platform from Shakespear as he from Homer, and with no thought of pretending to express the Mommsenite view of

Cæsar any better than Shakespear expressed a view which was not even Plutarchian, and must, I fear, be referred to the tradition in stage conquerors established by Marlowe's Tamerlane as much as to the chivalrous conception of heroism dramatized in Henry V.

For my own part, I can avouch that such powers of invention, humor and stage ingenuity as I have been able to exercise in Plays Pleasant and Unpleasant, and in these Three Plays for Puritans, availed me not at all until I saw the old facts in a new light. Technically, I do not find myself able to proceed otherwise than as former playwrights have done. True, my plays have the latest mechanical improvements : the action is not carried on by impossible soliloquys and asides ; and my people get on and off the stage without requiring four doors to a room which in real life would have only one. But my stories are the old stories ; my characters are the familiar harlequin and columbine, clown and pantaloon (note the harlequin's leap in the third act of Cæsar and Cleopatra) ; my stage tricks and suspenses and thrills and jests are the ones in vogue when I was a boy, by which time my grandfather was tired of them. To the young people who make their acquaintance for the first time in my plays, they may be as novel as Cyrano's nose to those who have never seen Punch ; whilst to older play-goers the unexpectedness of my attempt to substitute natural history for conventional ethics and romantic logic may so transfigure the eternal stage puppets and their inevitable dilemmas as to make their identification impossible for the moment. If so, so much the better for me : I shall perhaps enjoy a few years of immortality. But the whirligig of time will soon bring my audiences to my own point of view ; and then the next Shakespear that comes along will turn these petty tentatives of mine into masterpieces final for their epoch. By that time my twentieth century characteristics will pass unnoticed as a matter of course, whilst the eighteenth century artificiality that marks the work of every literary Irishman of my generation will seem antiquated and silly. It is a dangerous thing to be hailed at once, as a few rash admirers have hailed me, as above all things original : what the world calls originality is only an unaccustomed method of tickling it. Meyerbeer seemed prodigiously original to the Parisians when he first burst on them. Today, he is only the crow who followed Beethoven's plough. I am a crow who has followed many ploughs. No doubt I seem prodigiously clever to those who have never hopped, hungry and curious, across the fields of philosophy, politics, and art. Karl Marx said of Stuart Mill that his eminence was due to the flatness of the surrounding country. In these days of Free Schools, universal reading, cheap newspapers, and the inevitable ensuing demand for notabilities of all sorts, literary, military, political and fashionable, to write paragraphs about, that sort of eminence is within the reach of very moderate ability. Reputations are cheap nowadays. Even were they dear, it would still be impossible for any public-spirited citizen of the world to hope that his reputation might endure ; for this would be to hope that the flood of general enlightenment may never rise above his miserable high-watermark. I hate to think that Shakespear has lasted 300 years, though he got no further than Koheleth the Preacher, who died many centuries before him ; or that Plato, more than 2000 years old, is still ahead of our voters. We must hurry on : we must get rid of reputations : they are weeds in the soil of ignorance. Cultivate that soil, and they will flower more beautifully, but only as annuals. If this preface will at all help to get rid of mine, the writing of it will have been well worth the pains.

SURREY, 1900

THE DEVIL'S DISCIPLE

A MELODRAMA

1897

THE DEVIL'S DISCIPLE

ACT I

At the most wretched hour between a black night and a wintry morning in the year 1777, Mrs Dudgeon, of New Hampshire, is sitting up in the kitchen and general dwelling room of her farm house on the outskirts of the town of Webster-bridge. She is not a prepossessing woman. No woman looks her best after sitting up all night ; and Mrs Dudgeon's face, even at its best, is grimly trenched by the channels into which the barren forms and observances of a dead Puritanism can pen a bitter temper and a fierce pride. She is an elderly matron who has worked hard and got nothing by it except dominion and detestation in her sordid home, and an unquestioned reputation for piety and respectability among her neighbors, to whom drink and debauchery are still so much more tempting than religion and rectitude, that they conceive goodness simply as self-denial. This conception is easily extended to others-denial, and finally generalized as covering anything disagreeable. So Mrs Dudgeon, being exceedingly disagreeable, is held to be exceedingly good. Short of flat felony, she enjoys complete license except for amiable weaknesses of any sort, and is consequently, without knowing it, the most licentious woman in the parish on the strength of never having broken the seventh commandment or missed a Sunday at the Presbyterian church.
The year 1777 is the one in which the passions roused by the breaking-off of the American colonies from England, more by their own weight than by their own will, boiled up to shooting point, the shooting being idealized to the English mind as suppression of rebellion and maintenance of British dominion, and to the American as defence of liberty, resistance to tyranny, and self-sacrifice on the altar of the Rights of Man. Into the merits of these idealizations it is not here necessary to inquire : suffice it to say, without prejudice, that they have convinced both Americans and English that the most high-

43

minded course for them to pursue is to kill as many of one another as possible, and that military operations to that end are in full swing, morally supported by confident requests from the clergy of both sides for the blessing of God on their arms.

Under such circumstances many other women besides this disagreeable Mrs Dudgeon find themselves sitting up all night waiting for news. Like her, too, they fall asleep towards morning at the risk of nodding themselves into the kitchen fire. Mrs Dudgeon sleeps with a shawl over her head, and her feet on a broad fender of iron laths, the step of the domestic altar of the fireplace, with its huge hobs and boiler, and its hinged arm above the smoky mantelshelf for roasting. The plain kitchen table is opposite the fire, at her elbow, with a candle on it in a tin sconce. Her chair, like all the others in the room, is uncushioned and unpainted ; but as it has a round railed back and a seat conventionally moulded to the sitter's curves, it is comparatively a chair of state. The room has three doors, one on the same side as the fireplace, near the corner, leading to the best bedroom ; one, at the opposite end of the opposite wall, leading to the scullery and washhouse ; and the house-door, with its latch, heavy lock, and clumsy wooden bar, in the front wall, between the window in its middle and the corner next the bedroom door. Between the door and the window a rack of pegs suggests to the deductive observer that the men of the house are all away, as there are no hats or coats on them. On the other side of the window the clock hangs on a nail, with its white wooden dial, black iron weights, and brass pendulum. Between the clock and the corner, a big cupboard, locked, stands on a dwarf dresser full of common crockery.

On the side opposite the fireplace, between the door and the corner, a shamelessly ugly black horsehair sofa stands against the wall. An inspection of its stridulous surface shews that Mrs Dudgeon is not alone. A girl of sixteen or seventeen has fallen asleep on it. She is a wild, timid looking creature with black hair and tanned skin. Her frock, a scanty garment, is rent, weather-stained, berrystained, and by no means scrupulously clean. It hangs on her with a freedom which,

*taken with her brown legs and bare feet, suggests no great
stock of underclothing.*

*Suddenly there comes a tapping at the door, not loud
enough to wake the sleepers. Then knocking, which disturbs
Mrs Dudgeon a little. Finally the latch is tried, whereupon
she springs up at once.*

MRS DUDGEON [*threateningly*] Well, why dont you open
the door ? [*She sees that the girl is asleep, and immediately
raises a clamor of heartfelt vexation*]. Well, dear, dear me !
Now this is— [*shaking her*] wake up, wake up : do you
hear ?

THE GIRL [*sitting up*] What is it ?

MRS DUDGEON. Wake up ; and be ashamed of yourself,
you unfeeling sinful girl, falling asleep like that, and your
father hardly cold in his grave.

THE GIRL [*half asleep still*] I didnt mean to. I dropped
off—

MRS DUDGEON [*cutting her short*] Oh yes, youve plenty of
excuses, I daresay. Dropped off ! [*Fiercely, as the knocking
recommences*] Why dont you get up and let your uncle in ?
after me waiting up all night for him ! [*She pushes her
rudely off the sofa*]. There : I'll open the door : much good
you are to wait up. Go and mend that fire a bit.

*The girl, cowed and wretched, goes to the fire and puts a
log on. Mrs Dudgeon unbars the door and opens it, letting
into the stuffy kitchen a little of the freshness and a great
deal of the chill of the dawn, also her second son Christy, a
fattish, stupid, fair-haired, roundfaced man of about 22,
muffled in a plaid shawl and grey overcoat. He hurries,
shivering, to the fire, leaving Mrs Dudgeon to shut the door.*

CHRISTY [*at the fire*] F—f—f ! but it is cold. [*Seeing the
girl, and staring lumpishly at her*] Why, who are you ?

THE GIRL [*shyly*] Essie.

MRS DUDGEON. Oh, you may well ask. [*To Essie*] Go
to your room, child, and lie down, since you havnt feeling
enough to keep you awake. Your history isnt fit for your
own ears to hear.

ESSIE. I—

MRS DUDGEON [*peremptorily*] Dont answer me, Miss ; but shew your obedience by doing what I tell you. [*Essie, almost in tears, crosses the room to the door near the sofa*]. And dont forget your prayers. [*Essie goes out*]. She'd have gone to bed last night just as if nothing had happened if I'd let her.

CHRISTY [*phlegmatically*] Well, she cant be expected to feel Uncle Peter's death like one of the family.

MRS DUDGEON. What are you talking about, child ? Isnt she his daughter—the punishment of his wickedness and shame ? [*She assaults her chair by sitting down*].

CHRISTY [*staring*] Uncle Peter's daughter !

MRS DUDGEON. Why else should she be here ? D'ye think Ive not had enough trouble and care put upon me bringing up my own girls, let alone you and your good-for-nothing brother, without having your uncle's bastards—

CHRISTY [*interrupting her with an apprehensive glance at the door by which Essie went out*] Sh ! She may hear you.

MRS DUDGEON [*raising her voice*] Let her hear me. People who fear God dont fear to give the devil's work its right name. [*Christy, soullessly indifferent to the strife of Good and Evil, stares at the fire, warming himself*]. Well, how long are you going to stare there like a stuck pig ? What news have you for me ?

CHRISTY [*taking off his hat and shawl and going to the rack to hang them up*] The minister is to break the news to you. He'll be here presently.

MRS DUDGEON. Break what news ?

CHRISTY [*standing on tiptoe, from boyish habit, to hang his hat up, though he is quite tall enough to reach the peg, and speaking with callous placidity, considering the nature of the announcement*] Father's dead too.

MRS DUDGEON [*stupent*] Your father !

CHRISTY [*sulkily, coming back to the fire and warming himself again, attending much more to the fire than to his mother*] Well, it's not my fault. When we got to Nevins-town we found him ill in bed. He didnt know us at first.

The minister sat up with him and sent me away. He died in the night.

MRS DUDGEON [*bursting into dry angry tears*] Well, I do think this is hard on me—very hard on me. His brother, that was a disgrace to us all his life, gets hanged on the public gallows as a rebel ; and your father, instead of staying at home where his duty was, with his own family, goes after him and dies, leaving everything on my shoulders. After sending this girl to me to take care of, too ! [*She plucks her shawl vexedly over her ears*]. It's sinful, so it is : downright sinful.

CHRISTY [*with a slow, bovine cheerfulness, after a pause*] I think it's going to be a fine morning, after all.

MRS DUDGEON [*railing at him*] A fine morning ! And your father newly dead ! Wheres your feelings, child ?

CHRISTY [*obstinately*] Well, I didnt mean any harm. I suppose a man may make a remark about the weather even if his father's dead.

MRS DUDGEON [*bitterly*] A nice comfort my children are to me ! One son a fool, and the other a lost sinner thats left his home to live with smugglers and gypsies and villains, the scum of the earth !

Someone knocks.

CHRISTY [*without moving*] Thats the minister.

MRS DUDGEON [*sharply*] Well, arnt you going to let Mr Anderson in ?

Christy goes sheepishly to the door. Mrs Dudgeon buries her face in her hands, as it is her duty as a widow to be overcome with grief. Christy opens the door, and admits the minister, Anthony Anderson, a shrewd, genial, ready Presbyterian divine of about 50, with something of the authority of his profession in his bearing. But it is an altogether secular authority, sweetened by a conciliatory, sensible manner not at all suggestive of a quite thorough-going other-worldliness. He is a strong, healthy man too, with a thick sanguine neck ; and his keen, cheerful mouth cuts into somewhat fleshy corners. No doubt an excellent parson, but still a man capable of making the most of this world, and perhaps a little apologetically conscious of getting on better with it than a sound Presbyterian ought.

ANDERSON [*to Christy, at the door, looking at Mrs Dudgeon whilst he takes off his cloak*] Have you told her?

CHRISTY. She made me. [*He shuts the door ; yawns ; and loafs across to the sofa, where he sits down and presently drops off to sleep*].

Anderson looks compassionately at Mrs Dudgeon. Then he hangs his cloak and hat on the rack. Mrs Dudgeon dries her eyes and looks up at him.

ANDERSON. Sister : the Lord has laid his hand very heavily upon you.

MRS DUDGEON [*with intensely recalcitrant resignation*] It's His will, I suppose ; and I must bow to it. But I do think it hard. What call had Timothy to go to Springtown, and remind everybody that he belonged to a man that was being hanged ?—and [*spitefully*] that deserved it, if ever a man did.

ANDERSON [*gently*] They were brothers, Mrs Dudgeon.

MRS DUDGEON. Timothy never acknowledged him as his brother after we were married : he had too much respect for me to insult me with such a brother. Would such a selfish wretch as Peter have come thirty miles to see Timothy hanged, do you think ? Not thirty yards, not he. However, I must bear my cross as best I may : least said is soonest mended.

ANDERSON [*very grave, coming down to the fire to stand with his back to it*] Your eldest son was present at the execution, Mrs Dudgeon.

MRS DUDGEON [*disagreeably surprised*] Richard ?

ANDERSON [*nodding*] Yes.

MRS DUDGEON [*vindictively*] Let it be a warning to him. He may end that way himself, the wicked, dissolute, godless—[*she suddenly stops ; her voice fails ; and she asks, with evident dread*] Did Timothy see him ?

ANDERSON. Yes.

MRS DUDGEON [*holding her breath*] Well ?

ANDERSON. He only saw him in the crowd : they did not speak. [*Mrs Dudgeon, greatly relieved, exhales the pent up breath and sits at her ease again*] Your husband was greatly touched and impressed by his brother's awful death. [*Mrs Dudgeon sneers. Anderson breaks off to demand with some indignation*] Well, wasnt it only natural, Mrs Dudgeon? He softened towards his prodigal son in that moment. He sent for him to come to see him.

MRS DUDGEON [*her alarm renewed*] Sent for Richard !

ANDERSON. Yes ; but Richard would not come. He sent his father a message ; but I'm sorry to say it was a wicked message—an awful message.

MRS DUDGEON. What was it ?

ANDERSON. That he would stand by his wicked uncle and stand against his good parents, in this world and the next.

MRS DUDGEON [*implacably*] He will be punished for it. He will be punished for it—in both worlds.

ANDERSON. That is not in our hands, Mrs Dudgeon.

MRS DUDGEON. Did I say it was, Mr Anderson ? We are told that the wicked shall be punished. Why should we do our duty and keep God's law if there is to be no difference made between us and those who follow their own likings and dislikings, and make a jest of us and of their Maker's word ?

ANDERSON. Well, Richard's earthly father has been merciful to him ; and his heavenly judge is the father of us all.

MRS DUDGEON [*forgetting herself*] Richard's earthly father was a softheaded—

ANDERSON [*shocked*] Oh !

MRS DUDGEON [*with a touch of shame*] Well, I am Richard's mother. If I am against him who has any right to be for him ? [*Trying to conciliate him*] Wont you sit down, Mr Anderson ? I should have asked you before ; but I'm so troubled.

ANDERSON. Thank you. [*He takes a chair from beside the fireplace, and turns it so that he can sit comfortably at the fire. When he is seated he adds, in the tone of a man who knows that he is opening a difficult subject*] Has Christy told you about the new will ?

MRS DUDGEON [*all her fears returning*] The new will !

Did Timothy—? [*She breaks off, gasping, unable to complete the question*].

ANDERSON. Yes. In his last hours he changed his mind.

MRS DUDGEON [*white with intense rage*] And you let him rob me ?

ANDERSON. I had no power to prevent him giving what was his to his own son.

MRS DUDGEON. He had nothing of his own. His money was the money I brought him as my marriage portion. It was for me to deal with my own money and my own son. He dare not have done it if I had been with him ; and well he knew it. That was why he stole away like a thief to take advantage of the law to rob me by making a new will behind my back. The more shame on you, Mr Anderson, —you, a minister of the gospel—to act as his accomplice in such a crime.

ANDERSON [*rising*] I will take no offence at what you say in the first bitterness of your grief.

MRS DUDGEON [*contemptuously*] Grief !

ANDERSON. Well, of your disappointment, if you can find it in your heart to think that the better word.

MRS DUDGEON. My heart ! My heart ! And since when, pray, have you begun to hold up our hearts as trustworthy guides for us ?

ANDERSON [*rather guiltily*] I—er—

MRS DUDGEON [*vehemently*] Dont lie, Mr Anderson. We are told that the heart of man is deceitful above all things, and desperately wicked. My heart belonged, not to Timothy, but to that poor wretched brother of his that has just ended his days with a rope round his neck—aye, to Peter Dudgeon. You know it : old Eli Hawkins, the man to whose pulpit you succeeded, though you are not worthy to loose his shoe latchet, told it you when he gave over our souls into your charge. He warned me and strengthened me against my heart, and made me marry a Godfearing man—as he thought. What else but that discipline has made me the woman I am ? And you, you, who followed your heart in your marriage, you talk to me of what I find in my heart. Go home to your pretty wife, man ; and leave me to my prayers. [*She turns from him and leans with her elbows on the table, brooding over her wrongs and taking no further notice of him*].

ANDERSON [*willing enough to escape*] The Lord forbid that I should come between you and the source of all comfort ! [*He goes to the rack for his coat and hat*].

MRS DUDGEON [*without looking at him*] The Lord will know what to forbid and what to allow without your help.

ANDERSON. And whom to forgive, I hope—Eli Hawkins and myself, if we have ever set up our preaching against His law. [*He fastens his cloak, and is now ready to go*]. Just one word—on necessary business, Mrs Dudgeon. There is the reading of the will to be gone through ; and Richard has a right to be present. He is in the town ; but he has the grace to say that he does not want to force himself in here.

MRS DUDGEON. He shall come here. Does he expect us to leave his father's house for his convenience ? Let them all come, and come quickly, and go quickly. They shall not make the will an excuse to shirk half their day's work. I shall be ready, never fear.

ANDERSON [*coming back a step or two*] Mrs Dudgeon : I used to have some little influence with you. When did I lose it ?

MRS DUDGEON [*still without turning to him*] When you married for love. Now youre answered.

ANDERSON. Yes : I am answered. [*He goes out, musing*].

MRS DUDGEON [*to herself, thinking of her husband*] Thief ! Thief ! [*She shakes herself angrily out of her chair ; throws back the shawl from her head ; and sets to work to prepare the room for the reading of the will, beginning by replacing Anderson's chair against the wall and pushing back her own to the window. Then she calls, in her hard, driving, wrathful way*] Christy. [*No answer : he is fast asleep*]. Christy. [*She shakes him roughly*]. Get up out of that ; and be ashamed of yourself—sleeping, and your father dead ! [*She returns to the table ; puts the candle on the mantelshelf ;*

and takes from the table drawer a red table cloth which she spreads].

CHRISTY [*rising reluctantly*] Well, do you suppose we are never going to sleep until we are out of mourning ?

MRS DUDGEON. I want none of your sulks. Here : help me to set this table. [*They place the table in the middle of the room, with Christy's end towards the fireplace and Mrs Dudgeon's towards the sofa. Christy drops the table as soon as possible, and goes to the fire, leaving his mother to make the final adjustments of its position*]. We shall have the minister back here with the lawyer and all the family to read the will before you have done toasting yourself. Go and wake that girl ; and then light the stove in the shed : you cant have your breakfast here. And mind you wash yourself, and make yourself fit to receive the company. [*She punctuates these orders by going to the cupboard ; unlocking it ; and producing a decanter of wine, which has no doubt stood there untouched since the last state occasion in the family, and some glasses, which she sets on the table. Also two green ware plates, on one of which she puts a barn-brack with a knife beside it. On the other she shakes some biscuits out of a tin, putting back one or two, and counting the rest*]. Now mind : there are ten biscuits there : let there be ten there when I come back after dressing myself. And keep your fingers off the raisins in that cake. And tell Essie the same. I suppose I can trust you to bring in the case of stuffed birds without breaking the glass ? [*She replaces the tin in the cupboard, which she locks, pocketing the key carefully*].

CHRISTY [*lingering at the fire*] Youd better put the ink-stand instead, for the lawyer.

MRS DUDGEON. Thats no answer to make to me, sir. Go and do as youre told. [*Christy turns sullenly to obey*]. Stop : take down that shutter before you go, and let the daylight in : you cant expect me to do all the heavy work of the house with a great lout like you idling about.

Christy takes the window bar out of its clamps, and puts it aside ; then opens the shutter, shewing the grey morning.

Mrs Dudgeon takes the sconce from the mantelshelf ; blows out the candle ; extinguishes the snuff by pinching it with her fingers, first licking them for the purpose : and replaces the sconce on the shelf.

CHRISTY [*looking through the window*] Heres the minister's wife.

MRS DUDGEON [*displeased*] What ! Is she coming here ?

CHRISTY. Yes.

MRS DUDGEON. What does she want troubling me at this hour, before I am properly dressed to receive people ?

CHRISTY. Youd better ask her.

MRS DUDGEON [*threateningly*] Youd better keep a civil tongue in your head. [*He goes sulkily towards the door. She comes after him, plying him with instructions*]. Tell that girl to come to me as soon as she's had her breakfast. And tell her to make herself fit to be seen before the people. [*Christy goes out and slams the door in her face*]. Nice manners, that ! [*Someone knocks at the house door : she turns and cries inhospitably*] Come in. [*Judith Anderson, the minister's wife, comes in. Judith is more than twenty years younger than her husband, though she will never be as young as he in vitality. She is pretty and proper and ladylike, and has been admired and petted into an opinion of herself sufficiently favorable to give her a self-assurance which serves her instead of strength. She has a pretty taste in dress, and in her face the pretty lines of a sentimental character formed by dreams. Even her little self-complacency is pretty, like a child's vanity. Rather a pathetic creature to any sympathetic observer who knows how rough a place the world is. One feels, on the whole, that Anderson might have chosen worse, and that she, needing protection, could not have chosen better*]. Oh, it's you, is it, Mrs Anderson ?

JUDITH [*very politely—almost patronizingly*] Yes. Can I do anything for you, Mrs Dudgeon ? Can I help to get the place ready before they come to read the will ?

MRS DUDGEON [*stiffly*] Thank you, Mrs Anderson, my house is always ready for anyone to come into.

MRS ANDERSON [*with complacent amiability*] Yes, indeed

it is. Perhaps you had rather I did not intrude on you just now.

MRS DUDGEON. Oh, one more or less will make no difference this morning, Mrs Anderson. Now that youre here, youd better stay. If you wouldnt mind shutting the door ! [*Judith smiles, implying " How stupid of me ! " and shuts it with an exasperating air of doing something pretty and becoming*]. Thats better. I must go and tidy myself a bit. I suppose you dont mind stopping here to receive anyone that comes until I'm ready.

JUDITH [*graciously giving her leave*] Oh yes, certainly. Leave that to me, Mrs Dudgeon ; and take your time. [*She hangs her cloak and bonnet on the rack*].

MRS DUDGEON [*half sneering*] I thought that would be more in your way than getting the house ready. [*Essie comes back*]. Oh, here you are ! [*Severely*] Come here : let me see you. [*Essie timidly goes to her. Mrs Dudgeon takes her roughly by the arm and pulls her round to inspect the results of her attempt to clean and tidy herself—results which shew little practice and less conviction*]. Mm ! Thats what you call doing your hair properly, I suppose. It's easy to see what you are, and how you were brought up. [*She throws her arm away, and goes on, peremptorily*] Now you listen to me and do as youre told. You sit down there in the corner by the fire ; and when the company comes dont dare to speak until youre spoken to. [*Essie creeps away to the fireplace*]. Your father's people had better see you and know youre there : theyre as much bound to keep you from starvation as I am. At any rate they might help. But let me have no chattering and making free with them, as if you were their equal. Do you hear ?

ESSIE. Yes.

MRS DUDGEON. Well, then go and do as youre told. [*Essie sits down miserably on the corner of the fender furthest from the door*]. Never mind her, Mrs Anderson : you know who she is and what she is. If she gives you any trouble, just tell me ; and I'll settle accounts with her. [*Mrs Dudgeon goes into the bedroom, shutting the door sharply behind her as if even it had to be made do its duty with a ruthless hand*].

JUDITH [*patronizing Essie, and arranging the cake and wine on the table more becomingly*] You must not mind if your aunt is strict with you. She is a very good woman, and desires your good too.

ESSIE [*in listless misery*] Yes.

JUDITH [*annoyed with Essie for her failure to be consoled and edified, and to appreciate the kindly condescension of the remark*] You are not going to be sullen, I hope, Essie.

ESSIE. No.

JUDITH. Thats a good girl ! [*She places a couple of chairs at the table with their backs to the window, with a pleasant sense of being a more thoughtful housekeeper than Mrs Dudgeon*]. Do you know any of your father's relatives ?

ESSIE. No. They wouldnt have anything to do with him : they were too religious. Father used to talk about Dick Dudgeon ; but I never saw him.

JUDITH [*ostentatiously shocked*] Dick Dudgeon ! Essie : do you wish to be a really respectable and grateful girl, and to make a place for yourself here by steady good conduct ?

ESSIE [*very half-heartedly*] Yes.

JUDITH. Then you must never mention the name of Richard Dudgeon—never even think about him. He is a bad man.

ESSIE. What has he done ?

JUDITH. You must not ask questions about him, Essie. You are too young to know what it is to be a bad man. But he is a smuggler ; and he lives with gypsies ; and he has no love for his mother and his family ; and he wrestles and plays games on Sunday instead of going to church. Never let him into your presence, if you can help it, Essie ; and try to keep yourself and all womanhood unspotted by contact with such men.

ESSIE. Yes.

JUDITH [*again displeased*] I am afraid you say Yes and

No without thinking very deeply.

ESSIE. Yes. At least I mean—

JUDITH [*severely*] What do you mean?

ESSIE [*almost crying*] Only—my father was a smuggler;
and— [*Someone knocks*].

JUDITH. They are beginning to come. Now remember
your aunt's directions, Essie; and be a good girl. [*Christy
comes back with the stand of stuffed birds under a glass case,
and an inkstand, which he places on the table*]. Good
morning, Mr Dudgeon. Will you open the door, please:
the people have come.

CHRISTY. Good morning. [*He opens the house door*].

*The morning is now fairly bright and warm; and Anderson,
who is the first to enter, has left his cloak at home. He is
accompanied by Lawyer Hawkins, a brisk, middleaged man in
brown riding gaiters and yellow breeches, looking as much
squire as solicitor. He and Anderson are allowed precedence
as representing the learned professions. After them comes
the family, headed by the senior uncle, William Dudgeon, a
large, shapeless man, bottle-nosed and evidently no ascetic
at table. His clothes are not the clothes, nor his anxious wife
the wife, of a prosperous man. The junior uncle, Titus
Dudgeon, is a wiry little terrier of a man, with an immense
and visibly purseproud wife, both free from the cares of the
William household.*

*Hawkins at once goes briskly to the table and takes the
chair nearest the sofa, Christy having left the inkstand there.
He puts his hat on the floor beside him, and produces the will.
Uncle William comes to the fire and stands on the hearth
warming his coat tails, leaving Mrs William derelict near
the door. Uncle Titus, who is the lady's man of the family,
rescues her by giving her his disengaged arm and bringing her
to the sofa, where he sits down warmly between his own lady
and his brother's. Anderson hangs up his hat and waits for
a word with Judith.*

JUDITH. She will be here in a moment. Ask them to
wait. [*She taps at the bedroom door. Receiving an answer
from within, she opens it and passes through*].

ANDERSON [*taking his place at the table at the opposite
end to Hawkins*] Our poor afflicted sister will be with us in
a moment. Are we all here?

CHRISTY [*at the house door, which he has just shut*] All
except Dick.

*The callousness with which Christy names the reprobate
jars on the moral sense of the family. Uncle William shakes
his head slowly and repeatedly. Mrs Titus catches her breath
convulsively through her nose. Her husband speaks.*

UNCLE TITUS. Well, I hope he will have the grace not to
come. I hope so.

*The Dudgeons all murmur assent, except Christy, who
goes to the window and posts himself there, looking out.
Hawkins smiles secretively as if he knew something that would
change their tune if they knew it. Anderson is uneasy : the
love of solemn family councils, especially funeral ones, is not
in his nature. Judith appears at the bedroom door.*

JUDITH [*with gentle impressiveness*] Friends, Mrs Dudgeon. [*She takes the chair from beside the fireplace ; and
places it for Mrs Dudgeon, who comes from the bedroom in
black, with a clean handkerchief to her eyes. All rise, except
Essie. Mrs Titus and Mrs William produce equally clean
handkerchiefs and weep. It is an affecting moment*].

UNCLE WILLIAM. Would it comfort you, sister, if we were
to offer up a prayer?

UNCLE TITUS. Or sing a hymn?

ANDERSON [*rather hastily*] I have been with our sister
this morning already, friends. In our hearts we ask a
blessing.

ALL [*except Essie*] Amen.

*They all sit down, except Judith, who stands behind Mrs
Dudgeon's chair.*

JUDITH [*to Essie*] Essie : did you say Amen?

ESSIE [*scaredly*] No.

JUDITH. Then say it, like a good girl.

ESSIE. Amen.

UNCLE WILLIAM [*encouragingly*] Thats right : thats right.
We know who you are ; but we are willing to be kind to

you if you are a good girl and deserve it. We are all equal before the Throne.

This republican sentiment does not please the women, who are convinced that the Throne is precisely the place where their superiority, often questioned in this world, will be recognized and rewarded.

CHRISTY [*at the window*] Heres Dick.

Anderson and Hawkins look round sociably. Essie, with a gleam of interest breaking through her misery, looks up. Christy grins and gapes expectantly at the door. The rest are petrified with the intensity of their sense of Virtue menaced with outrage by the approach of flaunting Vice. The reprobate appears in the doorway, graced beyond his alleged merits by the morning sunlight. He is certainly the best looking member of the family ; but his expression is reckless and sardonic, his manner defiant and satirical, his dress picturesquely careless. Only, his forehead and mouth betray an extraordinary steadfastness ; and his eyes are the eyes of a fanatic.

RICHARD [*on the threshold, taking off his hat*] Ladies and gentlemen : your servant, your very humble servant. [*With this comprehensive insult, he throws his hat to Christy with a suddenness that makes him jump like a negligent wicket keeper, and comes into the middle of the room, where he turns and deliberately surveys the company*]. How happy you all look ! how glad to see me ! [*He turns towards Mrs Dudgeon's chair ; and his lip rolls up horribly from his dog tooth as he meets her look of undisguised hatred*]. Well, mother : keeping up appearances as usual ? thats right, thats right. [*Judith pointedly moves away from his neighborhood to the other side of the kitchen, holding her skirt instinctively as if to save it from contamination. Uncle Titus promptly marks his approval of her action by rising from the sofa, and placing a chair for her to sit down upon*]. What ! Uncle William ! I havnt seen you since you gave up drinking. [*Poor Uncle William, shamed, would protest ; but Richard claps him heartily on his shoulder, adding*] you have given it up, havnt you ? [*releasing him with a playful push*] of course you have : quite right too : you overdid it. [*He turns away from Uncle*

William and makes for the sofa]. And now, where is that upright horsedealer Uncle Titus ? Uncle Titus : come forth. [*He comes upon him holding the chair as Judith sits down*]. As usual, looking after the ladies !

UNCLE TITUS [*indignantly*] Be ashamed of yourself, sir—

RICHARD [*interrupting him and shaking his hand in spite of him*] I am : I am ; but I am proud of my uncle—proud of all my relatives—[*again surveying them*] who could look at them and not be proud and joyful ? [*Uncle Titus, overborne, resumes his seat on the sofa. Richard turns to the table*]. Ah, Mr Anderson, still at the good work, still shepherding them. Keep them up to the mark, minister, keep them up to the mark. Come ! [*with a spring he seats himself on the table and takes up the decanter*] clink a glass with me, Pastor, for the sake of old times.

ANDERSON. You know, I think, Mr Dudgeon, that I do not drink before dinner.

RICHARD. You will, some day, Pastor : Uncle William used to drink before breakfast. Come : it will give your sermons unction. [*He smells the wine and makes a wry face*]. But do not begin on my mother's company sherry. I stole some when I was six years old ; and I have been a temperate man ever since. [*He puts the decanter down and changes the subject*]. So I hear you are married, Pastor, and that your wife has a most ungodly allowance of good looks.

ANDERSON [*quietly indicating Judith*] Sir : you are in the presence of my wife. [*Judith rises and stands with stony propriety*].

RICHARD [*quickly slipping down from the table with instinctive good manners*] Your servant, madam : no offence. [*He looks at her earnestly*]. You deserve your reputation ; but I'm sorry to see by your expression that youre a good woman. [*She looks shocked, and sits down amid a murmur of indignant sympathy from his relatives. Anderson, sensible enough to know that these demonstrations can only gratify and encourage a man who is deliberately trying to provoke them, remains perfectly goodhumored*]. All the same, Pastor, I respect you more than I did before. By the way, did I hear, or did I not, that our late lamented Uncle Peter, though unmarried, was a father?

UNCLE TITUS. He had only one irregular child, sir.

RICHARD. Only one! He thinks one a mere trifle! I blush for you, Uncle Titus.

ANDERSON. Mr Dudgeon: you are in the presence of your mother and her grief.

RICHARD. It touches me profoundly, Pastor. By the way, what has become of the irregular child?

ANDERSON [*pointing to Essie*] There, sir, listening to you.

RICHARD [*shocked into sincerity*] What! Why the devil didnt you tell me that before? Children suffer enough in this house without—[*He hurries remorsefully to Essie*]. Come, little cousin! never mind me: it was not meant to hurt you. [*She looks up gratefully at him. Her tearstained face affects him violently; and he bursts out, in a transport of wrath*] Who has been making her cry? Who has been ill-treating her? By God—

MRS DUDGEON [*rising and confronting him*] Silence your blasphemous tongue. I will bear no more of this. Leave my house.

RICHARD. How do you know it's your house until the will is read? [*They look at one another for a moment with intense hatred; and then she sinks, checkmated, into her chair. Richard goes boldly up past Anderson to the window, where he takes the railed chair in his hand*]. Ladies and gentlemen: as the eldest son of my late father, and the unworthy head of this household, I bid you welcome. By your leave, Minister Anderson: by your leave, Lawyer Hawkins. The head of the table for the head of the family. [*He places the chair at the table between the minister and the attorney; sits down between them; and addresses the assembly with a presidential air*]. We meet on a melancholy occasion: a father dead! an uncle actually hanged. and probably damned. [*He shakes his head deploringly. The relatives freeze with horror*]. Thats right: pull your longest faces [*his voice suddenly sweetens gravely as his glance lights on Essie*] provided only there is hope in the eyes of the child.

[*Briskly*] Now then, Lawyer Hawkins : business, business. Get on with the will, man.

TITUS. Do not let yourself be ordered or hurried, Mr Hawkins.

HAWKINS [*very politely and willingly*] Mr Dudgeon means no offence, I feel sure. I will not keep you one second, Mr Dudgeon. Just while I get my glasses—[*he fumbles for them. The Dudgeons look at one another with misgiving*].

RICHARD. Aha ! They notice your civility, Mr Hawkins. They are prepared for the worst. A glass of wine to clear your voice before you begin. [*He pours out one for him and hands it ; then pours one for himself*].

HAWKINS. Thank you, Mr Dudgeon. Your good health, sir.

RICHARD. Yours, sir. [*With the glass half way to his lips, he checks himself, giving a dubious glance at the wine, and adds, with quaint intensity*] Will anyone oblige me with a glass of water ?

Essie, who has been hanging on his every word and move-ment, rises stealthily and slips out behind Mrs Dudgeon through the bedroom door, returning presently with a jug and going out of the house as quietly as possible.

HAWKINS. The will is not exactly in proper legal phrase-ology.

RICHARD. No : my father died without the consolations of the law.

HAWKINS. Good again, Mr Dudgeon, good again. [*Preparing to read*] Are you ready, sir ?

RICHARD. Ready, aye ready. For what we are about to receive, may the Lord make us truly thankful. Go ahead.

HAWKINS [*reading*] " This is the last will and testament of me Timothy Dudgeon on my deathbed at Nevinstown on the road from Springtown to Websterbridge on this twenty-fourth day of September, one thousand seven hundred and seventy seven. I hereby revoke all former wills made by me and declare that I am of sound mind and know well what I am doing and that this is my real will according to my own wish and affections."

RICHARD [*glancing at his mother*] Aha !

HAWKINS [*shaking his head*] Bad phraseology, sir, wrong phraseology. " I give and bequeath a hundred pounds to my younger son Christopher Dudgeon, fifty pounds to be paid to him on the day of his marriage to Sarah Wilkins if she will have him, and ten pounds on the birth of each of his children up to the number of five."

RICHARD. How if she wont have him ?

CHRISTY. She will if I have fifty pounds.

RICHARD. Good, my brother. Proceed.

HAWKINS. " I give and bequeath to my wife Annie Dudgeon, born Annie Primrose "—you see he did not know the law, Mr Dudgeon : your mother was not born Annie : she was christened so—" an annuity of fifty-two pounds a year for life [*Mrs Dudgeon, with all eyes on her, holds herself convulsively rigid*] to be paid out of the interest on her own money "—there's a way to put it, Mr Dudgeon ! Her own money !

MRS DUDGEON. A very good way to put God's truth. It was every penny my own. Fifty-two pounds a year !

HAWKINS. " And I recommend her for her goodness and piety to the forgiving care of her children, having stood between them and her as far as I could to the best of my ability."

MRS DUDGEON. And this is my reward ! [*Raging inwardly*] You know what I think, Mr Anderson : you know the word I gave to it.

ANDERSON. It cannot be helped, Mrs Dudgeon. We must take what comes to us. [*To Hawkins*]. Go on, sir.

HAWKINS. " I give and bequeath my house at Webster-bridge with the land belonging to it and all the rest of my property soever to my eldest son and heir, Richard Dudgeon."

RICHARD. Oho ! The fatted calf, Minister, the fatted calf.

HAWKINS. " On these conditions—"

RICHARD. The devil ! Are there conditions ?

HAWKINS. " To wit : first, that he shall not let my

brother Peter's natural child starve or be driven by want
to an evil life."

RICHARD [*emphatically, striking his fist on the table*]
Agreed.

*Mrs Dudgeon, turning to look malignantly at Essie, misses
her and looks quickly round to see where she has moved to ;
then, seeing that she has left the room without leave, closes
her lips vengefully.*

HAWKINS. " Second, that he shall be a good friend to
my old horse Jim "—[*again shaking his head*] he should
have written James, sir.

RICHARD. James shall live in clover. Go on.

HAWKINS.—" and keep my deaf farm labourer Prodger
Feston in his service."

RICHARD. Prodger Feston shall get drunk every Saturday.

HAWKINS. " Third, that he make Christy a present on
his marriage out of the ornaments in the best room."

RICHARD [*holding up the stuffed birds*] Here you are,
Christy.

CHRISTY [*disappointed*] I'd rather have the china peacocks.

RICHARD. You shall have both. [*Christy is greatly
pleased*]. Go on.

HAWKINS. " Fourthly and lastly, that he try to live at
peace with his mother as far as she will consent to it."

RICHARD [*dubiously*] Hm ! Anything more, Mr Hawkins?

HAWKINS [*solemnly*] " Finally I give and bequeath my
soul into my Maker's hands, humbly asking forgiveness for
all my sins and mistakes, and hoping that He will so guide
my son that it may not be said that I have done wrong in
trusting to him rather than to others in the perplexity of my
last hour in this strange place."

ANDERSON. Amen.

THE UNCLES AND AUNTS. Amen.

RICHARD. My mother does not say Amen.

MRS DUDGEON [*rising, unable to give up her property
without a struggle*] Mr Hawkins : is that a proper will ?
Remember, I have his rightful, legal will, drawn up by
yourself, leaving all to me.

HAWKINS. This is a very wrongly and irregularly worded will, Mrs Dudgeon : though [*turning politely to Richard*] it contains in my judgment an excellent disposal of his property.

ANDERSON [*interposing before Mrs Dudgeon can retort*] That is not what you are asked, Mr Hawkins. Is it a legal will ?

HAWKINS. The courts will sustain it against the other.

ANDERSON. But why, if the other is more lawfully worded ?

HAWKINS. Because, sir, the courts will sustain the claim of a man—and that man the eldest son—against any woman, if they can. I warned you, Mrs Dudgeon, when you got me to draw that other will, that it was not a wise will, and that though you might make him sign it, he would never be easy until he revoked it. But you wouldnt take advice ; and now Mr Richard is cock of the walk. [*He takes his hat from the floor ; rises ; and begins pocketing his papers and spectacles*].

This is the signal for the breaking-up of the party. Anderson takes his hat from the rack and joins Uncle William at the fire. Titus fetches Judith her things from the rack. The three on the sofa rise and chat with Hawkins. Mrs Dudgeon, now an intruder in her own house, stands inert, crushed by the weight of the law on women, accepting it, as she has been trained to accept all monstrous calamities, as proofs of the greatness of the power that inflicts them, and of her own wormlike insignificance. For at this time, remember, Mary Wollstonecraft is as yet only a girl of eighteen, and her Vindication of the Rights of Women is still fourteen years off. Mrs Dudgeon is rescued from her apathy by Essie, who comes back with the jug full of water. She is taking it to Richard when Mrs Dudgeon stops her.

MRS DUDGEON [*threatening her*] Where have you been ? [*Essie, appalled, tries to answer, but cannot*]. How dare you go out by yourself after the orders I gave you ?

ESSIE. He asked for a drink—[*she stops, her tongue cleaving to her palate with terror*].

JUDITH [*with gentler severity*] Who asked for a drink? [*Essie, speechless, points to Richard*].

RICHARD. What! I!

JUDITH [*shocked*] Oh Essie, Essie!

RICHARD. I believe I did. [*He takes a glass and holds it to Essie to be filled. Her hand shakes*]. What! afraid of me?

ESSIE [*quickly*] No. I—[*She pours out the water*].

RICHARD [*tasting it*] Ah, youve been up the street to the market gate spring to get that. [*He takes a draught*]. Delicious! Thank you. [*Unfortunately, at this moment he chances to catch sight of Judith's face, which expresses the most prudish disapproval of his evident attraction for Essie, who is devouring him with her grateful eyes. His mocking expression returns instantly. He puts down the glass; deliberately winds his arm round Essie's shoulders; and brings her into the middle of the company. Mrs Dudgeon being in Essie's way as they come past the table, he says*] By your leave, mother [*and compels her to make way for them*]. What do they call you? Bessie?

ESSIE. Essie.

RICHARD. Essie, to be sure. Are you a good girl, Essie?

ESSIE [*greatly disappointed that he, of all people, should begin at her in this way*] Yes. [*She looks doubtfully at Judith*]. I think so. I mean I—I hope so.

RICHARD. Essie: did you ever hear of a person called the devil?

ANDERSON [*revolted*] Shame on you, sir, with a mere child—

RICHARD. By your leave, Minister: I do not interfere with your sermons: do not you interrupt mine. [*To Essie*] Do you know what they call me, Essie?

ESSIE. Dick.

RICHARD [*amused: patting her on the shoulder*] Yes, Dick; but something else too. They call me the Devil's Disciple.

ESSIE. Why do you let them?

RICHARD [*seriously*] Because it's true. I was brought up in the other service; but I knew from the first that the

Devil was my natural master and captain and friend. I
saw that he was in the right, and that the world cringed to
his conqueror only through fear. I prayed secretly to him ;
and he comforted me, and saved me from having my spirit
broken in this house of children's tears. I promised him
my soul, and swore an oath that I would stand up for him
in this world and stand by him in the next. [*Solemnly*]
That promise and that oath made a man of me. From this
day this house is his home ; and no child shall cry in it :
this hearth is his altar ; and no soul shall ever cower over
it in the dark evenings and be afraid. Now [*turning forcibly
on the rest*] which of you good men will take this child and
rescue her from the house of the devil ?

JUDITH [*coming to Essie and throwing a protecting arm
about her*] I will. You should be burnt alive.

ESSIE. But I dont want to. [*She shrinks back, leaving
Richard and Judith face to face*].

RICHARD [*to Judith*] Actually doesnt want to, most
virtuous lady !

UNCLE TITUS. Have a care, Richard Dudgeon. The law—

RICHARD [*turning threateningly on him*] Have a care, you.
In an hour from this there will be no law here but martial
law. I passed the soldiers within six miles on my way here :
before noon Major Swindon's gallows for rebels will be up
in the market place.

ANDERSON [*calmly*] What have we to fear from that, sir ?

RICHARD. More than you think. He hanged the wrong
man at Springtown: he thought Uncle Peter was respectable,
because the Dudgeons had a good name. But his next
example will be the best man in the town to whom he can
bring home a rebellious word. Well, we're all rebels ; and
you know it.

ALL THE MEN [*except Anderson*] No, no, no !

RICHARD. Yes, you are. You havnt damned King
George up hill and down dale as I have ; but youve prayed
for his defeat ; and you, Anthony Anderson, have conducted the service, and sold your family bible to buy a pair
of pistols. They maynt hang me, perhaps ; because the

moral effect of the Devil's Disciple dancing on nothing wouldnt help them. But a minister ! [*Judith, dismayed, clings to Anderson*] or a lawyer ! [*Hawkins smiles like a man able to take care of himself*] or an upright horsedealer ! [*Uncle Titus snarls at him in rage and terror*] or a reformed drunkard ! [*Uncle William, utterly unnerved, moans and wobbles with fear*] eh ? Would that shew that King George meant business—ha ?

ANDERSON [*perfectly self-possessed*] Come, my dear : he is only trying to frighten you. There is no danger. [*He takes her out of the house. The rest crowd to the door to follow him, except Essie, who remains near Richard*].

RICHARD [*boisterously derisive*] Now then : how many of you will stay with me ; run up the American flag on the devil's house ; and make a fight for freedom ? [*They scramble out, Christy among them, hustling one another in their haste*] Ha ha ! Long live the devil ! [*To Mrs Dudgeon, who is following them*] What, mother ! Are you off too ?

MRS DUDGEON [*deadly pale, with her hand on her heart as if she had received a deathblow*] My curse on you ! My dying curse ! [*She goes out*].

RICHARD [*calling after her*] It will bring me luck. Ha ha ha !

ESSIE [*anxiously*] Maynt I stay ?

RICHARD [*turning to her*] What ! Have they forgotten to save your soul in their anxiety about their own bodies ? Oh yes : you may stay. [*He turns excitedly away again and shakes his fist after them. His left fist, also clenched, hangs down. Essie seizes it and kisses it, her tears falling on it. He starts and looks at it*]. Tears ! The devil's baptism ! [*She falls on her knees, sobbing. He stoops good-naturedly to raise her, saying*] Oh yes, you may cry that way, Essie, if you like.

*Minister Anderson's house is in the main street of Webster-
bridge, not far from the town hall. To the eye of the eighteenth
century New Englander, it is much grander than the plain
farmhouse of the Dudgeons ; but it is so plain itself that a
modern house agent would let both at about the same rent.
The chief dwelling room has the same sort of kitchen fireplace,
with boiler, toaster hanging on the bars, movable iron griddle
socketed to the hob, hook above for roasting, and broad
fender, on which stand a kettle and a plate of buttered toast.
The door, between the fireplace and the corner, has neither
panels, fingerplates nor handles : it is made of plain boards,
and fastens with a latch. The table is a kitchen table, with
a treacle colored cover of American cloth, chapped at the
corners by draping. The tea service on it consists of two thick
cups and saucers of the plainest ware, with milk jug and bowl
to match, each large enough to contain nearly a quart, on a
black japanned tray, and, in the middle of the table, a wooden
trencher with a big loaf upon it, and a square half pound block
of butter in a crock. The big oak press facing the fire from
the opposite side of the room, is for use and storage, not for
ornament ; and the minister's house coat hangs on a peg
from its door, shewing that he is out ; for when he is in, it is
his best coat that hangs there. His big riding boots stand
beside the press, evidently in their usual place, and rather
proud of themselves. In fact, the evolution of the minister's
kitchen, dining room and drawing room into three separate
apartments has not yet taken place ; and so, from the point
of view of our pampered period, he is no better off than the
Dudgeons.*

*But there is a difference, for all that. To begin with, Mrs
Anderson is a pleasanter person to live with than Mrs Dudgeon.
To which Mrs Dudgeon would at once reply, with reason, that
Mrs Anderson has no children to look after ; no poultry, pigs
nor cattle ; a steady and sufficient income not directly
dependent on harvests and prices at fairs ; an affectionate*

husband who is a tower of strength to her : in short, that life is as easy at the minister's house as it is hard at the farm. This is true ; but to explain a fact is not to alter it ; and however little credit Mrs Anderson may deserve for making her home happier, she has certainly succeeded in doing it. The outward and visible signs of her superior social pretensions are, a drugget on the floor, a plaster ceiling between the timbers, and chairs which, though not upholstered, are stained and polished. The fine arts are represented by a mezzotint portrait of some Presbyterian divine, a copperplate of Raphael's St Paul preaching at Athens, a rococo presentation clock on the mantelshelf, flanked by a couple of miniatures, a pair of crockery dogs with baskets in their mouths, and, at the corners, two large cowrie shells. A pretty feature of the room is the low wide latticed window, nearly its whole width, with little red curtains running on a rod half way up it to serve as a blind. There is no sofa ; but one of the seats, standing near the press, has a railed back and is long enough to accommodate two people easily. On the whole, it is rather the sort of room that the nineteenth century has ended in struggling to get back to under the leadership of Mr Philip Webb and his disciples in domestic architecture, though no genteel clergyman would have tolerated it fifty years ago.

The evening has closed in ; and the room is dark except for the cosy firelight and the dim oil lamps seen through the window in the wet street, where there is a quiet, steady, warm, windless downpour of rain. As the town clock strikes the quarter, Judith comes in with a couple of candles in earthenware candlesticks, and sets them on the table. Her self-conscious airs of the morning are gone : she is anxious and frightened. She goes to the window and peers into the street. The first thing she sees there is her husband, hurrying home through the rain. She gives a little gasp of relief, not very far removed from a sob, and turns to the door. Anderson comes in, wrapped in a very wet cloak.

JUDITH [*running to him*] Oh, here you are at last, at last ! [*She attempts to embrace him*].

ANDERSON [*keeping her off*] Take care, my love : I'm wet. Wait till I get my cloak off. [*He places a chair with its back to the fire ; hangs his cloak on it to dry ; shakes the rain from his hat and puts it on the fender ; and at last turns with his hands outstretched to Judith*]. Now ! [*She flies into his arms*]. I am not late, am I ? The town clock struck the quarter as I came in at the front door. And the town clock is always fast.

JUDITH. I'm sure it's slow this evening. I'm so glad youre back.

ANDERSON [*taking her more closely in his arms*] Anxious, my dear ?

JUDITH. A little.

ANDERSON. Why, youve been crying.

JUDITH. Only a little. Never mind : it's all over now. [*A bugle call is heard in the distance. She starts in terror and retreats to the long seat, listening*]. What's that ?

ANDERSON [*following her tenderly to the seat and making her sit down with him*] Only King George, my dear. He's returning to barracks, or having his roll called, or getting ready for tea, or booting or saddling or something. Soldiers dont ring the bell or call over the banisters when they want anything : they send a boy out with a bugle to disturb the whole town.

JUDITH. Do you think there is really any danger ?

ANDERSON. Not the least in the world.

JUDITH. You say that to comfort me, not because you believe it.

ANDERSON. My dear : in this world there is always danger for those who are afraid of it. Theres a danger that the house will catch fire in the night ; but we shant sleep any the less soundly for that.

JUDITH. Yes, I know what you always say ; and youre quite right. Oh, quite right : I know it. But—I suppose I'm not brave : thats all. My heart shrinks every time I think of the soldiers.

ANDERSON. Never mind that, dear : bravery is none the worse for costing a little pain.

JUDITH. Yes, I suppose so. [*Embracing him again*] Oh how brave you are, my dear ! [*With tears in her eyes*] Well, I'll be brave too : you shant be ashamed of your wife.

ANDERSON. Thats right. Now you make me happy. Well, well ! [*He rises and goes cheerily to the fire to dry his shoes*]. I called on Richard Dudgeon on my way back ; but he wasnt in.

JUDITH [*rising in consternation*] You called on that man !

ANDERSON [*reassuring her*] Oh, nothing happened, dearie. He was out.

JUDITH [*almost in tears, as if the visit were a personal humiliation to her*] But why did you go there ?

ANDERSON [*gravely*] Well, it is all the talk that Major Swindon is going to do what he did in Springtown—make an example of some notorious rebel, as he calls us. He pounced on Peter Dudgeon as the worst character there ; and it is the general belief that he will pounce on Richard as the worst here.

JUDITH. But Richard said—

ANDERSON [*goodhumoredly cutting her short*] Pooh ! Richard said ! He said what he thought would frighten you and frighten me, my dear. He said what perhaps (God forgive him !) he would like to believe. It's a terrible thing to think of what death must mean for a man like that. I felt that I must warn him. I left a message for him.

JUDITH [*querulously*] What message ?

ANDERSON. Only that I should be glad to see him for a moment on a matter of importance to himself, and that if he would look in here when he was passing he would be welcome.

JUDITH [*aghast*] You asked that man to come here !

ANDERSON. I did.

JUDITH [*sinking on the seat and clasping her hands*] I hope he wont come ! Oh, I pray that he may not come !

ANDERSON. Why ? Dont you want him to be warned ?

JUDITH. He must know his danger. Oh, Tony, is it wrong to hate a blasphemer and a villain ? I do hate him. I cant get him out of my mind : I know he will bring harm

with him. He insulted you : he insulted me : he insulted
his mother.

ANDERSON [*quaintly*] Well, dear, lets forgive him ; and
then it wont matter.

JUDITH. Oh, I know it's wrong to hate anybody ; but—

ANDERSON [*going over to her with humorous tenderness*]
Come, dear, youre not so wicked as you think. The worst
sin towards our fellow creatures is not to hate them, but to
be indifferent to them ; thats the essence of inhumanity.
After all, my dear, if you watch people carefully, youll be
surprised to find how like hate is to love. [*She starts,
strangely touched—even appalled. He is amused at her*].
Yes : I'm quite in earnest. Think of how some of our
married friends worry one another, tax one another, are
jealous of one another, cant bear to let one another out of
sight for a day, are more like jailers and slave-owners than
lovers. Think of those very same people with their enemies,
scrupulous, lofty, self-respecting, determined to be independent of one another, careful of how they speak of one
another—pooh ! havnt you often thought that if they only
knew it, they were better friends to their enemies than to
their own husbands and wives ? Come : depend on it, my
dear, you are really fonder of Richard than you are of me,
if you only knew it. Eh !

JUDITH. Oh, dont say that : dont say that, Tony,
even in jest. You dont know what a horrible feeling it
gives me.

ANDERSON [*laughing*] Well, well : never mind, pet. He's
a bad man ; and you hate him as he deserves. And youre
going to make the tea, arnt you ?

JUDITH [*remorsefully*] Oh yes, I forgot. Ive been keeping
you waiting all this time. [*She goes to the fire and puts on
the kettle*].

ANDERSON [*going to the press and taking his coat off*]
Have you stitched up the shoulder of my old coat ?

JUDITH. Yes, dear. [*She goes to the table, and sets about
putting the tea into the teapot from the caddy*].

ANDERSON [*as he changes his coat for the older one hanging*

on the press, and replaces it by the one he has just taken off]
Did anyone call when I was out ?

JUDITH. No, only— [*Someone knocks at the door. With
a start which betrays her intense nervousness, she retreats to
the further end of the table with the tea caddy and spoon in
her hands, exclaiming*] Who's that ?

ANDERSON [*going to her and patting her encouragingly on
the shoulder*] All right, pet, all right. He wont eat you,
whoever he is. [*She tries to smile, and nearly makes herself
cry. He goes to the door and opens it. Richard is there,
without overcoat or cloak*]. You might have raised the latch
and come in, Mr Dudgeon. Nobody stands on much
ceremony with us. [*Hospitably*] Come in. [*Richard comes
in carelessly and stands at the table, looking round the room
with a slight pucker of his nose at the mezzotinted divine on
the wall. Judith keeps her eyes on the tea caddy*]. Is it still
raining ? [*He shuts the door*].

RICHARD. Raining like the very [*his eye catches Judith's
as she looks quickly and haughtily up*]—I beg your pardon ;
but [*shewing that his coat is wet*] you see— !

ANDERSON. Take it off, sir ; and let it hang before the
fire a while : my wife will excuse your shirtsleeves. Judith :
put in another spoonful of tea for Mr Dudgeon.

RICHARD [*eyeing him cynically*] The magic of property,
Pastor ! Are even you civil to me now that I have succeeded
to my father's estate ?

Judith throws down the spoon indignantly.

ANDERSON [*quite unruffled, and helping Richard off with
his coat*] I think, sir, that since you accept my hospitality,
you cannot have so bad an opinion of it. Sit down. [*With
the coat in his hand, he points to the railed seat. Richard,
in his shirtsleeves, looks at him half quarrelsomely for a
moment ; then, with a nod, acknowledges that the minister
has got the better of him, and sits down on the seat. Anderson
pushes his cloak into a heap on the seat of the chair at the
fire, and hangs Richard's coat on the back in its place*].

RICHARD. I come, sir, on your own invitation. You left
word you had something important to tell me.

ANDERSON. I have a warning which it is my duty to give you.

RICHARD [*quickly rising*] You want to preach to me. Excuse me : I prefer a walk in the rain [*he makes for his coat*].

ANDERSON [*stopping him*] Dont be alarmed, sir : I am no great preacher. You are quite safe. [*Richard smiles in spite of himself. His glance softens : he even makes a gesture of excuse. Anderson, seeing that he has tamed him, now addresses him earnestly*] Mr Dudgeon : you are in danger in this town.

RICHARD. What danger ?

ANDERSON. Your uncle's danger. Major Swindon's gallows.

RICHARD. It is you who are in danger. I warned you—

ANDERSON [*interrupting him goodhumoredly but authoritatively*] Yes, yes, Mr Dudgeon ; but they do not think so in the town. And even if I were in danger, I have duties here which I must not forsake. But you are a free man. Why should you run any risk ?

RICHARD. Do you think I should be any great loss, Minister ?

ANDERSON. I think that a man's life is worth saving, whoever it belongs to. [*Richard makes him an ironical bow. Anderson returns the bow humorously*]. Come : youll have a cup of tea, to prevent you catching cold ?

RICHARD. I observe that Mrs Anderson is not quite so pressing as you are, Pastor.

JUDITH [*almost stifled with resentment, which she has been expecting her husband to share and express for her at every insult of Richard's*] You are welcome for my husband's sake. [*She brings the teapot to the fireplace and sets it on the hob*].

RICHARD. I know I am not welcome for my own, madam. [*He rises*]. But I think I will not break bread here, Minister.

ANDERSON [*cheerily*] Give me a good reason for that.

RICHARD. Because there is something in you that I

respect, and that makes me desire to have you for my enemy.

ANDERSON. Thats well said. On those terms, sir, I will accept your enmity or any man's. Judith : Mr Dudgeon will stay to tea. Sit down : it will take a few minutes to draw by the fire. [*Richard glances at him with a troubled face ; then sits down with his head bent, to hide a convulsive swelling of his throat*]. I was just saying to my wife, Mr Dudgeon, that enmity— [*She grasps his hand and looks imploringly at him, doing both with an intensity that checks him at once*]. Well, well, I mustnt tell you, I see ; but it was nothing that need leave us worse friend—enemies, I mean. Judith is a great enemy of yours.

RICHARD. If all my enemies were like Mrs Anderson, I should be the best Christian in America.

ANDERSON [*gratified, patting her hand*] You hear that, Judith ? Mr Dudgeon knows how to turn a compliment.

The latch is lifted from without.

JUDITH [*starting*] Who is that ?

Christy comes in.

CHRISTY [*stopping and staring at Richard*] Oh, are you here ?

RICHARD. Yes. Begone, you fool : Mrs Anderson doesnt want the whole family to tea at once.

CHRISTY [*coming further in*] Mother's very ill.

RICHARD. Well, does she want to see me ?

CHRISTY. No.

RICHARD. I thought not.

CHRISTY. She wants to see the minister—at once.

JUDITH [*to Anderson*] Oh, not before youve had some tea.

ANDERSON. I shall enjoy it more when I come back, dear. [*He is about to take up his cloak*].

CHRISTY. The rain's over.

ANDERSON [*dropping the cloak and picking up his hat from the fender*] Where is your mother, Christy ?

CHRISTY. At Uncle Titus's.

ANDERSON. Have you fetched the doctor ?

CHRISTY. No : she didnt tell me to.

ANDERSON. Go on there at once : I'll overtake you on his doorstep. [*Christy turns to go*]. Wait a moment. Your brother must be anxious to know the particulars.

RICHARD. Psha ! not I : he doesnt know ; and I dont care. [*Violently*] Be off, you oaf. [*Christy runs out. Richard adds, a little shamefacedly*] We shall know soon enough.

ANDERSON. Well, perhaps you will let me bring you the news myself. Judith : will you give Mr Dudgeon his tea, and keep him here until I return.

JUDITH [*white and trembling*] Must I—

ANDERSON [*taking her hands and interrupting her to cover her agitation*] My dear : I can depend on you ?

JUDITH [*with a piteous effort to be worthy of his trust*] Yes.

ANDERSON [*pressing her hand against his cheek*] You will not mind two old people like us, Mr Dudgeon. [*Going*] I shall not say good evening : you will be here when I come back. [*He goes out*].

They watch him pass the window, and then look at each other dumbly, quite disconcerted. Richard, noting the quiver of her lips, is the first to pull himself together.

RICHARD. Mrs Anderson : I am perfectly aware of the nature of your sentiments towards me. I shall not intrude on you. Good evening. [*Again he starts for the fireplace to get his coat*].

JUDITH [*getting between him and the coat*] No, no. Dont go : please dont go.

RICHARD [*roughly*] Why ? You dont want me here.

JUDITH. Yes, I— [*Wringing her hands in despair*] Oh, if I tell you the truth, you will use it to torment me.

RICHARD [*indignantly*] Torment ! What right have you to say that ? Do you expect me to stay after that ?

JUDITH. I want you to stay ; but [*suddenly raging at him like an angry child*] it is not because I like you.

RICHARD. Indeed !

JUDITH. Yes : I had rather you did go than mistake me about that. I hate and dread you ; and my husband knows it. If you are not here when he comes back, he will believe that I disobeyed him and drove you away.

RICHARD [*ironically*] Whereas, of course, you have really been so kind and hospitable and charming to me that I only want to go away out of mere contrariness, eh?

Judith, unable to bear it, sinks on the chair and bursts into tears.

RICHARD. Stop, stop, stop, I tell you. Dont do that. [*Putting his hand to his breast as if to a wound*] He wrung my heart by being a man. Need you tear it by being a woman? Has he not raised you above my insults, like himself? [*She stops crying, and recovers herself somewhat, looking at him with a scared curiosity*]. There: thats right. [*Sympathetically*] Youre better now, arnt you? [*He puts his hand encouragingly on her shoulder. She instantly rises haughtily, and stares at him defiantly. He at once drops into his usual sardonic tone*]. Ah, thats better. You are yourself again: so is Richard. Well, shall we go to tea like a quiet respectable couple, and wait for your husband's return?

JUDITH [*rather ashamed of herself*] If you please. I—I am sorry to have been so foolish. [*She stoops to take up the plate of toast from the fender*].

RICHARD. I am sorry, for your sake, that I am—what I am. Allow me. [*He takes the plate from her and goes with it to the table*].

JUDITH [*following with the teapot*] Will you sit down? [*He sits down at the end of the table nearest the press. There is a plate and knife laid there. The other plate is laid near it: but Judith stays at the opposite end of the table, next the fire, and takes her place there, drawing the tray towards her*]. Do you take sugar?

RICHARD. No: but plenty of milk. Let me give you some toast. [*He puts some on the second plate, and hands it to her, with the knife. The action shews quickly how well he knows that she has avoided her usual place so as to be as far from him as possible*].

JUDITH [*consciously*] Thanks. [*She gives him his tea*]. Wont you help yourself?

RICHARD. Thanks. [*He puts a piece of toast on his own plate; and she pours out tea for herself*].

JUDITH [*observing that he tastes nothing*] Dont you like it ? You are not eating anything.

RICHARD. Neither are you.

JUDITH [*nervously*] I never care much for my tea. Please dont mind me.

RICHARD [*looking dreamily round*] I am thinking. It is all so strange to me. I can see the beauty and peace of this home : I think I have never been more at rest in my life than at this moment ; and yet I know quite well I could never live here. It's not in my nature, I suppose, to be domesticated. But it's very beautiful : it's almost holy. [*He muses a moment, and then laughs softly*].

JUDITH [*quickly*] Why do you laugh ?

RICHARD. I was thinking that if any stranger came in here now, he would take us for man and wife.

JUDITH [*taking offence*] You mean, I suppose, that you are more my age than he is.

RICHARD [*staring at this unexpected turn*] I never thought of such a thing. [*Sardonic again*]. I see there is another side to domestic joy.

JUDITH [*angrily*] I would rather have a husband whom everybody respects than—than—

RICHARD. Than the devil's disciple. You are right ; but I daresay your love helps him to be a good man, just as your hate helps me to be a bad one.

JUDITH. My husband has been very good to you. He has forgiven you for insulting him, and is trying to save you. Can you not forgive him for being so much better than you are ? How dare you belittle him by putting yourself in his place ?

RICHARD. Did I ?

JUDITH. Yes, you did. You said that if anybody came in they would take us for man and— [*She stops, terror-stricken, as a squad of soldiers tramps past the window*]. The English soldiers ! Oh, what do they—

RICHARD [*listening*] Sh !

A VOICE [*outside*] Halt ! Four outside : two in with me. *Judith half rises, listening and looking with dilated eyes at*

*Richard, who takes up his cup prosaically, and is drinking his
tea when the latch goes up with a sharp click, and an English
sergeant walks into the room with two privates, who post
themselves at the door. He comes promptly to the table
between them.*

THE SERGEANT. Sorry to disturb you, mum. Duty!
Anthony Anderson : I arrest you in King George's name
as a rebel.

JUDITH [*pointing at Richard*] But that is not— [*He looks
up quickly at her, with a face of iron. She stops her mouth
hastily with the hand she has raised to indicate him, and stands
staring affrightedly*].

THE SERGEANT. Come, parson : put your coat on and
come along.

RICHARD. Yes : I'll come. [*He rises and takes a step
towards his own coat ; then recollects himself, and, with his
back to the sergeant, moves his gaze slowly round the room
without turning his head until he sees Anderson's black coat
hanging up on the press. He goes composedly to it ; takes
it down ; and puts it on. The idea of himself as a parson
tickles him : he looks down at the black sleeve on his arm,
and then smiles slyly at Judith, whose white face shews him
that what she is painfully struggling to grasp is not the humor
of the situation but its horror. He turns to the sergeant, who
is approaching him with a pair of handcuffs hidden behind
him, and says lightly*] Did you ever arrest a man of my cloth
before, Sergeant ?

THE SERGEANT [*instinctively respectful, half to the black
coat, and to Richard's good breeding*] Well, no sir. At least,
only an army chaplain. [*Shewing the handcuffs*]. I'm sorry
sir ; but duty—

RICHARD. Just so, Sergeant. Well, I'm not ashamed of
them : thank you kindly for the apology. [*He holds out
his hands*].

SERGEANT [*not availing himself of the offer*] One gentleman to another, sir. Wouldnt you like to say a word to
your missis, sir, before you go ?

RICHARD [*smiling*] Oh, we shall meet again before—eh ?

[*meaning " before you hang me "*].

SERGEANT [*loudly, with ostentatious cheerfulness*] Oh, of course, of course. No call for the lady to distress herself. Still— [*in a lower voice, intended for Richard alone*] your last chance, sir.

They look at one another significantly for a moment. Then Richard exhales a deep breath and turns towards Judith.

RICHARD [*very distinctly*] My love. [*She looks at him, pitiably pale, and tries to answer, but cannot—tries also to come to him, but cannot trust herself to stand without the support of the table*]. This gallant gentleman is good enough to allow us a moment of leavetaking. [*The sergeant retires delicately and joins his men near the door*]. He is trying to spare you the truth ; but you had better know it. Are you listening to me ? [*She signifies assent*]. Do you understand that I am going to my death ? [*She signifies that she understands*]. Remember, you must find our friend who was with us just now. Do you understand ? [*She signifies yes*]. See that you get him safely out of harm's way. Dont for your life let him know of my danger ; but if he finds it out, tell him that he cannot save me : they would hang him ; and they would not spare me. And tell him that I am steadfast in my religion as he is in his, and that he may depend on me to the death. [*He turns to go, and meets the eyes of the sergeant, who looks a little suspicious. He considers a moment, and then, turning roguishly to Judith with something of a smile breaking through his earnestness, says*] And now, my dear, I am afraid the sergeant will not believe that you love me like a wife unless you give one kiss before I go.

He approaches her and holds out his arms. She quits the table and almost falls into them.

JUDITH [*the words choking her*] I ought to—it's murder—
RICHARD. No : only a kiss [*softly to her*] for his sake.
JUDITH. I cant. You must—
RICHARD [*folding her in his arms with an impulse of compassion for her distress*] My poor girl !

Judith, with a sudden effort, throws her arms round him ;

kisses him ; and swoons away, dropping from his arms to the ground as if the kiss had killed her.

RICHARD [*going quickly to the sergeant*] Now, Sergeant : quick, before she comes to. The handcuffs. [*He puts out his hands*].

SERGEANT [*pocketing them*] Never mind, sir : I'll trust you. Youre a game one. You ought to a bin a soldier, sir. Between them two, please. [*The soldiers place themselves one before Richard and one behind him. The sergeant opens the door*].

RICHARD [*taking a last look round him*] Goodbye, wife : goodbye, home. Muffle the drums, and quick march !

*The sergeant signs to the leading soldier to march. They file out quickly.*******************When Anderson returns from Mrs Dudgeon's, he is astonished to find the room apparently empty and almost in darkness except for the glow from the fire ; for one of the candles has burnt out, and the other is at its last flicker.*

ANDERSON. Why, what on earth— ? [*Calling*] Judith, Judith ! [*He listens : there is no answer*]. Hm ! [*He goes to the cupboard ; takes a candle from the drawer ; lights it at the flicker of the expiring one on the table ; and looks wonderingly at the untasted meal by its light. Then he sticks it in the candlestick ; takes off his hat ; and scratches his head, much puzzled. This action causes him to look at the floor for the first time ; and there he sees Judith lying motionless with her eyes closed. He runs to her and stoops beside her, lifting her head*]. Judith.

JUDITH [*waking ; for her swoon has passed into the sleep of exhaustion after suffering*] Yes. Did you call ? Whats the matter ?

ANDERSON. Ive just come in and found you lying here with the candles burnt out and the tea poured out and cold. What has happened ?

JUDITH [*still astray*] I dont know. Have I been asleep ? I suppose— [*She stops blankly*], I dont know.

ANDERSON [*groaning*] Heaven forgive me, I left you alone with that scoundrel. [*Judith remembers. With an agonized cry, she clutches his shoulders and drags herself to her feet as he rises with her. He clasps her tenderly in his arms*]. My poor pet !

JUDITH [*frantically clinging to him*] What shall I do ? Oh my God, what shall I do ?

ANDERSON. Never mind, never mind, my dearest dear : it was my fault. Come : youre safe now ; and youre not hurt, are you ? [*He takes his arms from her to see whether she can stand*]. There : thats right, thats right. If only you are not hurt, nothing else matters.

JUDITH. No, no, no : I'm not hurt.

ANDERSON. Thank Heaven for that ! Come now : [*leading her to the railed seat and making her sit down beside him*] sit down and rest : you can tell me about it tomorrow. Or [*misunderstanding her distress*] you shall not tell me at all if it worries you. There, there ! [*Cheerfully*] I'll make you some fresh tea : that will set you up again. [*He goes to the table, and empties the teapot into the slop bowl*].

JUDITH [*in a strained tone*] Tony.

ANDERSON. Yes, dear ?

JUDITH. Do you think we are only in a dream now ?

ANDERSON [*glancing round at her for a moment with a pang of anxiety, though he goes on steadily and cheerfully putting fresh tea into the pot*] Perhaps so, pet. But you may as well dream a cup of tea when youre about it.

JUDITH. Oh stop, stop. You dont know— [*Distracted, she buries her face in her knotted hands*].

ANDERSON [*breaking down and coming to her*] My dear, what is it ? I cant bear it any longer : you must tell me. It was all my fault : I was mad to trust him.

JUDITH. No : dont say that. You mustnt say that. He —oh no, no : I cant. Tony : dont speak to me. Take my hands—both my hands. [*He takes them, wondering*]. Make me think of you, not of him. Theres danger, frightful danger ; but it is your danger ; and I cant keep thinking of it : I cant, I cant : my mind goes back to his danger. He must be saved—no : you must be saved : you, you, you. [*She springs up as if to do something or go somewhere, exclaiming*] Oh, Heaven help me !

ANDERSON [*keeping his seat and holding her hands with resolute composure*] Calmly, calmly, my pet. Youre quite distracted.

JUDITH. I may well be. I dont know what to do. I dont know what to do. [*Tearing her hands away*]. I must save him. [*Anderson rises in alarm as she runs wildly to the door. It is opened in her face by Essie, who hurries in full of anxiety. The surprise is so disagreeable to Judith that it brings her to her senses. Her tone is sharp and angry as she demands*] What do you want ?

ESSIE. I was to come to you.

ANDERSON. Who told you to ?

ESSIE [*staring at him, as if his presence astonished her*] Are you here ?

JUDITH. Of course. Dont be foolish, child.

ANDERSON. Gently, dearest : youll frighten her. [*Going between them*]. Come here, Essie. [*She comes to him*]. Who sent you ?

ESSIE. Dick. He sent me word by a soldier. I was to come here at once and do whatever Mrs Anderson told me.

ANDERSON [*enlightened*] A soldier ! Ah, I see it all now ! They have arrested Richard. [*Judith makes a gesture of despair*].

ESSIE. No. I asked the soldier. Dick's safe. But the soldier said you had been taken.

ANDERSON. I ! [*Bewildered, he turns to Judith for an explanation*].

JUDITH [*coaxingly*] All right, dear : I understand. [*To Essie*] Thank you, Essie, for coming : but I dont need you now. You may go home.

ESSIE [*suspicious*] Are you sure Dick has not been touched? Perhaps he told the soldier to say it was the minister. [*Anxiously*] Mrs Anderson : do you think it can have been that ?

ANDERSON. Tell her the truth if it is so, Judith. She will learn it from the first neighbor she meets in the street. [*Judith turns away and covers her eyes with her hands*].

ESSIE [*wailing*] But what will they do to him? Oh, what will they do to him? Will they hang him? [*Judith shudders convulsively, and throws herself into the chair in which Richard sat at the tea table*].

ANDERSON [*patting Essie's shoulder and trying to comfort her*] I hope not. I hope not. Perhaps if youre very quiet and patient, we may be able to help him in some way.

ESSIE. Yes—help him—yes, yes, yes. I'll be good.

ANDERSON. I must go to him at once, Judith.

JUDITH [*springing up*] Oh no. You must go away—far away, to some place of safety.

ANDERSON. Pooh!

JUDITH [*passionately*] Do you want to kill me? Do you think I can bear to live for days and days with every knock at the door—every footstep—giving me a spasm of terror? to lie awake for nights and nights in an agony of dread, listening for them to come and arrest you?

ANDERSON. Do you think it would be better to know that I had run away from my post at the first sign of danger?

JUDITH [*bitterly*] Oh, you wont go. I know it. Youll stay; and I shall go mad.

ANDERSON. My dear, your duty—

JUDITH [*fiercely*] What do I care about my duty?

ANDERSON [*shocked*] Judith!

JUDITH. I am doing my duty. I am clinging to my duty. My duty is to get you away, to save you, to leave him to his fate [*Essie utters a cry of distress and sinks on the chair at the fire, sobbing silently*] My instinct is the same as hers—to save him above all things, though it would be so much better for him to die! so much greater! But I know you will take your own way as he took it. I have no power. [*She sits down sullenly on the railed seat*] I'm only a woman: I can do nothing but sit here and suffer. Only, tell him I tried to save you—that I did my best to save you.

ANDERSON. My dear, I am afraid he will be thinking more of his own danger than of mine.

JUDITH. Stop; or I shall hate you.

ANDERSON [*remonstrating*] Come, come, come! How

am I to leave you if you talk like this ? You are quite out of your senses. [*He turns to Essie*] Essie.

ESSIE [*eagerly rising and drying her eyes*] Yes ?

ANDERSON. Just wait outside a moment, like a good girl : Mrs Anderson is not well. [*Essie looks doubtful*]. Never fear : I'll come to you presently ; and I'll go to Dick.

ESSIE. You are sure you will go to him ? [*Whispering*]. You wont let her prevent you ?

ANDERSON [*smiling*] No, no : it's all right. All right. [*She goes*]. Thats a good girl. [*He closes the door, and returns to Judith*].

JUDITH [*seated—rigid*] You are going to your death.

ANDERSON [*quaintly*] Then I shall go in my best coat, dear. [*He turns to the press, beginning to take off his coat*]. Where—? [*He stares at the empty nail for a moment ; then looks quickly round to the fire ; strides across to it ; and lifts Richard's coat*]. Why, my dear, it seems that he has gone in my best coat.

JUDITH [*still motionless*] Yes.

ANDERSON. Did the soldiers make a mistake ?

JUDITH. Yes : they made a mistake.

ANDERSON. He might have told them. Poor fellow, he was too upset, I suppose.

JUDITH. Yes : he might have told them. So might I.

ANDERSON. Well, it's all very puzzling—almost funny. It's curious how these little things strike us even in the most— [*He breaks off and begins putting on Richard's coat*] I'd better take him his own coat. I know what he'll say— [*imitating Richard's sardonic manner*] " Anxious about my soul, Pastor, and also about your best coat." Eh ?

JUDITH. Yes, that is just what he will say to you. [*Vacantly*] It doesnt matter : I shall never see either of you again.

ANDERSON [*rallying her*] Oh pooh, pooh, pooh ! [*He sits down beside her*]. Is this how you keep your promise that I shant be ashamed of my brave wife ?

JUDITH. No : this is how I break it. I cannot keep my promises to him : why should I keep my promises to you ?

ANDERSON. Dont speak so strangely, my love. It sounds insincere to me. [*She looks unutterable reproach at him*]. Yes, dear, nonsense is always insincere ; and my dearest is talking nonsense. Just nonsense. [*Her face darkens into dumb obstinacy. She stares straight before her, and does not look at him again, absorbed in Richard's fate. He scans her face ; sees that his rallying has produced no effect ; and gives it up, making no further effort to conceal his anxiety*]. I wish I knew what has frightened you so. Was there a struggle ? Did he fight ?

JUDITH. No. He smiled.

ANDERSON. Did he realize his danger, do you think ?

JUDITH. He realized yours.

ANDERSON. Mine !

JUDITH [*monotonously*] He said " See that you get him safely out of harm's way." I promised : I cant keep my promise. He said, " Dont for your life let him know of my danger." Ive told you of it. He said that if you found it out, you could not save him—that they will hang him and not spare you.

ANDERSON [*rising in generous indignation*] And you think that I will let a man with that much good in him die like a dog, when a few words might make him die like a Christian. I'm ashamed of you, Judith.

JUDITH. He will be steadfast in his religion as you are in yours ; and you may depend on him to the death. He said so.

ANDERSON. God forgive him ! What else did he say ?

JUDITH. He said goodbye.

ANDERSON [*fidgeting nervously to and fro in great concern*] Poor fellow, poor fellow ! You said goodbye to him in all kindness and charity, Judith, I hope.

JUDITH. I kissed him.

ANDERSON. What ! Judith !

JUDITH. Are you angry ?

ANDERSON. No, no. You were right : you were right. Poor fellow, poor fellow ! [*Greatly distressed*] To be hanged like that at his age ! And then did they take him away ?

JUDITH [*wearily*] Then you were here : thats the next
thing I remember. I suppose I fainted. Now bid me goodbye, Tony. Perhaps I shall faint again. I wish I could die.

ANDERSON. No, no, my dear : you must pull yourself
together and be sensible. I am in no danger—not the least
in the world.

JUDITH [*solemnly*] You are going to your death, Tony—
your sure death, if God will let innocent men be murdered.
They will not let you see him : they will arrest you the
moment you give your name. It was for you the soldiers
came.

ANDERSON [*thunderstruck*] For me !!! [*His fists clinch;
his neck thickens ; his face reddens ; the fleshy purses under
his eyes become injected with hot blood ; the man of peace
vanishes, transfigured into a choleric and formidable man of
war. Still, she does not come out of her absorption to look
at him : her eyes are steadfast wtih a mechanical reflection
of Richard's steadfastness*].

JUDITH. He took your place : he is dying to save you.
That is why he went in your coat. That is why I kissed him.

ANDERSON [*exploding*] Blood an' owns ! [*His voice is
rough and dominant, his gesture full of brute energy*]. Here !
Essie, Essie !

ESSIE [*running in*] Yes.

ANDERSON [*impetuously*] Off with you as hard as you can
run, to the inn. Tell them to saddle the fastest and strongest
horse they have [*Judith rises breathless, and stares at him
incredulously*]—the chestnut mare, if she's fresh—without a
moment's delay. Go into the stable yard and tell the black
man there that I'll give him a silver dollar if the horse is
waiting for me when I come, and that I am close on your
heels. Away with you. [*His energy sends Essie flying from
the room. He pounces on his riding boots ; rushes with them
to the chair at the fire ; and begins pulling them on*].

JUDITH [*unable to believe such a thing of him*] You are
not going to him !

ANDERSON [*busy with the boots*] Going to him ! What
good would that do ? [*Growling to himself as he gets the*

first boot on with a wrench] I'll go to them, so I will. [*To Judith peremptorily*] Get me the pistols : I want them. And money, money : I want money—all the money in the house. [*He stoops over the other boot, grumbling*]. A great satisfaction it would be to him to have my company on the gallows. [*He pulls on the boot*].

JUDITH. You are deserting him, then ?

ANDERSON. Hold your tongue, woman ; and get me the pistols. [*She goes to the press and takes from it a leather belt with two pistols, a powder horn, and a bag of bullets attached to it. She throws it on the table. Then she unlocks a drawer in the press and takes out a purse. Anderson grabs the belt and buckles it on, saying*] If they took him for me in my coat, perhaps theyll take me for him in his. [*Hitching the belt into its place*] Do I look like him ?

JUDITH [*turning with the purse in her hand*] Horribly unlike him.

ANDERSON [*snatching the purse from her and emptying it on the table*] Hm ! We shall see.

JUDITH [*sitting down helplessly*] Is it of any use to pray, do you think, Tony ?

ANDERSON [*counting the money*] Pray ! Can we pray Swindon's rope off Richard's neck ?

JUDITH. God may soften Major Swindon's heart.

ANDERSON [*contemptuously—pocketing a handful of money*] Let him, then. I am not God ; and I must go to work another way. [*Judith gasps at the blasphemy. He throws the purse on the table*]. Keep that. Ive taken 25 dollars.

JUDITH. Have you forgotten even that you are a minister?

ANDERSON. Minister be—faugh ! My hat : wheres my hat ? [*He snatches up hat and cloak, and puts both on in hot haste*] Now listen, you. If you can get a word with him by pretending youre his wife, tell him to hold his tongue until morning : that will give me all the start I need.

JUDITH [*solemnly*] You may depend on him to the death.

ANDERSON. Youre a fool, a fool, Judith. [*For a moment checking the torrent of his haste, and speaking with something of his old quiet and impressive conviction*] You dont know the man youre married to. [*Essie returns. He swoops at her at once*]. Well : is the horse ready ?

ESSIE [*breathless*] It will be ready when you come.

ANDERSON. Good. [*He makes for the door*].

JUDITH [*rising and stretching out her arms after him involuntarily*] Wont you say goodbye ?

ANDERSON. And waste another half minute ! Psha ! [*He rushes out like an avalanche*].

ESSIE [*hurrying to Judith*] He has gone to save Richard, hasnt he ?

JUDITH. To save Richard ! No : Richard has saved him. He has gone to save himself. Richard must die.

Essie screams with terror and falls on her knees, hiding her face. Judith, without heeding her, looks rigidly straight in front of her, at the vision of Richard, dying.

ACT III

Early next morning the sergeant, at the British head-
quarters in the Town Hall, unlocks the door of a little empty
panelled waiting room, and invites Judith to enter. She has
had a bad night, probably a rather delirious one; for even in
the reality of the raw morning, her fixed gaze comes back at
moments when her attention is not strongly held.

The sergeant considers that her feelings do her credit, and
is sympathetic in an encouraging military way. Being a fine
figure of a man, vain of his uniform and of his rank, he feels
specially qualified, in a respectful way, to console her.

SERGEANT. You can have a quiet word with him here,
mum.

JUDITH. Shall I have long to wait?

SERGEANT. No, mum, not a minute. We kep him in the
Bridewell for the night; and he's just been brought over
here for the court martial. Dont fret, mum: he slep like a
child, and has made a rare good breakfast.

JUDITH [incredulously] He is in good spirits!

SERGEANT. Tip top, mum. The chaplain looked in to
see him last night; and he won seventeen shillings off him
at spoil five. He spent it among us like the gentleman he is.
Duty's duty, mum, of course; but youre among friends
here. [The tramp of a couple of soldiers is heard approaching].
There: I think he's coming. [Richard comes in, without a
sign of care or captivity in his bearing. The sergeant nods to
the two soldiers, and shews them the key of the room in his
hand. They withdraw]. Your good lady, sir.

RICHARD [going to her] What! My wife. My adored
one. [He takes her hand and kisses it with a perverse, raffish
gallantry]. How long do you allow a brokenhearted husband for leave-taking, Sergeant?

SERGEANT. As long as we can, sir. We shall not disturb
you till the court sits.

RICHARD. But it has struck the hour.

SERGEANT. So it has, sir ; but theres a delay. General Burgoyne's just arrived—Gentlemanly Johnny we call him, sir—and he wont have done finding fault with everything this side of half past. I know him, sir : I served with him in Portugal. You may count on twenty minutes, sir ; and by your leave I wont waste any more of them. [*He goes out, locking the door. Richard immediately drops his raffish manner and turns to Judith with considerate sincerity*].

RICHARD. Mrs Anderson : this visit is very kind of you. And how are you after last night ? I had to leave you before you recovered ; but I sent word to Essie to go and look after you. Did she understand the message ?

JUDITH [*breathless and urgent*] Oh, dont think of me : I havnt come here to talk about myself. Are they going to to—[*meaning " to hang you "*] ?

RICHARD [*whimsically*] At noon, punctually. At least, that was when they disposed of Uncle Peter. [*She shudders*]. Is your husband safe ? Is he on the wing ?

JUDITH. He is no longer my husband.

RICHARD [*opening his eyes wide*] Eh ?

JUDITH. I disobeyed you. I told him everything. I expected him to come here and save you. I wanted him to come here and save you. He ran away instead.

RICHARD. Well, thats what I meant him to do. What good would his staying have done ? Theyd only have hanged us both.

JUDITH [*with reproachful earnestness*] Richard Dudgeon : on your honor, what would you have done in his place ?

RICHARD. Exactly what he has done, of course.

JUDITH. Oh, why will you not be simple with me—honest and straightforward ? If you are so selfish as that, why did you let them take you last night ?

RICHARD [*gaily*] Upon my life, Mrs Anderson, I dont know. Ive been asking myself that question ever since ; and I can find no manner of reason for acting as I did.

JUDITH. You know you did it for his sake, believing he was a more worthy man than yourself.

RICHARD [*laughing*] Oho ! No : thats a very pretty

reason, I must say ; but I'm not so modest as that. No : it wasnt for his sake.

JUDITH [*after a pause, during which she looks shame-facedly at him, blushing painfully*] Was it for my sake ?

RICHARD [*gallantly*] Well, you had a hand in it. It must have been a little for your sake. You let them take me, at all events.

JUDITH. Oh, do you think I have not been telling myself that all night ? Your death will be at my door. [*Impulsively, she gives him her hand, and adds, with intense earnestness*] If I could save you as you saved him, I would do it, no matter how cruel the death was.

RICHARD [*holding her hand and smiling, but keeping her almost at arms length*] I am very sure I shouldnt let you.

JUDITH. Dont you see that I can save you ?

RICHARD. How ? by changing clothes with me, eh ?

JUDITH [*disengaging her hand to touch his lips with it*] Dont [*meaning " Dont jest "*]. No : by telling the Court who you really are.

RICHARD [*frowning*] No use : they wouldnt spare me ; and it would spoil half his chance of escaping. They are determined to cow us by making an example of somebody on that gallows today. Well, let us cow them by showing that we can stand by one another to the death. That is the only force that can send Burgoyne back across the Atlantic and make America a nation.

JUDITH [*impatiently*] Oh, what does all that matter ?

RICHARD [*laughing*] True : what does it matter ? what does anything matter ? You see, men have these strange notions, Mrs Anderson ; and women see the folly of them.

JUDITH. Women have to lose those they love through them.

RICHARD. They can easily get fresh lovers.

JUDITH [*revolted*] Oh ! [*Vehemently*] Do you realize that you are going to kill yourself ?

RICHARD. The only man I have any right to kill, Mrs Anderson. Dont be concerned : no woman will lose her lover through my death. [*Smiling*] Bless you, nobody cares for me. Have you heard that my mother is dead?

JUDITH. Dead!

RICHARD. Of heart disease—in the night. Her last word to me was her curse: I dont think I could have borne her blessing. My other relatives will not grieve much on my account. Essie will cry for a day or two; but I have provided for her: I made my own will last night.

JUDITH [*stonily, after a moment's silence*] And I!

RICHARD [*surprised*] You?

JUDITH. Yes, I. Am I not to care at all?

RICHARD [*gaily and bluntly*] Not a scrap. Oh, you expressed your feelings towards me very frankly yesterday. What happened may have softened you for the moment; but believe me, Mrs Anderson, you dont like a bone in my skin or a hair on my head. I shall be as good a riddance at 12 today as I should have been at 12 yesterday.

JUDITH [*her voice trembling*] What can I do to shew you that you are mistaken.

RICHARD. Dont trouble. I'll give you credit for liking me a little better than you did. All I say is that my death will not break your heart.

JUDITH [*almost in a whisper*] How do you know? [*She puts her hands on his shoulders and looks intently at him*].

RICHARD [*amazed—divining the truth*] Mrs Anderson! [*The bell of the town clock strikes the quarter. He collects himself, and removes her hands, saying rather coldly*] Excuse me: they will be here for me presently. It is too late.

JUDITH. It is not too late. Call me as witness: they will never kill you when they know how heroically you have acted.

RICHARD [*with some scorn*] Indeed! But if I dont go through with it, where will the heroism be? I shall simply have tricked them; and theyll hang me for that like a dog. Serve me right too!

JUDITH [*wildly*] Oh, I believe you want to die.

RICHARD [*obstinately*] No I dont.

JUDITH. Then why not try to save yourself? I implore you—listen. You said just now that you saved him for my sake—yes [*clutching him as he recoils with a gesture of denial*] a little for my sake. Well, save yourself for my sake. And I will go with you to the end of the world.

RICHARD [*taking her by the wrists and holding her a little way from him, looking steadily at her*] Judith.

JUDITH [*breathless—delighted at the name*] Yes.

RICHARD. If I said—to please you—that I did what I did ever so little for your sake, I lied as men always lie to women. You know how much I have lived with worthless men—aye, and worthless women too. Well, they could all rise to some sort of goodness and kindness when they were in love [*the word love comes from him with true Puritan scorn*]. That has taught me to set very little store by the goodness that only comes out red hot. What I did last night, I did in cold blood, caring not half so much for your husband, or [*ruthlessly*] for you [*she droops, stricken*] as I do for myself. I had no motive and no interest : all I can tell you is that when it came to the point whether I would take my neck out of the noose and put another man's into it, I could not do it. I dont know why not : I see myself as a fool for my pains ; but I could not and I cannot. I have been brought up standing by the law of my own nature ; and I may not go against it, gallows or no gallows. [*She has slowly raised her head and is now looking full at him*]. I should have done the same for any other man in the town, or any other man's wife. [*Releasing her*] Do you understand that ?

JUDITH. Yes : you mean that you do not love me.

RICHARD [*revolted—with fierce contempt*] Is that all it means to you ?

JUDITH. What more—what worse—can it mean to me? [*The sergeant knocks. The blow on the door jars on her heart*]. Oh, one moment more. [*She throws herself on her knees*]. I pray to you—

RICHARD. Hush ! [*Calling*] Come in. [*The sergeant unlocks the door and opens it. The guard is with him*].

SERGEANT [*coming in*] Time's up, sir.

RICHARD. Quite ready, Sergeant. Now, my dear. [*He attempts to raise her*].

JUDITH [*clinging to him*] Only one thing more—I entreat, I implore you. Let me be present in the court. I have seen Major Swindon: he said I should be allowed if you asked it. You will ask it. It is my last request : I shall never ask you anything again. [*She clasps his knee*]. I beg and pray it of you.

RICHARD. If I do, will you be silent ?

JUDITH. Yes.

RICHARD. You will keep faith ?

JUDITH. I will keep—[*She breaks down, sobbing*].

RICHARD [*taking her arm to lift her*] Just—her other arm, Sergeant.

They go out, she sobbing convulsively, supported by the two men.

Meanwhile, the Council Chamber is ready for the court martial. It is a large, lofty room, with a chair of state in the middle under a tall canopy with a gilt crown, and maroon curtains with the royal monogram G.R. In front of the chair is a table, also draped in maroon, with a bell, a heavy ink-stand, and writing materials on it. Several chairs are set at the table. The door is at the right hand of the occupant of the chair of state when it has an occupant : at present it is empty. Major Swindon, a pale, sandy-haired, very conscientious looking man of about 45, sits at the end of the table with his back to the door, writing. He is alone until the sergeant announces the General in a subdued manner which suggests that Gentlemanly Johnny has been making his presence felt rather heavily.

SERGEANT. The General, sir.

Swindon rises hastily. The general comes in : the sergeant goes out. General Burgoyne is 55, and very well preserved. He is a man of fashion, gallant enough to have made a distinguished marriage by an elopement, witty enough to write successful comedies, aristocratically-connected enough to have had opportunities of high military distinction. His eyes, large, brilliant, apprehensive, and intelligent, are his most remarkable feature : without them his fine nose and small mouth would suggest rather more fastidiousness and less

*force than go to the making of a first rate general. Just now
the eyes are angry and tragic, and the mouth and nostrils tense.*

BURGOYNE. Major Swindon, I presume.

SWINDON. Yes. General Burgoyne, if I mistake not.
[*They bow to one another ceremoniously*]. I am glad to have
the support of your presence this morning. It is not par-
ticularly lively business, hanging this poor devil of a
minister.

BURGOYNE [*throwing himself into Swindon's chair*] No,
sir, it is not. It is making too much of the fellow to execute
him : what more could you have done if he had been a
member of the Church of England? Martyrdom, sir, is
what these people like : it is the only way in which a man
can become famous without ability. However, you have
committed us to hanging him ; and the sooner he is hanged
the better.

SWINDON. We have arranged it for 12 o'clock. Nothing
remains to be done except to try him.

BURGOYNE [*looking at him with suppressed anger*] Nothing—except to save your own necks, perhaps. Have you
heard the news from Springtown?

SWINDON. Nothing special. The latest reports are satisfactory.

BURGOYNE [*rising in amazement*] Satisfactory, sir ! Satisfactory !! [*He stares at him for a moment, and then adds,
with grim intensity*] I am glad you take that view of them.

SWINDON [*puzzled*] Do I understand that in your
opinion—

BURGOYNE. I do not express my opinion. I never stoop
to that habit of profane language which unfortunately
coarsens our profession. If I did, sir, perhaps I should be
able to express my opinion of the news from Springtown—
the news which you [*severely*] have apparently not heard.
How soon do you get news from your supports here ?—in
the course of a month, eh ?

SWINDON [*turning sulky*] I suppose the reports have been
taken to you, sir, instead of to me. Is there anything serious?

BURGOYNE [*taking a report from his pocket and holding it*

up] Springtown's in the hands of the rebels. [*He throws the report on the table*].

SWINDON [*aghast*] Since yesterday !

BURGOYNE. Since two o'clock this morning. Perhaps we shall be in their hands before two o'clock tomorrow morning. Have you thought of that ?

SWINDON [*confidently*] As to that, General, the British soldier will give a good account of himself.

BURGOYNE [*bitterly*] And therefore, I suppose, sir, the British officer need not know his business : the British soldier will get him out of all his blunders with the bayonet. In future, sir, I must ask you to be a little less generous with the blood of your men, and a little more generous with your own brains.

SWINDON. I am sorry I cannot pretend to your intellectual eminence, sir. I can only do my best, and rely on the devotion of my countrymen.

BURGOYNE [*suddenly becoming suavely sarcastic*] May I ask are you writing a melodrama, Major Swindon ?

SWINDON [*flushing*] No, sir.

BURGOYNE. What a pity ! What a pity ! [*Dropping his sarcastic tone and facing him suddenly and seriously*] Do you at all realize, sir, that we have nothing standing between us and destruction but our own bluff and the sheepishness of these colonists ? They are men of the same English stock as ourselves : six to one of us [*repeating it emphatically*] six to one, sir ; and nearly half our troops are Hessians, Brunswickers, German dragoons, and Indians with scalping knives. These are the countrymen on whose devotion you rely ! Suppose the colonists find a leader ! Suppose the news from Springtown should turn out to mean that they have already found a leader ! What shall we do then ? Eh ?

SWINDON [*sullenly*] Our duty, sir, I presume.

BURGOYNE [*again sarcastic—giving him up as a fool*] Quite so, quite so. Thank you, Major Swindon, thank you. Now youve settled the question, sir—thrown a flood of light on the situation. What a comfort to me to feel that

T.P.—4

I have at my side so devoted and able an officer to support me in this emergency ! I think, sir, it will probably relieve both our feelings if we proceed to hang this dissenter without further delay [*he strikes the bell*] especially as I am debarred by my principles from the customary military vent for my feelings. [*The sergeant appears*]. Bring your man in.

SERGEANT. Yes, sir.

BURGOYNE. And mention to any officer you may meet that the court cannot wait any longer for him.

SWINDON [*keeping his temper with difficulty*] The staff is perfectly ready, sir. They have been waiting your convenience for fully half an hour. Perfectly ready, sir.

BURGOYNE [*blandly*] So am I. [*Several officers come in and take their seats. One of them sits at the end of the table furthest from the door, and acts throughout as clerk of the court, making notes of the proceedings. The uniforms are those of the 9th, 20th, 21st, 24th, 47th, 53rd, and 62nd British Infantry. One officer is a Major General of the Royal Artillery. There are also German officers of the Hessian Rifles, and of German dragoon and Brunswicker regiments*]. Oh, good morning, gentlemen. Sorry to disturb you, I am sure. Very good of you to spare us a few moments.

SWINDON. Will you preside, sir ?

BURGOYNE [*becoming additionally polished, lofty, sarcastic, and urbane now that he is in public*] No, sir : I feel my own deficiencies too keenly to presume so far. If you will kindly allow me, I will sit at the feet of Gamaliel. [*He takes the chair at the end of the table next the door, and motions Swindon to the chair of state, waiting for him to be seated before sitting down himself*].

SWINDON [*greatly annoyed*] As you please, sir, I am only trying to do my duty under excessively trying circumstances. [*He takes his place in the chair of state*].

Burgoyne, relaxing his studied demeanor for the moment, sits down and begins to read the report with knitted brows and careworn looks, reflecting on his desperate situation and Swindon's uselessness. Richard is brought in. Judith walks beside him. Two soldiers precede and two follow him, with the sergeant in command. They cross the room to the wall opposite the door; but when Richard has just passed before the chair of state the sergeant stops him with a touch on the arm, and posts himself behind him, at his elbow. Judith stands timidly at the wall. The four soldiers place themselves in a squad near her.

BURGOYNE [*looking up and seeing Judith*] Who is that woman?

SERGEANT. Prisoner's wife, sir.

SWINDON [*nervously*] She begged me to allow her to be present; and I thought—

BURGOYNE [*completing the sentence for him ironically*] You thought it would be a pleasure for her. Quite so, quite so. [*Blandly*] Give the lady a chair; and make her thoroughly comfortable.

The sergeant fetches a chair and places it near Richard.

JUDITH. Thank you, sir. [*She sits down after an awe-stricken curtsy to Burgoyne, which he acknowledges by a dignified bend of his head*].

SWINDON [*to Richard, sharply*] Your name, sir?

RICHARD [*affable, but obstinate*] Come: you dont mean to say that youve brought me here without knowing who I am?

SWINDON. As a matter of form, sir, give your name.

RICHARD. As a matter of form then, my name is Anthony Anderson, Presbyterian minister in this town.

BURGOYNE [*interested*] Indeed! Pray, Mr Anderson, what do you gentlemen believe?

RICHARD. I shall be happy to explain if time is allowed me. I cannot undertake to complete your conversion in less than a fortnight.

SWINDON [*snubbing him*] We are not here to discuss your views.

BURGOYNE [*with an elaborate bow to the unfortunate Swindon*] I stand rebuked.

SWINDON [*embarrassed*] Oh, not you, I as—

BURGOYNE. Dont mention it. [*To Richard, very politely*] Any political views, Mr Anderson?

RICHARD. I understand that that is just what we are here to find out.

SWINDON [*severely*] Do you mean to deny that you are a rebel?

RICHARD. I am an American, sir.

SWINDON. What do you expect me to think of that speech, Mr Anderson?

RICHARD. I never expect a soldier to think, sir.

Burgoyne is boundlessly delighted by this retort, which almost reconciles him to the loss of America.

SWINDON [*whitening with anger*] I advise you not to be insolent, prisoner.

RICHARD. You cant help yourself, General. When you make up your mind to hang a man, you put yourself at a disadvantage with him. Why should I be civil to you? I may as well be hanged for a sheep as a lamb.

SWINDON. You have no right to assume that the court has made up its mind without a fair trial. And you will please not address me as General. I am Major Swindon.

RICHARD. A thousand pardons. I thought I had the honor of addressing Gentlemanly Johnny.

Sensation among the officers. The sergeant has a narrow escape from a guffaw.

BURGOYNE [*with extreme suavity*] I believe I am Gentlemanly Johnny, sir, at your service. My more intimate friends call me General Burgoyne. [*Richard bows with perfect politeness*]. You will understand, sir, I hope, since you seem to be a gentleman and a man of some spirit in spite of your calling, that if we should have the misfortune to hang you, we shall do so as a mere matter of political necessity and military duty, without any personal ill-feeling.

RICHARD. Oh, quite so. That makes all the difference in the world, of course.

They all smile in spite of themselves; and some of the younger officers burst out laughing.

JUDITH [*her dread and horror deepening at every one of these jests and compliments*] How can you?

RICHARD. You promised to be silent.

BURGOYNE [*to Judith, with studied courtesy*] Believe me, Madam, your husband is placing us under the greatest obligation by taking this very disagreeable business so thoroughly in the spirit of a gentleman. Sergeant : give Mr Anderson a chair. [*The sergeant does so. Richard sits down*]. Now, Major Swindon : we are waiting for you.

SWINDON. You are aware, I presume, Mr Anderson, of your obligations as a subject of His Majesty King George the Third.

RICHARD. I am aware, sir, that His Majesty King George the Third is about to hang me because I object to Lord North's robbing me.

SWINDON. That is a treasonable speech, sir.

RICHARD [*briefly*] Yes. I meant it to be.

BURGOYNE [*strongly deprecating this line of defence, but still polite*] Dont you think, Mr Anderson, that this is rather —if you will excuse the word—a vulgar line to take ? Why should you cry out robbery because of a stamp duty and a tea duty and so forth ? After all, it is the essence of your position as a gentleman that you pay with a good grace.

RICHARD. It is not the money, General. But to be swindled by a pig-headed lunatic like King George—

SWINDON [*scandalized*] Chut, sir—silence !

SERGEANT [*in stentorian tones, greatly shocked*] Silence !

BURGOYNE [*unruffled*] Ah, that is another point of view. My position does not allow of my going into that, except in private. But [*shrugging his shoulders*] of course, Mr Anderson, if you are determined to be hanged [*Judith flinches*] theres nothing more to be said. An unusual taste ! however [*with a final shrug*]— !

SWINDON [*To Burgoyne*] Shall we call witnesses ?

RICHARD. What need is there of witnesses ? If the towns-people here had listened to me, you would have found the streets barricaded, the houses loopholed, and the people in arms to hold the town against you to the last man. But you arrived, unfortunately, before we had got out of the talking stage ; and then it was too late.

SWINDON [*severely*] Well, sir, we shall teach you and your

townspeople a lesson they will not forget. Have you anything more to say?

RICHARD. I think you might have the decency to treat me as a prisoner of war, and shoot me like a man instead of hanging me like a dog.

BURGOYNE [*sympathetically*] Now there, Mr Anderson, you talk like a civilian, if you will excuse my saying so. Have you any idea of the average marksmanship of the army of His Majesty King George the Third? If we make you up a firing party, what will happen? Half of them will miss you : the rest will make a mess of the business and leave you to the provo-marshal's pistol. Whereas we can hang you in a perfectly workmanlike and agreeable way. [*Kindly*] Let me persuade you to be hanged, Mr Anderson?

JUDITH [*sick with horror*] My God!

RICHARD [*To Judith*] Your promise! [*To Burgoyne*] Thank you, General : that view of the case did not occur to me before. To oblige you, I withdraw my objection to the rope. Hang me, by all means.

BURGOYNE [*smoothly*] Will 12 o'clock suit you, Mr Anderson?

RICHARD. I shall be at your disposal then, General.

BURGOYNE [*rising*] Nothing more to be said, gentlemen. [*They all rise*].

JUDITH [*rushing to the table*] Oh, you are not going to murder a man like that, without a proper trial—without thinking of what you are doing—without— [*she cannot find words*].

RICHARD. Is this how you keep your promise?

JUDITH. If I am not to speak, you must. Defend yourself : save yourself : tell them the truth.

RICHARD [*worriedly*] I have told them truth enough to hang me ten times over. If you say another word you will risk other lives ; but you will not save mine.

BURGOYNE. My good lady, our only desire is to save unpleasantness. What satisfaction would it give you to have a solemn fuss made, with my friend Swindon in a black cap and so forth? I am sure we are greatly indebted to the admirable tact and gentlemanly feeling shewn by your husband.

JUDITH [*throwing the words in his face*] Oh, you are mad. Is it nothing to you what wicked thing you do if only you do it like a gentleman? Is it nothing to you whether you are a murderer or not, if only you murder in a red coat? [*Desperately*] You shall not hang him : that man is not my husband.

The officers look at one another, and whisper : some of the Germans asking their neighbors to explain what the woman had said. Burgoyne, who has been visibly shaken by Judith's reproach, recovers himself promptly at this new development. Richard meanwhile raises his voice above the buzz.

RICHARD. I appeal to you, gentlemen, to put an end to this. She will not believe that she cannot save me. Break up the court.

BURGOYNE [*in a voice so quiet and firm that it restores silence at once*] One moment, Mr Anderson. One moment, gentlemen. [*He resumes his seat. Swindon and the officers follow his example*]. Let me understand you clearly, madam. Do you mean that this gentleman is not your husband, or merely—I wish to put this with all delicacy—that you are not his wife?

JUDITH. I dont know what you mean. I say that he is not my husband—that my husband has escaped. This man took his place to save him. Ask anyone in the town—send out into the street for the first person you find there, and bring him in as a witness. He will tell you that the prisoner is not Anthony Anderson.

BURGOYNE [*quietly, as before*] Sergeant.

SERGEANT. Yes, sir.

BURGOYNE. Go out into the street and bring in the first townsman you see there.

SERGEANT [*making for the door*] Yes, sir.

BURGOYNE [*as the sergeant passes*] The first clean, sober townsman you see.

SERGEANT. Yes, sir. [*He goes out*].

BURGOYNE. Sit down, Mr Anderson—if I may call you so for the present. [*Richard sits down*]. Sit down, madam, whilst we wait. Give the lady a newspaper.

RICHARD [*indignantly*] Shame !

BURGOYNE [*keenly, with a half smile*] If you are not her husband, sir, the case is not a serious one—for he r [*Richard bites his lip, silenced*].

JUDITH [*to Richard, as she returns to her seat*] I couldnt help it. [*He shakes his head. She sits down*].

BURGOYNE. You will understand of course, Mr Anderson, that you must not build on this little incident. We are bound to make an example of somebody.

RICHARD. I quite understand. I suppose theres no use in my explaining.

BURGOYNE. I think we should prefer independent testimony, if you dont mind.

The sergeant, with a packet of papers in his hand, returns conducting Christy, who is much scared.

SERGEANT [*giving Burgoyne the packet*] Dispatches, sir. Delivered by a corporal of the 33rd. Dead beat with hard riding, sir.

Burgoyne opens the dispatches, and presently becomes absorbed in them. They are so serious as to take his attention completely from the court martial.

THE SERGEANT [*to Christy*] Now then. Attention ; and take your hat off. [*He posts himself in charge of Christy, who stands on Burgoyne's side of the court*].

RICHARD [*in his usual bullying tone to Christy*] Dont be frightened, you fool : youre only wanted as a witness. Theyre not going to hang you.

SWINDON. Whats your name ?

CHRISTY. Christy.

RICHARD [*impatiently*] Christopher Dudgeon, you blatant idiot. Give your full name.

SWINDON. Be silent, prisoner. You must not prompt the witness.

RICHARD. Very well. But I warn you youll get nothing out of him unless you shake it out of him. He has been too well brought up by a pious mother to have any sense or manhood left in him.

BURGOYNE [*springing up and speaking to the sergeant in a startling voice*] Where is the man who brought these?

SERGEANT. In the guard-room, sir.

Burgoyne goes out with a haste that sets the officers exchanging looks.

SWINDON [*to Christy*] Do you know Anthony Anderson, the Presbyterian minister?

CHRISTY. Of course I do [*implying that Swindon must be an ass not to know it*].

SWINDON. Is he here?

CHRISTY [*staring round*] I dont know.

SWINDON. Do you see him?

CHRISTY. No.

SWINDON. You seem to know the prisoner?

CHRISTY. Do you mean Dick?

SWINDON. Which is Dick?

CHRISTY [*pointing to Richard*] Him.

SWINDON. What is his name?

CHRISTY. Dick.

RICHARD. Answer properly, you jumping jackass. What do they know about Dick?

CHRISTY. Well, you are Dick, aint you? What am I to say?

SWINDON. Address me, sir; and do you, prisoner, be silent. Tell us who the prisoner is.

CHRISTY. He's my brother Dick — Richard — Richard Dudgeon.

SWINDON. Your brother!

CHRISTY. Yes.

SWINDON. You are sure he is not Anderson.

CHRISTY. Who?

RICHARD [*exasperatedly*] Me, me, me, you—

SWINDON. Silence, sir.

SERGEANT [*shouting*] Silence.

RICHARD [*impatiently*] Yah! [*To Christy*] He wants to know am I Minister Anderson. Tell him, and stop grinning like a zany.

CHRISTY [*grinning more than ever*] You Pastor Anderson! [*To Swindon*] Why, Mr Anderson's a minister—a very good man ; and Dick's a bad character : the respectable people wont speak to him. He's the bad brother : I'm the good one. [*The officers laugh outright. The soldiers grin*].

SWINDON. Who arrested this man ?

SERGEANT. I did, sir. I found him in the minister's house, sitting at tea with the lady with his coat off, quite at home. If he isnt married to her, he ought to be.

SWINDON. Did he answer to the minister's name ?

SERGEANT. Yes, sir, but not to a minister's nature. You ask the chaplain, sir.

SWINDON [*to Richard, threateningly*] So, sir, you have attempted to cheat us. And your name is Richard Dudgeon?

RICHARD. Youve found it out at last, have you ?

SWINDON. Dudgeon is a name well known to us, eh ?

RICHARD. Yes : Peter Dudgeon, whom you murdered, was my uncle.

SWINDON. Hm ! [*He compresses his lips, and looks at Richard with vindictive gravity*].

CHRISTY. Are they going to hang you, Dick ?

RICHARD. Yes. Get out : theyve done with you.

CHRISTY. And I may keep the china peacocks ?

RICHARD [*jumping up*] Get out. Get out, you blithering baboon, you. [*Christy flies, panicstricken*].

SWINDON [*rising—all rise*] Since you have taken the minister's place, Richard Dudgeon, you shall go through with it. The execution will take place at 12 o'clock as arranged ; and unless Anderson surrenders before then, you shall take his place on the gallows. Sergeant : take your man out.

JUDITH [*distracted*] No, no—

SWINDON [*fiercely, dreading a renewal of her entreaties*] Take that woman away.

RICHARD [*springing across the table with a tiger-like bound, and seizing Swindon by the throat*] You infernal scoundrel—

The sergeant rushes to the rescue from one side, the soldiers from the other. They seize Richard and drag him back to his place. Swindon, who has been thrown supine on the table, rises, arranging his stock. He is about to speak, when he is anticipated by Burgoyne, who has just appeared at the door with two papers in his hand : a white letter and a blue dispatch.

BURGOYNE [*advancing to the table, elaborately cool*] What is this ? Whats happening ? Mr Anderson : I'm astonished at you.

RICHARD. I am sorry I disturbed you, General. I merely wanted to strangle your understrapper there. [*Breaking out violently at Swindon*] Why do you raise the devil in me by bullying the woman like that ? You oatmeal faced dog, I'd twist your cursed head off with the greatest satisfaction. [*He puts out his hands to the sergeant*] Here : handcuff me, will you ; or I'll not undertake to keep my fingers off him.

The sergeant takes out a pair of handcuffs and looks to Burgoyne for instructions.

BURGOYNE. Have you addressed profane language to the lady, Major Swindon ?

SWINDON [*very angry*] No, sir, certainly not. That question should not have been put to me. I ordered the woman to be removed, as she was disorderly ; and the fellow sprang at me. Put away those handcuffs. I am perfectly able to take care of myself.

RICHARD. Now you talk like a man, I have no quarrel with you.

BURGOYNE. Mr Anderson—

SWINDON. His name is Dudgeon, sir, Richard Dudgeon. He is an impostor.

BURGOYNE [*brusquely*] Nonsense, sir : you hanged Dudgeon at Springtown.

RICHARD. It was my uncle, General.

BURGOYNE. Oh, your uncle. [*To Swindon, handsomely*] I beg your pardon, Major Swindon. [*Swindon acknowledges the apology stiffly. Burgoyne turns to Richard*]. We are somewhat unfortunate in our relations with your family.

Well, Mr Dudgeon, what I wanted to ask you is this. Who is [*reading the name from the letter*] William Maindeck Parshotter?

RICHARD. He is the Mayor of Springtown.

BURGOYNE. Is William—Maindeck and so on—a man of his word?

RICHARD. Is he selling you anything?

BURGOYNE. No.

RICHARD. Then you may depend on him.

BURGOYNE. Thank you, Mr—'m Dudgeon. By the way, since you are not Mr Anderson, do we still—eh, Major Swindon? [*meaning " do we still hang him? "*]

RICHARD. The arrangements are unaltered, General.

BURGOYNE. Ah, indeed. I am sorry. Good morning, Mr Dudgeon. Good morning, madam.

RICHARD [*interrupting Judith almost fiercely as she is about to make some wild appeal, and taking her arm resolutely*] Not one word more. Come.

She looks imploringly at him, but is overborne by his determination. They are marched out by the four soldiers : the sergeant very sulky, walking between Swindon and Richard, whom he watches as if he were a dangerous animal.

BURGOYNE. Gentlemen : we need not detain you. Major Swindon: a word with you. [*The officers go out. Burgoyne waits with unruffled serenity until the last of them disappears. Then he becomes very grave, and addresses Swindon for the first time without his title*]. Swindon : do you know what this is [*shewing him the letter*]?

SWINDON. What?

BURGOYNE. A demand for a safe-conduct for an officer of their militia to come here and arrange terms with us.

SWINDON. Oh, they are giving in.

BURGOYNE. They add that they are sending the man who raised Springtown last night and drove us out; so that we may know that we are dealing with an officer of importance.

SWINDON. Pooh !

BURGOYNE. He will be fully empowered to arrange the terms of—guess what.

SWINDON. Their surrender, I hope.

BURGOYNE. No : our evacuation of the town. They offer us just six hours to clear out.

SWINDON. What monstrous impudence !

BURGOYNE. What shall we do, eh ?

SWINDON. March on Springtown and strike a decisive blow at once.

BURGOYNE [*quietly*] Hm ! [*Turning to the door*] Come to the adjutant's office.

SWINDON. What for ?

BURGOYNE. To write out that safe-conduct. [*He puts his hand to the door knob to open it*].

SWINDON [*who has not budged*] General Burgoyne.

BURGOYNE [*returning*] Sir ?

SWINDON. It is my duty to tell you, sir, that I do not consider the threats of a mob of rebellious tradesmen a sufficient reason for our giving way.

BURGOYNE [*imperturbable*] Suppose I resign my command to you, what will you do ?

SWINDON. I will undertake to do what we have marched south from Quebec to do, and what General Howe has marched north from New York to do : effect a junction at Albany and wipe out the rebel army with our united forces.

BURGOYNE [*enigmatically*] And will you wipe out our enemies in London, too ?

SWINDON. In London ! What enemies ?

BURGOYNE [*forcibly*] Jobbery and snobbery, incompetence and Red Tape. [*He holds up the dispatch and adds, with despair in his face and voice*] I have just learnt, sir, that General Howe is still in New York.

SWINDON [*thunderstruck*] Good God ! He has disobeyed orders !

BURGOYNE [*with sardonic calm*] He has received no orders, sir. Some gentleman in London forgot to dispatch them : he was leaving town for his holiday, I believe. To avoid upsetting his arrangements, England will lose her American colonies ; and in a few days you and I will be at Saratoga with 5,000 men to face 18,000 rebels in an impregnable position.

SWINDON [*appalled*] Impossible ?

BURGOYNE [*coldly*] I beg your pardon ?

SWINDON. I cant believe it ! What will History say ?

BURGOYNE. History, sir, will tell lies, as usual. Come : we must send the safe-conduct. [*He goes out*].

SWINDON [*following distractedly*] My God, my God ! We shall be wiped out.

As noon approaches there is excitement in the market place. The gallows which hangs there permanently for the terror of evildoers, with such minor advertizers and examples of crime as the pillory, the whipping post, and the stocks, has a new rope attached, with the noose hitched up to one of the uprights, out of reach of the boys. Its ladder, too, has been brought out and placed in position by the town beadle, who stands by to guard it from unauthorized climbing. The Websterbridge townsfolk are present in force, and in high spirits ; for the news has spread that it is the devil's disciple and not the minister that King George and his terrible general are about to hang : consequently the execution can be enjoyed without any misgiving as to its righteousness, or to the cowardice of allowing it to take place without a struggle. There is even some fear of a disappointment as midday approaches and the arrival of the beadle with the ladder remains the only sign of preparation. But at last reassuring shouts of Here they come : Here they are, are heard ; and a company of soldiers with fixed bayonets, half British infantry, half Hessians, tramp quickly into the middle of the market place, driving the crowd to the sides.

THE SERGEANT. Halt. Front. Dress. [*The soldiers change their column into a square enclosing the gallows, their petty officers, energetically led by the sergeant, hustling the persons who find themselves inside the square out at the corners*]. Now then ! Out of it with you : out of it. Some o youll get strung up yourselves presently. Form that square there, will you, you damned Hoosians. No use talkin German to them : talk to their toes with the butt ends of your muskets : theyll understand that. Get out of it, will you. [*He comes upon Judith, standing near the gallows*]. Now then : youve no call here.

JUDITH. May I not stay ? What harm am I doing ?

SERGEANT. I want none of your argufying. You ought to be ashamed of yourself, running to see a man hanged thats not your husband. And he's no better than yourself. I told my major he was a gentleman ; and then he goes and tries to strangle him, and calls his blessed Majesty a lunatic. So out of it with you, double quick.

JUDITH. Will you take these two silver dollars and let me stay ?

The sergeant, without an instant's hesitation, looks quickly and furtively round as he shoots the money dexterously into his pocket. Then he raises his voice in virtuous indignation.

THE SERGEANT. Me take money in the execution of my duty ! Certainly not. Now I'll tell you what I'll do, to teach you to corrupt the King's officer. I'll put you under arrest until the execution's over. You just stand there ; and dont let me see you as much as move from that spot until youre let. [*With a swift wink at her he points to the corner of the square behind the gallows on his right, and turns noisily away, shouting*] Now then, dress up and keep em back, will you.

Cries of Hush and Silence are heard among the townsfolk ; and the sound of a military band, playing the Dead March from Saul, is heard. The crowd becomes quiet at once ; and the sergeant and petty officers, hurrying to the back of the square, with a few whispered orders and some stealthy hustling cause it to open and admit the funeral procession, which is protected from the crowd by a double file of soldiers. First come Burgoyne and Swindon, who, on entering the square, glance with distaste at the gallows, and avoid passing under it by wheeling a little to the right and stationing themselves on that side. Then Mr Brudenell, the chaplain, in his surplice, with his prayer book open in his hand, walking beside Richard, who is moody and disorderly. He walks doggedly through the gallows framework, and posts himself a little in front of it. Behind him comes the executioner, a stalwart soldier in his shirtsleeves. Following him, two soldiers haul a light military waggon. Finally comes the band, which posts itself at the back of the square, and finishes the Dead March. Judith, watching Richard painfully, steals down to the gallows, and stands leaning against its right post. During the conversation which follows, the two soldiers place the cart under the gallows, and stand by the shafts, which point backwards. The executioner takes a set of steps from the cart and places it ready for the prisoner to mount. Then he climbs the tall ladder which stands against the gallows, and cuts the string by which the rope is hitched up ; so that the noose drops dangling over the cart, into which he steps as he descends.

RICHARD [*with suppressed impatience, to Brudenell*] Look here, sir : this is no place for a man of your profession. Hadnt you better go away ?

SWINDON. I appeal to you, prisoner, if you have any sense of decency left, to listen to the ministrations of the chaplain, and pay due heed to the solemnity of the occasion.

THE CHAPLAIN [*gently reproving Richard*] Try to control yourself, and submit to the divine will. [*He lifts his book to proceed with the service*].

RICHARD. Answer for your own will, sir, and those of your accomplices here [*indicating Burgoyne and Swindon*]: I see little divinity about them or you. You talk to me of Christianity when you are in the act of hanging your enemies. Was there ever such blasphemous nonsense ! [*To Swindon, more rudely*] Youve got up the solemnity of the occasion, as you call it, to impress the people with your own dignity— Handel's music and a clergyman to make murder look like piety ! Do you suppose *I* am going to help you ? Youve asked me to choose the rope because you dont know your own trade well enough to shoot me properly. Well, hang away and have done with it.

SWINDON [*to the chaplain*] Can you do nothing with him, Mr Brudenell ?

CHAPLAIN. I will try, sir. [*Beginning to read*] Man that is born of woman hath—

RICHARD [*fixing his eyes on him*] " Thou shalt not kill."
The book drops in Brudenell's hands.

CHAPLAIN [*confessing his embarrassment*] What am I to
say, Mr Dudgeon ?

RICHARD. Let me alone, man, cant you ?

BURGOYNE [*with extreme urbanity*] I think, Mr Brudenell,
that as the usual professional observations seem to strike
Mr Dudgeon as incongruous under the circumstances, you
had better omit them until—er—until Mr Dudgeon can no
longer be inconvenienced by them. [*Brudenell, with a shrug,
shuts his book and retires behind the gallows*]. You seem in a
hurry, Mr Dudgeon.

RICHARD [*with the horror of death upon him*] Do you think
this is a pleasant sort of thing to be kept waiting for ?
Youve made up your mind to commit murder : well, do it
and have done with it.

BURGOYNE. Mr Dudgeon : we are only doing this—

RICHARD. Because youre paid to do it.

SWINDON. You insolent— [*he swallows his rage*].

BURGOYNE [*with much charm of manner*] Ah, I am really
sorry that you should think that, Mr Dudgeon. If you
knew what my commission cost me, and what my pay is,
you would think better of me. I should be glad to part
from you on friendly terms.

RICHARD. Hark ye, General Burgoyne. If you think
that I like being hanged, youre mistaken. I dont like it ;
and I dont mean to pretend that I do. And if you think I'm
obliged to you for hanging me in a gentlemanly way, youre
wrong there too. I take the whole business in devilish bad
part ; and the only satisfaction I have in it is that youll feel
a good deal meaner than I'll look when it's over. [*He turns
away, and is striding to the cart when Judith advances and
interposes with her arms stretched out to him. Richard,
feeling that a very little will upset his self-possession, shrinks
from her, crying*] What are you doing here ? This is no
place for you. [*She makes a gesture as if to touch him. He
recoils impatiently*] No : go away, go away : youll unnerve
me. Take her away, will you.

JUDITH. Wont you bid me goodbye?

RICHARD [*allowing her to take his hand*] Oh goodbye, goodbye. Now go—go—quickly. [*She clings to his hand —will not be put off with so cold a last farewell—at last, as he tries to disengage himself, throws herself on his breast in agony*].

SWINDON [*angrily to the sergeant, who, alarmed at Judith's movement, has come from the back of the square to pull her back, and stopped irresolutely on finding that he is too late*] How is this? Why is she inside the lines?

SERGEANT [*guiltily*] I dunno, sir. She's that artful—cant keep her away.

BURGOYNE. You were bribed.

SERGEANT [*protesting*] No, sir—

SWINDON [*severely*] Fall back. [*He obeys*].

RICHARD [*imploringly to those around him, and finally to Burgoyne, as the least stolid of them*] Take her away. Do you think I want a woman near me now?

BURGOYNE [*going to Judith and taking her hand*] Here, madam : you had better keep inside the lines ; but stand here behind us ; and dont look.

Richard, with a great sobbing sigh of relief as she releases him and turns to Burgoyne, flies for refuge to the cart and mounts into it. The executioner takes off his coat and pinions him.

JUDITH [*resisting Burgoyne quietly and drawing her hand away*] No : I must stay. I wont look. [*She goes to the right of the gallows. She tries to look at Richard, but turns away with a frightful shudder, and falls on her knees in prayer. Brudenell comes towards her from the back of the square*].

BURGOYNE [*nodding approvingly as she kneels*] Ah, quite so. Do not disturb her, Mr Brudenell : that will do very nicely. [*Brudenell nods also, and withdraws a little, watching her sympathetically. Burgoyne resumes his former position, and takes out a handsome gold chronometer*]. Now then, are those preparations made? We must not detain Mr Dudgeon.

By this time Richard's hands are bound behind him ; and

the noose is round his neck. The two soldiers take the shafts of the waggon, ready to pull it away. The executioner, standing in the cart behind Richard, makes a sign to the sergeant.

SERGEANT [*to Burgoyne*] Ready, sir.

BURGOYNE. Have you anything more to say, Mr Dudgeon ? It wants two minutes of twelve still.

RICHARD [*in the strong voice of a man who has conquered the bitterness of death*] Your watch is two minutes slow by the town clock, which I can see from here, General. [*The town clock strikes the first stroke of twelve. Involuntarily the people flinch at the sound, and a subdued groan breaks from them*]. Amen ! my life for the world's future !

ANDERSON [*shouting as he rushes into the market place*] Amen ; and stop the execution. [*He bursts through the line of soldiers opposite Burgoyne, and rushes, panting, to the gallows*]. I am Anthony Anderson, the man you want.

The crowd, intensely excited, listens with all its ears. Judith, half rising, stares at him ; then lifts her hands like one whose dearest prayer has been granted.

SWINDON. Indeed. Then you are just in time to take your place on the gallows. Arrest him.

At a sign from the sergeant, two soldiers come forward to seize Anderson.

ANDERSON [*thrusting a paper under Swindon's nose*] Theres my safe-conduct, sir.

SWINDON [*taken aback*] Safe-conduct ! Are you— !

ANDERSON [*emphatically*] I am. [*The two soldiers take him by the elbows*]. Tell these men to take their hands off me.

SWINDON [*to the men*] Let him go

SERGEANT. Fall back.

The two men return to their places. The townsfolk raise a cheer ; and begin to exchange exultant looks, with a presentiment of triumph as they see their Pastor speaking with their enemies in the gate.

ANDERSON [*exhaling a deep breath of relief, and dabbing*

his perspiring brow with his handkerchief] Thank God, I was
in time !

BURGOYNE [*calm as ever, and still watch in hand*] Ample
time, sir. Plenty of time. I should never dream of hanging
any gentleman by an American clock. [*He puts up his
watch*].

ANDERSON. Yes : we are some minutes ahead of you
already, General. Now tell them to take the rope from the
neck of that American citizen.

BURGOYNE [*to the executioner in the cart—very politely*]
Kindly undo Mr Dudgeon.

*The executioner takes the rope from Richard's neck, unties
his hands, and helps him on with his coat.*

JUDITH [*stealing timidly to Anderson*] Tony.

ANDERSON [*putting his arm round her shoulders and
bantering her affectionately*] Well, what do you think of your
husband now, eh ?—eh ? ?—eh ? ? ?

JUDITH. I am ashamed— [*she hides her face against his
breast*].

BURGOYNE [*to Swindon*] You look disappointed, Major
Swindon.

SWINDON. You look defeated, General Burgoyne.

BURGOYNE. I am, sir ; and I am humane enough to be
glad of it. [*Richard jumps down from the cart, Brudenell
offering his hand to help him, and runs to Anderson, whose
left hand he shakes heartily, the right being occupied by
Judith*]. By the way, Mr Anderson, I do not quite understand. The safe-conduct was for a commander of the
militia. I understand you are a—[*He looks as pointedly as
his good manners permit at the riding boots, the pistols, and
Richard's coat, and adds*]—a clergyman.

ANDERSON [*between Judith and Richard*] Sir : it is in the
hour of trial that a man finds his true profession. This
foolish young man [*placing his hand on Richard's shoulder*]
boasted himself the Devil's Disciple ; but when the hour of
trial came to him, he found that it was his destiny to suffer
and be faithful to the death. I thought myself a decent
minister of the gospel of peace; but when the hour of trial

came to me, I found that it was my destiny to be a man of action, and that my place was amid the thunder of the captains and the shouting. So I am starting life at fifty as Captain Anthony Anderson of the Springtown militia; and the Devil's Disciple here will start presently as the Reverend Richard Dudgeon, and wag his pow in my old pulpit, and give good advice to this silly sentimental little wife of mine [*putting his other hand on her shoulder. She steals a glance at Richard to see how the prospect pleases him*]. Your mother told me, Richard, that I should never have chosen Judith if I'd been born for the ministry. I am afraid she was right ; so, by your leave, you may keep my coat and I'll keep yours.

RICHARD. Minister—I should say Captain. I have behaved like a fool.

JUDITH. Like a hero.

RICHARD. Much the same thing, perhaps. [*With some bitterness towards himself*] But no : if I had been any good, I should have done for you what you did for me, instead of making a vain sacrifice.

ANDERSON. Not vain, my boy. It takes all sorts to make a world—saints as well as soldiers. [*Turning to Burgoyne*] And now, General, time presses ; and America is in a hurry. Have you realized that though you may occupy towns and win battles, you cannot conquer a nation ?

BURGOYNE. My good sir, without a Conquest you cannot have an aristocracy. Come and settle the matter at my quarters.

ANDERSON. At your service, sir. [*To Richard*] See Judith home for me, will you, my boy. [*He hands her over to him*]. Now, General. [*He goes busily up the market place towards the Town Hall, leaving Judith and Richard together. Burgoyne follows him a step or two ; then checks himself and turns to Richard*].

BURGOYNE. Oh, by the way, Mr Dudgeon, I shall be glad to see you at lunch at half-past one. [*He pauses a moment, and adds, with politely veiled slyness*] Bring Mrs Anderson, if she will be so good. [*To Swindon, who is fuming*] Take it quietly, Major Swindon : your friend the British soldier can stand up to anything except the British War Office. [*He follows Anderson*].

SERGEANT [*to Swindon*] What orders, sir ?

SWINDON [*savagely*] Orders ! What use are orders now ! Theres no army. Back to quarters ; and be d— [*He turns on his heel and goes*].

SERGEANT [*pugnacious and patriotic, repudiating the idea of defeat*] 'Tention. Now then : cock up your chins, and shew em you dont care a damn for em. Slope arms ! Fours ! Wheel ! Quick march !

The drums mark time with a tremendous bang ; the band strikes up British Grenadiers ; and the Sergeant, Brudenell, and the English troops march off defiantly to their quarters. The townsfolk press in behind, and follow them up the market, jeering at them ; and the town band, a very primitive affair, brings up the rear, playing Yankee Doodle. Essie, who comes in with them, runs to Richard.

ESSIE. Oh, Dick !

RICHARD [*good-humoredly, but wilfully*] Now, now : come, come ! I dont mind being hanged : but I will not be cried over.

ESSIE. No, I promise. I'll be good. [*She trys to restrain her tears, but cannot*]. I—I want to see where the soldiers are going to. [*She goes a little way up the market, pretending to look after the crowd*].

JUDITH. Promise me you will never tell him.

RICHARD. Dont be afraid.

They shake hands on it.

ESSIE [*calling to them*] Theyre coming back. They want you.

Jubilation in the market. The townsfolk surge back again in wild enthusiasm with their band, and hoist Richard on their shoulders, cheering him.

NOTES TO THE DEVIL'S DISCIPLE

BURGOYNE

GENERAL JOHN BURGOYNE, who is presented in this play for the first time (as far as I am aware) on the English stage, is not a conventional stage soldier, but as faithful a portrait as it is in the nature of stage portraits to be. His objection to profane swearing is not borrowed from Mr Gilbert's H.M.S. Pinafore: it is taken from the Code of Instructions drawn up by himself for his officers when he introduced Light Horse into the English Army. His opinion that English soldiers should be treated as thinking beings was no doubt as unwelcome to the military authorities of his time, when nothing was thought of ordering a soldier a thousand lashes, as it will be to those modern victims of the flagellation neurosis who are so anxious to revive that discredited sport. His military reports are very clever as criticisms, and are humane and enlightened within certain aristocratic limits, best illustrated perhaps by his declaration, which now sounds so curious, that he should blush to ask for promotion on any other ground than that of family influence. As a parliamentary candidate, Burgoyne took our common expression " fighting an election " so very literally that he led his supporters to the poll at Preston in 1768 with a loaded pistol in each hand, and won the seat, though he was fined £1000, and denounced by Junius, for the pistols.

It is only within quite recent years that any general recognition has become possible for the feeling that led Burgoyne, a professed enemy of oppression in India and elsewhere, to accept his American command when so many other officers threw up their commissions rather than serve in a civil war against the Colonies. His biographer De Fonblanque, writing in 1876, evidently regarded his position as indefensible. Nowadays, it is sufficient to say that Burgoyne was an Imperialist. He sympathized with the

119

colonists; but when they proposed as a remedy the disruption of the Empire, he regarded that as a step backward in civilization. As he put it to the House of Commons, " while we remember that we are contending against brothers and fellow subjects, we must also remember that we are contending in this crisis for the fate of the British Empire." Eightyfour years after his defeat, his republican conquerors themselves engaged in a civil war for the integrity of their Union. In 1885 the Whigs who represented the anti-Burgoyne tradition of American Independence in English politics, abandoned Gladstone and made common cause with their political opponents in defence of the Union between England and Ireland. Only the other day England sent 200,000 men into the field south of the equator to fight out the question whether South Africa should develop as a Federation of British Colonies or as an independent Afrikander United States. In all these cases the Unionists who were detached from their parties were called renegades, as Burgoyne was. That, of course, is only one of the unfortunate consequences of the fact that mankind, being for the most part incapable of politics, accepts vituperation as an easy and congenial substitute. Whether Burgoyne or Washington, Lincoln or Davis, Gladstone or Bright, Mr Chamberlain or Mr Leonard Courtney was in the right will never be settled, because it will never be possible to prove that the government of the victor has been better for mankind than the government of the vanquished would have been. It is true that the victors have no doubt on the point ; but to the dramatist, that certainty of theirs is only part of the human comedy. The American Unionist is often a Separatist as to Ireland ; the English Unionist often sympathizes with the Polish Home Ruler ; and both English and American Unionists are apt to be Disruptionists as regards that Imperial Ancient of Days, the Empire of China. Both are Unionists concerning Canada, but with a difference as to the precise application to it of the Monroe doctrine. As for me, the dramatist, I smile, and lead the conversation back to Burgoyne.

Burgoyne's surrender at Saratoga made him that occasionally necessary part of our British system, a scapegoat. The explanation of his defeat given in the play (pp. 109-10) is founded on a passage quoted by De Fonblanque from Fitzmaurice's Life of Lord Shelburne, as follows : " Lord George Germain, having among other peculiarities a particular dislike to be put out of his way on any occasion, had arranged to call at his office on his way to the country to sign the dispatches; but as those addressed to Howe had not been fair-copied, and he was not disposed to be balked of his projected visit to Kent, they were not signed then and were forgotten on his return home." These were the dispatches instructing Sir William Howe, who was in New York, to effect a junction at Albany with Burgoyne, who had marched from Quebec for that purpose. Burgoyne got as far as Saratoga, where, failing the expected reinforcement, he was hopelessly outnumbered, and his officers picked off, Boer fashion, by the American farmer-sharp-shooters. His own collar was pierced by a bullet. The publicity of his defeat, however, was more than compensated at home by the fact that Lord George's trip to Kent had not been interfered with, and that nobody knew about the oversight of the dispatch. The policy of the English Government and Court for the next two years was simply concealment of Germain's neglect. Burgoyne's demand for an inquiry was defeated in the House of Commons by the court party; and when he at last obtained a committee, the king got rid of it by a prorogation. When Burgoyne realized what had happened about the instructions to Howe (the scene in which I have represented him as learning it before Saratoga is not historical : the truth did not dawn on him until many months afterwards) the king actually took advantage of his being a prisoner of war in England on parole, and ordered him to return to America into captivity. Burgoyne immediately resigned all his appointments ; and this practically closed his military career, though he was afterwards made Commander of the Forces in Ireland for the purpose of banishing him from parliament.

The episode illustrates the curious perversion of the English sense of honor when the privileges and prestige of the aristocracy are at stake. Mr Frank Harris said, after the disastrous battle of Modder River, that the English, having lost America a century ago because they preferred George III, were quite prepared to lose South Africa today because they preferred aristocratic commanders to successful ones. Horace Walpole, when the parliamentary recess came at a critical period of the War of Independence, said that the Lords could not be expected to lose their pheasant shooting for the sake of America. In the working class, which, like all classes, has its own official aristocracy, there is the same reluctance to discredit an institution or to " do a man out of his job." At bottom, of course, this apparently shameless sacrifice of great public interests to petty personal ones, is simply the preference of the ordinary man for the things he can feel and understand to the things that are beyond his capacity. It is stupidity, not dishonesty.

Burgoyne fell a victim to this stupidity in two ways. Not only was he thrown over, in spite of his high character and distinguished services, to screen a court favorite who had actually been cashiered for cowardice and misconduct in the field fifteen years before ; but his peculiar critical temperament and talent, artistic, satirical, rather histrionic, and his fastidious delicacy of sentiment, his fine spirit and humanity, were just the qualities to make him disliked by stupid people because of their dread of ironic criticism. Long after his death, Thackeray, who had an intense sense of human character, but was typically stupid in valuing and interpreting it, instinctively sneered at him and exulted in his defeat. That sneer represents the common English attitude towards the Burgoyne type. Every instance in which the critical genius is defeated and the stupid genius (for both temperaments have their genius) " muddles through all right," is popular in England. But Burgoyne's failure was not the work of his own temperament, but of the stupid temperament. What man could do under the circumstances he did, and did handsomely and loftily. He fell, and his ideal empire was dismembered, not through his own misconduct, but because Lord George Germain overestimated the importance of his Kentish holiday, and underestimated the difficulty of conquering those remote and inferior creatures, the colonists. And King George and the rest of the nation agreed, on the whole, with Germain. It is a significant point that in America, where Burgoyne was an enemy and an invader, he was admired and praised. The climate there is no doubt more favorable to intellectual vivacity.

I have described Burgoyne's temperament as rather histrionic ; and the reader will have observed that the Burgoyne of the Devil's Disciple is a man who plays his part in life, and makes all its points, in the manner of a born high comedian. If he had been killed at Saratoga, with all his comedies unwritten, and his plan for turning As You Like It into a Beggar's Opera unconceived, I should still have painted the same picture of him on the strength of his reply to the articles of capitulation proposed to him by the victorious Gates (an Englishman). Here they are :

PROPOSITION.	ANSWER.
1. General Burgoyne's army being reduced by repeated defeats, by desertion, sickness, etc., their provisions exhausted, their military horses, tents and baggage taken or destroyed, their retreat cut off, and their camp invested, they can only be allowed to surrender as prisoners of war.	Lieut - General Burgoyne's army, however reduced, will never admit that their retreat is cut off while they have arms in their hands.
2. The officers and soldiers may keep the baggage belonging to them. The Generals of the United States never permit individuals to be pillaged.	Noted.

3. The troops under his Excellency General Burgoyne will be conducted by the most convenient route to New England, marching by easy marches, and sufficiently provided for by the way.

Agreed.

4. The officers will be admitted on parole and will be treated with the liberality customary in such cases, so long as they, by proper behaviour, continue to deserve it ; but those who are apprehended having broke their parole, as some British officers have done, must expect to be close confined.

There being no officer in this army under, or capable of being under, the description of breaking parole, this article needs no answer.

5. All public stores, artillery, arms, ammunition, carriages, horses, etc., etc., must be delivered to commissaries appointed to receive them.

All public stores may be delivered, arms excepted.

6. These terms being agreed to and signed, the troops under his Excellency's, General Burgoyne's command, may be drawn up in their encampments, where they will be ordered to ground their arms, and may thereupon be marched to the river-side on their way to Bennington.

This article is inadmissible in any extremity. Sooner than this army will consent to ground their arms in their encampments, they will rush on the enemy determined to take no quarter.

And, later on, " If General Gates does not mean to recede from the 6th article, the treaty ends at once : the army will to a man proceed to any act of desperation sooner than submit to that article."

Here you have the man at his Burgoynest. Need I add that he had his own way ; and that when the actual cere-

mony of surrender came, he would have played poor
General Gates off the stage, had not that commander risen
to the occasion by handing him back his sword.

In connection with the reference to Indians with scalping
knives, who, with the troops hired from Germany, made
up about half Burgoyne's force, I may cite the case of
Jane McCrea, betrothed to one of Burgoyne's officers. A
Wyandotte chief attached to Burgoyne's force was bringing
her to the British camp as a prisoner of war, when another
party of Indians, sent by her betrothed, claimed her. The
Wyandotte settled the dispute by killing her and bringing
her scalp to Burgoyne. Burgoyne let the deed pass. Possibly
he feared that a massacre of whites on the Canadian border
by the Wyandottes would follow any attempt at punishment.
But his own proclamations had threatened just what the
savage chief executed.

BRUDENELL

Brudenell is also a real person. At least, an artillery
chaplain of that name distinguished himself at Saratoga
by reading the burial service over Major Fraser under
fire, and by a quite readable adventure, chronicled, with
exaggerations, by Burgoyne, concerning Lady Harriet
Acland. Others have narrated how Lady Harriet's husband
killed himself in a duel, by falling with his head against a
pebble ; and how Lady Harriet then married the warrior
chaplain. All this, however, is a tissue of romantic lies,
though it has been repeated in print as authentic history
from generation to generation, even to the first edition of
this book. As a matter of fact, Major Acland died in his
bed of a cold shortly after his return to England ; and Lady
Harriet remained a widow until her death in 1815.

The rest of the Devil's Disciple may have actually
occurred, like most stories invented by dramatists ; but I
cannot produce any documents. Major Swindon's name
is invented ; but the man, of course, is real. There are
dozens of him extant to this day.

CÆSAR AND CLEOPATRA

A HISTORY

1898

CÆSAR AND CLEOPATRA

PROLOGUE

In the doorway of the temple of Ra in Memphis. Deep gloom. An august personage with a hawk's head is mysteriously visible by his own light in the darkness within the temple. He surveys the modern audience with great contempt ; and finally speaks the following words to them.

Peace ! Be silent and hearken unto me, ye quaint little islanders. Give ear, ye men with white paper on your breasts and nothing written thereon (to signify the innocency of your minds). Hear me, ye women who adorn yourselves alluringly and conceal your thoughts from your men, leading them to believe that ye deem them wondrous strong and masterful whilst in truth ye hold them in your hearts as children without judgment. Look upon my hawk's head ; and know that I am Ra, who was once in Egypt a mighty god. Ye cannot kneel nor prostrate yourselves ; for ye are packed in rows without freedom to move, obstructing one another's vision ; neither do any of ye regard it as seemly to do ought until ye see all the rest do so too ; wherefore it commonly happens that in great emergencies ye do nothing, though each telleth his fellow that something must be done. I ask you not for worship, but for silence. Let not your men speak nor your women cough ; for I am come to draw you back two thousand years over the graves of sixty generations. Ye poor posterity, think not that ye are the first. Other fools before ye have seen the sun rise and set, and the moon change her shape and her hour. As they were so ye are ; and yet not so great ; for the pyramids my people built stand to this day ; whilst the dustheaps on which ye slave, and which ye call empires, scatter in the wind even as ye pile your dead sons' bodies on them to make yet more dust.

Hearken to me then, oh ye compulsorily educated ones.

Know that even as there is an old England and a new, and ye stand perplexed between the twain ; so in the days when I was worshipped was there an old Rome and a new, and men standing perplexed between them. And the old Rome was poor and little, and greedy and fierce, and evil in many ways ; but because its mind was little and its work was simple, it knew its own mind and did its own work ; and the gods pitied it and helped it and strengthened ĭt and shielded it ; for the gods are patient with littleness. Then the old Rome, like the beggar on horseback, presumed on the favor of the gods, and said, " Lo ! there is neither riches nor greatness in our littleness : the road to riches and greatness is through robbery of the poor and slaughter of the weak." So they robbed their own poor until they became great masters of that art, and knew by what laws it could be made to appear seemly and honest. And when they had squeezed their own poor dry, they robbed the poor of other lands, and added those lands to Rome until there came a new Rome, rich and huge. And I, Ra, laughed ; for the minds of the Romans remained the same size whilst their dominion spread over the earth.

Now mark me, that ye may understand what ye are presently to see. Whilst the Romans still stood between the old Rome and the new, there arose among them a mighty soldier : Pompey the Great. And the way of the soldier is the way of death ; but the way of the gods is the way of life ; and so it comes that a god at the end of his way is wise and a soldier at the end of his way is a fool. So Pompey held by the old Rome, in which only soldiers could become great ; but the gods turned to the new Rome, in which any man with wit enough could become what he would. And Pompey's friend Julius Cæsar was on the side of the gods ; for he saw that Rome had passed beyond the control of the little old Romans. This Cæsar was a great talker and a politician : he bought men with words and with gold, even as ye are bought. And when they would not be satisfied with words and gold, and demanded also the glories of war, Cæsar in his middle age turned his hand to that trade ; and they that were against him when he sought their welfare, bowed down before him when he became a slayer and a conqueror ; for such is the nature of you mortals. And as for Pompey, the gods grew tired of his triumphs and his airs of being himself a god ; for he talked of law and duty and other matters that concerned not a mere human worm. And the gods smiled on Cæsar ; for he lived the life they had given him boldly, and was not forever rebuking us for our indecent ways of creation, and hiding our handiwork as a shameful thing. Ye know well what I mean ; for this is one of your own sins.

And thus it fell out between the old Rome and the new, that Cæsar said, " Unless I break the law of old Rome, I cannot take my share in ruling her ; and the gift of ruling that the gods gave me will perish without fruit." But Pompey said, " The law is above all ; and if thou break it thou shalt die." Then said Cæsar, " I will break it : kill me who can." And he broke it. And Pompey went for him, as ye say, with a great army to slay him and uphold the old Rome. So Cæsar fled across the Adriatic sea ; for the high gods had a lesson to teach him, which lesson they shall also teach you in due time if ye continue to forget them and to worship that cad among gods, Mammon. Therefore before they raised Cæsar to be master of the world, they were minded to throw him down into the dust, even beneath the feet of Pompey, and blacken his face before the nations. And Pompey they raised higher than ever, he and his laws and his high mind that aped the gods, so that his fall might be the more terrible. And Pompey followed Cæsar, and overcame him with all the majesty of old Rome, and stood over him and over the whole world even as ye stand over it with your fleet that covers thirty miles of the sea. And when Cæsar was brought down to utter nothingness, he made a last stand to die honorably, and did not despair ; for he said, " Against me there is Pompey, and the old Rome, and the law and the legions : all all against me ; but high above these are the gods ; and Pompey is a fool." And the gods laughed and approved ; and on the field of

Pharsalia the impossible came to pass ; the blood and iron ye pin your faith on fell before the spirit of man ; for the spirit of man is the will of the gods ; and Pompey's power crumbled in his hand, even as the power of imperial Spain crumbled when it was set against your fathers in the days when England was little, and knew her own mind, and had a mind to know instead of a circulation of newspapers. Wherefore look to it, lest some little people whom ye would enslave rise up and become in the hand of God the scourge of your boastings and your injustices and your lusts and stupidities.

And now, would ye know the end of Pompey, or will ye sleep while a god speaks ? Heed my words well ; for Pompey went where ye have gone, even to Egypt, where there was a Roman occupation even as there was but now a British one. And Cæsar pursued Pompey to Egypt : a Roman fleeing, and a Roman pursuing : dog eating dog. And the Egyptians said, " Lo : these Romans which have lent money to our kings and levied a distraint upon us with their arms, call for ever upon us to be loyal to them by betraying our own country to them. But now behold two Romes ! Pompey's Rome and Cæsar's Rome ! To which of the twain shall we pretend to be loyal ? " So they turned in their perplexity to a soldier that had once served Pompey, and that knew the ways of Rome and was full of her lusts. And they said to him, " Lo : in thy country dog eats dog ; and both dogs are coming to eat us : what counsel hast thou to give us ? " And this soldier, whose name was Lucius Septimius, and whom ye shall presently see before ye, replied, " Ye shall diligently consider which is the bigger dog of the two ; and ye shall kill the other dog for his sake and thereby earn his favor." And the Egyptians said, " Thy counsel is expedient ; but if we kill a man outside the law we set ourselves in the place of the gods ; and this we dare not do. But thou, being a Roman, art accustomed to this kind of killing ; for thou hast imperial instincts. Wilt thou therefore kill the lesser dog for us ? " And he said, " I will ; for I have made my home in Egypt ; and I desire consideration and influence among you." And they said, "We knew well thou wouldst not do it for nothing : thou shalt have thy reward." Now when Pompey came, he came alone in a little galley, putting his trust in the law and the constitution. And it was plain to the people of Egypt that Pompey was now but a very small dog. So when he set his foot on the shore he was greeted by his old comrade Lucius Septimius, who welcomed him with one hand and with the other smote off his head, and kept it as it were a pickled cabbage to make a present to Cæsar. And mankind shuddered ; but the gods laughed ; for Septimius was but a knife that Pompey had sharpened ; and when it turned against his own throat they said that Pompey had better have made Septimius a ploughman than so brave and ready-handed a slayer. Therefore again I bid you beware, ye who would all be Pompeys if ye dared ; for war is a wolf that may come to your own door.

Are ye impatient with me ? Do ye crave for a story of an unchaste woman ? Hath the name of Cleopatra tempted ye hither ? Ye foolish ones ; Cleopatra is as yet but a child that is whipped by her nurse. And what I am about to shew you for the good of your souls is how Cæsar, seeking Pompey in Egypt, found Cleopatra ; and how he received that present of a pickled cabbage that was once the head of Pompey ; and what things happened between the old Cæsar and the child queen before he left Egypt and battled his way back to Rome to be slain there as Pompey was slain, by men in whom the spirit of Pompey still lived. All this ye shall see ; and ye shall marvel, after your ignorant manner, that men twenty centuries ago were already just such as you, and spoke and lived as ye speak and live, no worse and no better, no wiser and no sillier. And the two thousand years that have past are to me, the god Ra, but a moment ; nor is this day any other than the day in which Cæsar set foot in the land of my people. And now I leave you ; for ye are a dull folk, and instruction is wasted on you ; and I had not spoken so much but that it is in the nature of a god to struggle for ever with the dust and the darkness, and to drag from them, by the force of his longing for the divine, more life and more light.   Settle ye therefore in your seats and keep silent ; for ye are about to hear a man speak, and a great man he was, as ye count greatness. And fear not that I shall speak to you again : the rest of the story must ye learn from them that lived it.   Farewell ; and do not presume to applaud me.   [*The temple vanishes in utter darkness*].

[1912]

AN ALTERNATIVE TO THE PROLOGUE

An October night on the Syrian border of Egypt towards the end of the XXXIII Dynasty, in the year 706 by Roman computation, afterwards reckoned by Christian computation as 48 B.C. A great radiance of silver fire, the dawn of a moonlit night, is rising in the east. The stars and the cloudless sky are our own contemporaries, nineteen and a half centuries younger than we know them ; but you would not guess that from their appearance. Below them are two notable drawbacks of civilization : a palace, and soldiers. The palace, an old, low, Syrian building of whitened mud, is not so ugly as Buckingham Palace ; and the officers in the courtyard are more highly civilized than modern English officers : for example, they do not dig up the corpses of their dead enemies and mutilate them, as we dug up Cromwell and the Mahdi. They are in two groups : one intent on the gambling of their captain Belzanor, a warrior of fifty, who, with his spear on the ground beside his knee, is stooping to throw dice with a sly-looking young Persian recruit ; the other gathered about a guardsman who has just finished telling a naughty story (still current in English barracks) at which they are laughing uproariously. They are about a dozen in number, all highly aristocratic young Egyptian guardsmen, handsomely equipped with weapons and armor, very unEnglish in point of not being ashamed of and uncomfortable in their professional dress ; on the contrary, rather ostentatiously and arrogantly warlike, as valuing themselves on their military caste.

Belzanor is a typical veteran, tough and wilful ; prompt, capable and crafty where brute force will serve ; helpless and boyish when it will not : an effective sergeant, an incompetent general, a deplorable dictator. Would, if influentially connected, be employed in the two last capacities by a modern European State on the strength of his success in the first. Is rather to be pitied just now in view of the fact that Julius Cæsar is invading his country. Not knowing this, is intent on his game with the Persian, whom, as a foreigner, he considers quite capable of cheating him.

His subalterns are mostly handsome young fellows whose interest in the game and the story symbolize with tolerable completeness the main interests in life of which they are conscious. Their spears are leaning against the walls, or lying on the ground ready to their hands. The corner of the courtyard forms a triangle of which one side is the front of the palace, with a doorway, the other a wall with a gateway. The storytellers are on the palace side : the gamblers, on the gateway side. Close to the gateway, against the wall, is a stone block high enough to enable a Nubian sentinel, standing on it, to look over the wall. The yard is lighted by a torch stuck in the wall. As the laughter from the group round the storyteller dies away, the kneeling Persian, winning the throw, snatches up the stake from the ground.

BELZANOR. By Apis, Persian, thy gods are good to thee.

THE PERSIAN. Try yet again, O captain. Double or quits !

BELZANOR. No more. I am not in the vein.

THE SENTINEL [*poising his javelin as he peers over the wall*] Stand. Who goes there ?

They all start, listening. A strange voice replies from without.

VOICE. The bearer of evil tidings.

BELZANOR [*calling to the sentry*] Pass him.

THE SENTINEL [*grounding his javelin*] Draw near, O bearer of evil tidings.

BELZANOR [*pocketing the dice and picking up his spear*] Let us receive this man with honor. He bears evil tidings.

The guardsmen seize their spears and gather about the gate, leaving a way through for the new comer.

PERSIAN [*rising from his knee*] Are evil tidings, then, so honorable ?

BELZANOR. O barbarous Persian, hear my instruction. In Egypt the bearer of good tidings is sacrificed to the gods as a thank offering ; but no god will accept the blood of the messenger of evil. When we have good tidings, we are careful to send them in the mouth of the cheapest slave we can find. Evil tidings are borne by young noblemen who desire to bring themselves into notice. [*They join the rest at the gate*].

THE SENTINEL. Pass. O young captain ; and bow the head in the House of the Queen.

VOICE. Go anoint thy javelin with fat of swine, O Blackamoor : for before morning the Romans will make thee eat it to the very butt.

The owner of the voice, a fairhaired dandy, dressed in a different fashion from that affected by the guardsmen, but no less extravagantly, comes through the gateway laughing. He is somewhat battlestained ; and his left forearm, bandaged, comes through a torn sleeve. In his right hand he carries a Roman sword in its sheath. He swaggers down the courtyard, the Persian on his right, Belzanor on his left, and the guardsmen crowding down behind him.

BELZANOR. Who are thou that laughest in the House of Cleopatra the Queen, and in the teeth of Belzanor, the captain of her guard ?

THE NEW COMER. I am Bel Affris, descended from the gods.

BELZANOR [*ceremoniously*] Hail, cousin !

ALL [*except the Persian*] Hail, cousin !

PERSIAN. All the Queen's guards are descended from the gods, O stranger, save myself. I am Persian, and descended from many kings.

BEL AFFRIS [*to the guardsmen*] Hail, cousins ! [*To the Persian, condescendingly*] Hail, mortal !

BELZANOR. You have been in battle, Bel Affris ; and you are a soldier among soldiers. You will not let the Queen's women have the first of your tidings.

BEL AFFRIS. I have no tidings, except that we shall have our throats cut presently, women, soldiers, and all.

PERSIAN [*to Belzanor*] I told you so.

THE SENTINEL [*who has been listening*] Woe, alas !

BEL AFFRIS [*calling to him*] Peace, peace, poor Ethiop : destiny is with the gods who painted thee black. [*To*

Belzanor] What has this mortal [*indicating the Persian*] told you ?

BELZANOR. He says that the Roman Julius Cæsar, who has landed on our shores with a handful of followers, will make himself master of Egypt. He is afraid of the Roman soldiers. [*The guardsmen laugh with boisterous scorn*]. Peasants, brought up to scare crows and follow the plough ! Sons of smiths and millers and tanners ! And we nobles, consecrated to arms, descended from the gods !

PERSIAN. Belzanor : the gods are not always good to their poor relations.

BELZANOR [*hotly, to the Persian*] Man to man, are we worse than the slaves of Cæsar ?

BEL AFFRIS [*stepping between them*] Listen, cousin. Man to man, we Egyptians are as gods above the Romans.

THE GUARDSMEN [*exultantly*] Aha !

BEL AFFRIS. But this Cæsar does not pit man against man : he throws a legion at you where you are weakest as he throws a stone from a catapult ; and that legion is as a man with one head, a thousand arms, and no religion. I have fought against them ; and I know.

BELZANOR [*derisively*] Were you frightened, cousin ?

The guardsmen roar with laughter, their eyes sparkling at the wit of their captain.

BEL AFFRIS. No, cousin ; but I was beaten. They were frightened (perhaps) ; but they scattered us like chaff.

The guardsmen, much damped, utter a growl of contemptuous disgust.

BELZANOR. Could you not die ?

BEL AFFRIS. No : that was too easy to be worthy of a descendant of the gods. Besides, there was no time : all was over in a moment. The attack came just where we least expected it.

BELZANOR. That shews that the Romans are cowards.

BEL AFFRIS. They care nothing about cowardice, these Romans : they fight to win. The pride and honor of war are nothing to them.

PERSIAN. Tell us the tale of the battle. What befell ?

THE GUARDSMEN [*gathering eagerly round Bel Affris*] Ay : the tale of the battle.

BEL AFFRIS. Know then, that I am a novice in the guard of the temple of Ra in Memphis, serving neither Cleopatra nor her brother Ptolemy, but only the high gods. We went a journey to inquire of Ptolemy why he had driven Cleopatra into Syria, and how we of Egypt should deal with the Roman Pompey, newly come to our shores after his defeat by Cæsar at Pharsalia. What, think ye, did we learn ? Even that Cæsar is coming also in hot pursuit of his foe, and that Ptolemy has slain Pompey, whose severed head he holds in readiness to present to the conqueror. [*Sensation among the guardsmen*]. Nay, more : we found that Cæsar is already come ; for we had not made half a day's journey on our way back when we came upon a city rabble flying from his legions, whose landing they had gone out to withstand.

BELZANOR. And ye, the temple guard ! did ye not withstand these legions ?

BEL AFFRIS. What man could, that we did. But there came the sound of a trumpet whose voice was as the cursing of a black mountain. Then saw we a moving wall of shields coming towards us. You know how the heart burns when you charge a fortified wall ; but how if the fortified wall were to charge you ?

THE PERSIAN [*exulting in having told them so*] Did I not say it ?

BEL AFFRIS. When the wall came nigh, it changed into a line of men—common fellows enough, with helmets, leather tunics, and breastplates. Every man of them flung his javelin : the one that came my way drove through my shield as through a papyrus—lo there ! [*he points to the bandage on his left arm*] and would have gone through my neck had I not stooped. They were charging at the double then, and were upon us with short swords almost as soon as their javelins. When a man is close to you with such a sword, you can do nothing with our weapons : they are all too long.

THE PERSIAN. What did you do ?

BEL AFFRIS. Doubled my fist and smote my Roman on the sharpness of his jaw. He was but mortal after all : he lay down in a stupor ; and I took his sword and laid it on. [*Drawing the sword*] Lo ! a Roman sword with Roman blood on it !

THE GUARDSMEN [*approvingly*] Good ! [*They take the sword and hand it round, examining it curiously*].

THE PERSIAN. And your men ?

BEL AFFRIS. Fled. Scattered like sheep.

BELZANOR [*furiously*] The cowardly slaves ! Leaving the descendants of the gods to be butchered !

BEL AFFRIS [*with acid coolness*] The descendants of the gods did not stay to be butchered, cousin. The battle was not to the strong ; but the race was to the swift. The Romans who have no chariots, sent a cloud of horsemen in pursuit, and slew multitudes. Then our high priest's captain rallied a dozen descendants of the gods and exhorted us to die fighting. I said to myself : surely it is safer to stand than to lose my breath and be stabbed in the back ; so I joined our captain and stood. Then the Romans treated us with respect ; for no man attacks a lion when the field is full of sheep, except for the pride and honor of war, of which these Romans know nothing. So we escaped with our lives ; and I am come to warn you that you must open your gates to Cæsar ; for his advance guard is scarce an hour behind me ; and not an Egyptian warrior is left standing between you and his legions.

THE SENTINEL. Woe, alas ! [*He throws down his javelin and flies into the palace*].

BELZANOR. Nail him to the door, quick ! [*The guardsmen rush for him with their spears ; but he is too quick for them*]. Now this news will run through the palace like fire through stubble.

BEL AFFRIS. What shall we do to save the women from the Romans ?

BELZANOR. Why not kill them ?

PERSIAN. Because we should have to pay blood money

for some of them. Better let the Romans kill them : it is cheaper.

BELZANOR [*awestruck at his brain power*] O subtle one ! O serpent !

BEL AFFRIS. But your Queen ?

BELZANOR. True : we must carry off Cleopatra.

BEL AFFRIS. Will ye not await her command ?

BELZANOR. Command ! a girl of sixteen ! Not we. At Memphis ye deem her a Queen : here we know better. I will take her on the crupper of my horse. When we soldiers have carried her out of Cæsar's reach, then the priests and the nurses and the rest of them can pretend she is a queen again, and put their commands into her mouth.

PERSIAN. Listen to me, Belzanor.

BELZANOR. Speak, O subtle beyond thy years.

THE PERSIAN. Cleopatra's brother Ptolemy is at war with her. Let us sell her to him.

THE GUARDSMEN. O subtle one ! O serpent !

BELZANOR. We dare not. We are descended from the gods ; but Cleopatra is descended from the river Nile ; and the lands of our fathers will grow no grain if the Nile rises not to water them. Without our father's gifts we should live the lives of dogs.

PERSIAN. It is true : the Queen's guard cannot live on its pay. But hear me further, O ye kinsmen of Osiris.

THE GUARDSMEN. Speak, O subtle one. Hear the serpent begotten !

PERSIAN. Have I heretofore spoken truly to you of Cæsar, when you thought I mocked you ?

GUARDSMEN. Truly, truly.

BELZANOR [*reluctantly admitting it*] So Bel Affris says.

PERSIAN. Hear more of him, then. This Cæsar is a great lover of women : he makes them his friends and counsellors.

BELZANOR. Faugh ! This rule of women will be the ruin of Egypt.

THE PERSIAN. Let it rather be the ruin of Rome ! Cæsar grows old now : he is past fifty and full of labors and battles. He is too old for the young women ; and the old women are too wise to worship him.

BEL AFFRIS. Take heed, Persian. Cæsar is by this time almost within earshot.

PERSIAN. Cleopatra is not yet a woman : neither is she wise. But she already troubles men's wisdom.

BELZANOR. Ay : that is because she is descended from the river Nile and a black kitten of the sacred White Cat. What then ?

PERSIAN. Why, sell her secretly to Ptolemy, and then offer ourselves to Cæsar as volunteers to fight for the overthrow of her brother and the rescue of our Queen, the Great Granddaughter of the Nile.

THE GUARDSMEN. O serpent !

PERSIAN. He will listen to us if we come with her picture in our mouths. He will conquer and kill her brother, and reign in Egypt with Cleopatra for his Queen. And we shall be her guard.

GUARDSMEN. O subtlest of all the serpents ! O admiration ! O wisdom !

BEL AFFRIS. He will also have arrived before you have done talking, O word spinner.

BELZANOR. That is true. [*An affrighted uproar in the palace interrupts him*]. Quick : the flight has begun : guard the door. [*They rush to the door and form a cordon before it with their spears. A mob of women-servants and nurses surges out. Those in front recoil from the spears, screaming to those behind to keep back. Belzanor's voice dominates the disturbance as he shouts*] Back there. In again, unprofitable cattle.

THE GUARDSMEN. Back, unprofitable cattle.

BELZANOR. Send us out Ftatateeta, the Queen's chief nurse.

THE WOMEN [*calling into the palace*] Ftatateeta, Ftatateeta. Come, come. Speak to Belzanor.

A WOMAN. Oh, keep back. You are thrusting me on the spearheads.

A huge grim woman, her face covered with a network of

tiny wrinkles, and her eyes old, large, and wise ; sinewy handed, very tall, very strong ; with the mouth of a blood-hound and the jaws of a bulldog, appears on the threshold. She is dressed like a person of consequence in the palace, and confronts the guardsmen insolently.

FTATATEETA. Make way for the Queen's chief nurse.

BELZANOR [*with solemn arrogance*] Ftatateeta : I am Belzanor, the captain of the Queen's guard, descended from the gods.

FTATATEETA [*retorting his arrogance with interest*] Belzanor : I am Ftatateeta, the Queen's chief nurse ; and your divine ancestors were proud to be painted on the wall in the pyramids of the kings whom my fathers served.

The women laugh triumphantly.

BELZANOR [*with grim humor*] Ftatateeta : daughter of a long-tongued, swivel-eyed chameleon, the Romans are at hand. [*A cry of terror from the women : they would fly but for the spears*]. Not even the descendants of the gods can resist them ; for they have each man seven arms, each carrying seven spears. The blood in their veins is boiling quicksilver ; and their wives become mothers in three hours, and are slain and eaten the next day.

A shudder of horror from the women. Ftatateeta, despising them and scorning the soldiers, pushes her way through the crowd and confronts the spear points undismayed.

FTATATEETA. Then fly and save yourselves, O cowardly sons of the cheap clay gods that are sold to fish porters ; and leave us to shift for ourselves.

BELZANOR. Not until you have first done our bidding, O terror of manhood. Bring out Cleopatra the Queen to us ; and then go whither you will.

FTATATEETA [*with a derisive laugh*] Now I know why the gods have taken her out of our hands. [*The guardsmen start and look at one another*]. Know, thou foolish soldier, that the Queen has been missing since an hour past sundown.

BELZANOR [*furiously*] Hag : you have hidden her to sell to Cæsar or her brother. [*He grasps her by the left wrist, and drags her, helped by a few of the guard, to the middle of the courtyard, where, as they fling her on her knees, he draws a murderous looking knife*]. Where is she ? Where is she ? or— [*he threatens to cut her throat*].

FTATATEETA [*savagely*] Touch me, dog ; and the Nile will not rise on your fields for seven times seven years of famine.

BELZANOR [*frightened, but desperate*] I will sacrifice : I will pay. Or stay. [*To the Persian*] You, O subtle one : your father's lands lie far from the Nile. Slay her.

PERSIAN [*threatening her with his knife*] Persia has but one god ; yet he loves the blood of old women. Where is Cleopatra ?

FTATATEETA. Persian : as Osiris lives, I do not know. I chid her for bringing evil days upon us by talking to the sacred cats of the priests, and carrying them in her arms. I told her she would be left alone here when the Romans came as a punishment for her disobedience. And now she is gone—run away—hidden. I speak the truth. I call Osiris to witness—

THE WOMEN [*protesting officiously*] She speaks the truth, Belzanor.

BELZANOR. You have frightened the child : she is hiding. Search—quick—into the palace—search every corner.

The guards, led by Belzanor, shoulder their way into the palace through the flying crowd of women, who escape through the courtyard gate.

FTATATEETA [*screaming*] Sacrilege ! Men in the Queen's chambers ! Sa— [*her voice dies away as the Persian puts his knife to her throat*].

BEL AFFRIS [*laying a hand on Ftatateeta's left shoulder*] Forbear her yet a moment, Persian. [*To Ftatateeta, very significantly*] Mother : your gods are asleep or away hunting ; and the sword is at your throat. Bring us to where the Queen is hid, and you shall live.

FTATATEETA [*contemptuously*] Who shall stay the sword in the hand of a fool, if the high gods put it there ? Listen to me, ye young men without understanding. Cleopatra fears me ; but she fears the Romans more. There is but one power greater in her eyes than the wrath of the Queen's nurse and the cruelty of Cæsar ; and that is the power of the Sphinx that sits in the desert watching the way to the sea. What she would have it know, she tells into the ears of the sacred cats ; and on her birthday she sacrifices to it and decks it with poppies. Go ye therefore into the desert and seek Cleopatra in the shadow of the Sphinx ; and on your heads see to it that no harm comes to her.

BEL AFFRIS [to the Persian] May we believe this, O subtle one ?

PERSIAN. Which way come the Romans ?

BEL AFFRIS. Over the desert, from the sea, by this very Sphinx.

PERSIAN [to Ftatateeta] O mother of guile ! O aspic's tongue ! You have made up this tale so that we two may go into the desert and perish on the spears of the Romans. [Lifting his knife] Taste death.

FTATATEETA. Not from thee, baby. [She snatches his ankle from under him and flies stooping along the palace wall, vanishing in the darkness within its precinct. Bel Affris roars with laughter as the Persian tumbles. The guardsmen rush out of the palace with Belzanor and a mob of fugitives, mostly carrying bundles].

PERSIAN. Have you found Cleopatra ?

BELZANOR. She is gone. We have searched every corner.

THE NUBIAN SENTINEL [appearing at the door of the palace] Woe ! Alas ! Fly, fly !

BELZANOR. What is the matter now ?

THE NUBIAN SENTINEL. The sacred white cat has been stolen.

ALL. Woe ! woe ! [General panic. They all fly with cries of consternation. The torch is thrown down and extinguished in the rush. The noise of the fugitives dies away. Darkness and dead silence].

ACT I

The same darkness into which the temple of Ra and the Syrian palace vanished. The same silence. Suspense. Then the blackness and stillness break softly into silver mist and strange airs as the windswept harp of Memnon plays at the dawning of the moon. It rises full over the desert ; and a vast horizon comes into relief, broken by a huge shape which soon reveals itself in the spreading radiance as a Sphinx pedestalled on the sands. The light still clears, until the upraised eyes of the image are distinguished looking straight forward and upward in infinite fearless vigil, and a mass of color between its great paws defines itself as a heap of red poppies on which a girl lies motionless, her silken vest heaving gently and regularly with the breathing of a dreamless sleeper, and her braided hair glittering in a shaft of moonlight like a bird's wing.

Suddenly there comes from afar a vaguely fearful sound (it might be the bellow of a Minotaur softened by great distance) and Memnon's music stops. Silence : then a few faint high-ringing trumpet notes. Then silence again. Then a man comes from the south with stealing steps, ravished by the mystery of the night, all wonder, and halts, lost in contemplation, opposite the left flank of the Sphinx, whose bosom, with its burden, is hidden from him by its massive shoulder.

THE MAN. Hail, Sphinx : salutation from Julius Cæsar ! I have wandered in many lands, seeking the lost regions from which my birth into this world exiled me, and the company of creatures such as I myself. I have found flocks and pastures, men and cities, but no other Cæsar, no air native to me, no man kindred to me, none who can do my day's deed, and think my night's thought. In the little world yonder, Sphinx, my place is as high as yours in this great desert ; only I wander, and you sit still ; I conquer, and you endure ; I work and wonder, you watch and wait ; I look up and am dazzled, look down and am darkened, look round and am puzzled, whilst your eyes never turn from looking out—out of the world—to the lost region—the home from which we have strayed. Sphinx, you and I, strangers to the race of men, are no strangers to one another: have I not been conscious of you and of this place since I was born? Rome is a madman's dream : this is my Reality. These starry lamps of yours I have seen from afar in Gaul, in Britain, in Spain, in Thessaly, signalling great secrets to some eternal sentinel below, whose post I never could find. And here at last is their sentinel—an image of the constant and immortal part of my life, silent, full of thoughts, alone in the silver desert. Sphinx, Sphinx : I have climbed mountains at night to hear in the distance the stealthy footfall of the winds that chase your sands in forbidden play— our invisible children, O Sphinx, laughing in whispers. My way hither was the way of destiny ; for I am he of whose genius you are the symbol : part brute, part woman, and part god—nothing of man in me at all. Have I read your riddle, Sphinx?

THE GIRL [*who has wakened, and peeped cautiously from her nest to see who is speaking*] Old gentleman.

CÆSAR [*starting violently, and clutching his sword*] Immortal gods !

THE GIRL. Old gentleman : dont run away.

CÆSAR [*stupefied*] "Old gentleman : dont run away" ! ! ! This ! to Julius Cæsar !

THE GIRL [*urgently*] Old gentleman.

CÆSAR. Sphinx : you presume on your centuries. I am younger than you, though your voice is but a girl's voice as yet.

THE GIRL. Climb up here, quickly ; or the Romans will come and eat you.

CÆSAR [*running forward past the Sphinx's shoulder, and seeing her*] A child at its breast ! a divine child !

THE GIRL. Come up quickly. You must get up at its side and creep round.

CÆSAR [*amazed*] Who are you?

THE GIRL. Cleopatra, Queen of Egypt.

CÆSAR. Queen of the Gypsies, you mean.

CLEOPATRA. You must not be disrespectful to me, or the Sphinx will let the Romans eat you. Come up. It is quite cosy here.

CÆSAR [to himself] What a dream ! What a magnificent dream ! Only let me not wake, and I will conquer ten continents to pay for dreaming it out to the end. [He climbs to the Sphinx's flank, and presently reappears to her on the pedestal, stepping round its right shoulder].

CLEOPATRA. Take care. Thats right. Now sit down : you may have its other paw. [She seats herself comfortably on its left paw]. It is very powerful and will protect us ; but [shivering, and with plaintive loneliness] it would not take any notice of me or keep me company. I am glad you have come : I was very lonely. Did you happen to see a white cat anywhere ?

CÆSAR [sitting slowly down on the right paw in extreme wonderment] Have you lost one ?

CLEOPATRA. Yes : the sacred white cat : is it not dreadful ? I brought him here to sacrifice him to the Sphinx ; but when we got a little way from the city a black cat called him, and he jumped out of my arms and ran away to it. Do you think that the black cat can have been my great-great-great-grandmother ?

CÆSAR [staring at her] Your great-great-great-grandmother ! Well, why not ? Nothing would surprise me on this night of nights.

CLEOPATRA. I think it must have been. My great-grandmother's great-grandmother was a black kitten of the sacred white cat ; and the river Nile made her his seventh wife. That is why my hair is so wavy. And I always want to be let do as I like, no matter whether it is the will of the gods or not : that is because my blood is made with Nile water.

CÆSAR. What are you doing here at this time of night ? Do you live here ?

CLEOPATRA. Of course not : I am the Queen ; and I shall live in the palace at Alexandria when I have killed my brother, who drove me out of it. When I am old enough I shall do just what I like. I shall be able to poison the slaves and see them wriggle, and pretend to Ftatateeta that she is going to be put into the fiery furnace.

CÆSAR. Hm ! Meanwhile why are you not at home and in bed ?

CLEOPATRA. Because the Romans are coming to eat us all. You are not at home and in bed either.

CÆSAR [with conviction] Yes I am. I live in a tent ; and I am now in that tent, fast asleep and dreaming. Do you suppose that I believe you are real, you impossible little dream witch ?

CLEOPATRA [giggling and leaning trustfully towards him] You are a funny old gentleman. I like you.

CÆSAR. Ah, that spoils the dream. Why dont you dream that I am young ?

CLEOPATRA. I wish you were ; only I think I should be more afraid of you. I like men, especially young men with round strong arms ; but I am afraid of them. You are old and rather thin and stringy ; but you have a nice voice ; and I like to have somebody to talk to, though I think you are a little mad. It is the moon that makes you talk to yourself in that silly way.

CÆSAR. What ! you heard that, did you ? I was saying my prayers to the great Sphinx.

CLEOPATRA. But this isnt the great Sphinx.

CÆSAR [much disappointed, looking up at the statue] What !

CLEOPATRA. This is only a dear little kitten of a Sphinx. Why, the great Sphinx is so big that it has a temple between its paws. This is my pet Sphinx. Tell me : do you think the Romans have any sorcerers who could take us away from the Sphinx by magic ?

CÆSAR. Why ? Are you afraid of the Romans ?

CLEOPATRA [very seriously] Oh, they would eat us if they caught us. They are barbarians. Their chief is called Julius Cæsar. His father was a tiger and his mother a burning mountain ; and his nose is like an elephant's trunk. [Cæsar involuntarily rubs his nose]. They all have long noses, and ivory tusks, and little tails, and seven arms with a hundred arrows in each ; and they live on human flesh.

CÆSAR. Would you like me to shew you a real Roman ?

CLEOPATRA [*terrified*] No. You are frightening me.

CÆSAR. No matter : this is only a dream—

CLEOPATRA [*excitedly*] It is not a dream : it is not a dream. See, see. [*She plucks a pin from her hair and jabs it repeatedly into his arm*].

CÆSAR. Ffff—Stop. [*Wrathfully*] How dare you ?

CLEOPATRA [*abashed*] You said you were dreaming. [*Whimpering*] I only wanted to shew you—

CÆSAR [*gently*] Come, come : dont cry. A queen mustnt cry. [*He rubs his arm, wondering at the reality of the smart*]. Am I awake ? [*He strikes his hand against the Sphinx to test its solidity. It feels so real that he begins to be alarmed, and says perplexedly*] Yes, I— [*quite panicstricken*] no : impossible : madness, madness ! [*Desperately*] Back to camp— to camp. [*He rises to spring down from the pedestal*].

CLEOPATRA [*flinging her arms in terror round him*] No : you shant leave me. No, no, no : dont go. I'm afraid— afraid of the Romans.

CÆSAR [*as the conviction that he is really awake forces itself on him*] Cleopatra : can you see my face well ?

CLEOPATRA. Yes. It is so white in the moonlight.

CÆSAR. Are you sure it is the moonlight that makes me look whiter than an Egyptian ? [*Grimly*] Do you notice that I have a rather long nose ?

CLEOPATRA [*recoiling, paralysed by a terrible suspicion*] Oh !

CÆSAR. It is a Roman nose, Cleopatra.

CLEOPATRA. Ah ! [*With a piercing scream she springs up ; darts round the left shoulder of the Sphinx ; scrambles down to the sand ; and falls on her knees in frantic supplication, shrieking*] Bite him in two, Sphinx : bite him in two. I meant to sacrifice the white cat—I did indeed—I [*Cæsar, who has slipped down from the pedestal, touches her on the shoulder*]—Ah ! [*She buries her head in her arms*].

CÆSAR. Cleopatra : shall I teach you a way to prevent Cæsar from eating you ?

CLEOPATRA [*clinging to him piteously*] Oh do, do, do. I will steal Ftatateeta's jewels and give them to you. I will make the river Nile water your lands twice a year.

CÆSAR. Peace, peace, my child. Your gods are afraid of the Romans : you see the Sphinx dare not bite me, nor prevent me carrying you off to Julius Cæsar.

CLEOPATRA [*in pleading murmurings*] You wont, you wont. You said you wouldnt.

CÆSAR. Cæsar never eats women.

CLEOPATRA [*springing up full of hope*] What !

CÆSAR [*impressively*] But he eats girls [*she relapses*] and cats. Now you are a silly little girl ; and you are descended from the black kitten. You are both a girl and a cat.

CLEOPATRA [*trembling*] And will he eat me ?

CÆSAR. Yes ; unless you make him believe that you are a woman.

CLEOPATRA. Oh, you must get a sorcerer to make a woman of me. Are you a sorcerer ?

CÆSAR. Perhaps. But it will take a long time ; and this very night you must stand face to face with Cæsar in the palace of your fathers.

CLEOPATRA. No, no. I darent.

CÆSAR. Whatever dread may be in your soul—however terrible Cæsar may be to you—you must confront him as a brave woman and a great queen ; and you must feel no fear. If your hand shakes : if your voice quavers ; then —night and death ! [*She moans*]. But if he thinks you worthy to rule, he will set you on the throne by his side and make you the real ruler of Egypt.

CLEOPATRA [*despairingly*] No : he will find me out : he will find me out.

CÆSAR [*rather mournfully*] He is easily deceived by women. Their eyes dazzle him ; and he sees them not as they are, but as he wishes them to appear to him.

CLEOPATRA [*hopefully*] Then we will cheat him. I will

put on Ftatateeta's head-dress ; and he will think me quite an old woman.

CÆSAR. If you do that he will eat you at one mouthful.

CLEOPATRA. But I will give him a cake with my magic opal and seven hairs of the white cat baked in it ; and—

CÆSAR [*abruptly*] Pah ! you are a little fool. He will eat your cake and you too. [*He turns contemptuously from her*].

CLEOPATRA [*running after him and clinging to him*] Oh please, please ! I will do whatever you tell me. I will be good. I will be your slave. [*Again the terrible bellowing note sounds across the desert, now closer at hand. It is the bucina, the Roman war trumpet*].

CÆSAR. Hark !

CLEOPATRA [*trembling*] What was that ?

CÆSAR. Cæsar's voice.

CLEOPATRA [*pulling at his hand*] Let us run away. Come. Oh, come.

CÆSAR. You are safe with me until you stand on your throne to receive Cæsar. Now lead me thither.

CLEOPATRA [*only too glad to get away*] I will, I will. [*Again the bucina*]. Oh come, come, come : the gods are angry. Do you feel the earth shaking ?

CÆSAR. It is the tread of Cæsar's legions.

CLEOPATRA [*drawing him away*] This way, quickly. And let us look for the white cat as we go. It is he that has turned you into a Roman.

CÆSAR. Incorrigible, oh, incorrigible ! Away ! [*He follows her, the bucina sounding louder as they steal across the desert. The moonlight wanes : the horizon again shews black against the sky, broken only by the fantastic silhouette of the Sphinx. The sky itself vanishes in darkness, from which there is no relief until the gleam of a distant torch falls on great Egyptian pillars supporting the roof of a majestic corridor. At the further end of this corridor a Nubian slave appears carrying the torch. Cæsar, still led by Cleopatra, follows him. They come down the corridor, Cæsar peering keenly about at the strange architecture, and at the pillar shadows between which, as the passing torch makes them*] *hurry noiselessly backwards, figures of men with wings and hawks' heads, and vast black marble cats, seem to flit in and out of ambush. Further along, the wall turns a corner and makes a spacious transept in which Cæsar sees, on his right, a throne, and behind the throne a door. On each side of the throne is a slender pillar with a lamp on it*].

CÆSAR. What place is this ?

CLEOPATRA. This is where I sit on the throne when I am allowed to wear my crown and robes. [*The slave holds his torch to shew the throne*].

CÆSAR. Order the slave to light the lamps.

CLEOPATRA [*shyly*] Do you think I may ?

CÆSAR. Of course. You are the Queen. [*She hesitates*]. Go on.

CLEOPATRA [*timidly, to the slave*] Light all the lamps.

FTATATEETA [*suddenly coming from behind the throne*] Stop. [*The slave stops. She turns sternly to Cleopatra, who quails like a naughty child*]. Who is this you have with you ; and how dare you order the lamps to be lighted without my permission ? [*Cleopatra is dumb with apprehension*].

CÆSAR. Who is she ?

CLEOPATRA. Ftatateeta.

FTATATEETA [*arrogantly*] Chief nurse to—

CÆSAR [*cutting her short*] I speak to the Queen. Be silent. [*To Cleopatra*] Is this how your servants know their places ? Send her away ; and do you [*to the slave*] do as the Queen has bidden. [*The slave lights the lamps. Meanwhile Cleopatra stands hesitating, afraid of Ftatateeta*]. You are the Queen : send her away.

CLEOPATRA [*cajoling*] Ftatateeta, dear : you must go away—just for a little.

CÆSAR. You are not commanding her to go away : you are begging her. You are no Queen. You will be eaten. Farewell. [*He turns to go*].

CLEOPATRA [*clutching him*] No, no, no. Dont leave me.

CÆSAR. A Roman does not stay with queens who are afraid of their slaves.

CLEOPATRA. I am not afraid. Indeed I am not afraid.

FTATATEETA. We shall see who is afraid here. [*Menacingly*] Cleopatra—

CÆSAR. On your knees, woman : am I also a child that you dare trifle with me ? [*He points to the floor at Cleopatra's feet. Ftatateeta, half cowed, half savage, hesitates. Cæsar calls to the Nubian*] Slave. [*The Nubian comes to him*] Can you cut off a head ? [*The Nubian nods and grins ecstatically, showing all his teeth. Cæsar takes his sword by the scabbard, ready to offer the hilt to the Nubian, and turns again to Ftatateeta, repeating his gesture*]. Have you remembered yourself, mistress ?

Ftatateeta, crushed, kneels before Cleopatra, who can hardly believe her eyes.

FTATATEETA [*hoarsely*] O Queen, forget not thy servant in the days of thy greatness.

CLEOPATRA [*blazing with excitement*] Go. Begone. Go away. [*Ftatateeta rises with stooped head, and moves backwards towards the door. Cleopatra watches her submission eagerly, almost clapping her hands, which are trembling. Suddenly she cries*] Give me something to beat her with. [*She snatches a snake-skin from the throne and dashes after Ftatateeta, whirling it like a scourge in the air. Cæsar makes a bound and manages to catch her and hold her while Ftatateeta escapes*].

CÆSAR. You scratch, kitten, do you ?

CLEOPATRA [*breaking from him*] I will beat somebody. I will beat him. [*She attacks the slave*]. There, there, there ! [*The slave flies for his life up the corridor and vanishes. She throws the snake-skin away and jumps on the step of the throne with her arms waving, crying*] I am a real Queen at last—a real, real Queen ! Cleopatra the Queen ! [*Cæsar shakes his head dubiously, the advantage of the change seeming open to question from the point of view of the general welfare of Egypt. She turns and looks at him exultantly. Then she jumps down from the steps, runs to him, and flings her arms round him rapturously, crying*] Oh, I love you for making me a Queen.

CÆSAR. But queens love only kings.

CLEOPATRA. I will make all the men I love kings. I will make you a king. I will have many young kings, with round, strong arms ; and when I am tired of them I will whip them to death ; but you shall always be my king : my nice, kind, wise, good old king.

CÆSAR. Oh, my wrinkles, my wrinkles ! And my child's heart ! You will be the most dangerous of all Cæsar's conquests.

CLEOPATRA [appalled] Cæsar ! I forgot Cæsar. [Anxiously] You will tell him that I am a Queen, will you not ?—a real Queen. Listen ! [stealthily coaxing him] : let us run away and hide until Cæsar is gone.

CÆSAR. If you fear Cæsar, you are no true queen ; and though you were to hide beneath a pyramid, he would go straight to it and lift it with one hand. And then— ! [he chops his teeth together].

CLEOPATRA [trembling] Oh !

CÆSAR. Be afraid if you dare. [The note of the bucina resounds again in the distance. She moans with fear. Cæsar exults in it, exclaiming] Aha ! Cæsar approaches the throne of Cleopatra. Come : take your place. [He takes her hand and leads her to the throne. She is too downcast to speak]. Ho, there, Teetatota. How do you call your slaves ?

CLEOPATRA [spiritlessly, as she sinks on the throne and cowers there, shaking] Clap your hands.

He claps his hands. Ftatateeta returns.

CÆSAR. Bring the Queen's robes, and her crown, and her women ; and prepare her.

CLEOPATRA [eagerly—recovering herself a little] Yes, the crown, Ftatateeta : I shall wear the crown.

FTATATEETA. For whom must the Queen put on her state ?

CÆSAR. For a citizen of Rome. A king of kings, Totateeta.

CLEOPATRA [stamping at her] How dare you ask questions? Go and do as you are told. [Ftatateeta goes out with a grim smile. Cleopatra goes on eagerly, to Cæsar] Cæsar will know that I am a Queen when he sees my crown and robes, will he not ?

CÆSAR. No. How shall he know that you are not a slave dressed up in the Queen's ornaments ?

CLEOPATRA. You must tell him.

CÆSAR. He will not ask me. He will know Cleopatra by her pride, her courage, her majesty, and her beauty. [*She looks very doubtful*] Are you trembling ?

CLEOPATRA [*shivering with dread*] No, I—I— [*in a very sickly voice*] No.

Ftatateeta and three women come in with the regalia.

FTATATEETA. Of all the Queen's women, these three alone are left. The rest are fled. [*They begin to deck Cleopatra, who submits, pale and motionless*].

CÆSAR. Good, good. Three are enough. Poor Cæsar generally has to dress himself.

FTATATEETA [*contemptuously*] The queen of Egypt is not a Roman barbarian. [*To Cleopatra*] Be brave, my nursling. Hold up your head before this stranger.

CÆSAR [*admiring Cleopatra, and placing the crown on her head*] Is it sweet or bitter to be a Queen, Cleopatra ?

CLEOPATRA. Bitter.

CÆSAR. Cast out fear ; and you will conquer Cæsar. Tota : are the Romans at hand ?

FTATATEETA. They are at hand ; and the guard has fled

THE WOMEN [*wailing subduedly*] Woe to us !

The Nubian comes running down the hall.

NUBIAN. The Romans are in the courtyard. [*He bolts through the door. With a shriek, the women fly after him Ftatateeta's jaw expresses savage resolution : she does not budge. Cleopatra can hardly restrain herself from following them. Cæsar grips her wrist, and looks steadfastly at her. She stands like a martyr*].

CÆSAR. The Queen must face Cæsar alone. Answer " So be it."

CLEOPATRA [*white*] So be it.

CÆSAR [*releasing her*] Good.

A tramp and tumult of armed men is heard. Cleopatra's terror increases. The bucina sounds close at hand, followed by a formidable clangor of trumpets. This is too much for

Cleopatra : she utters a cry and darts towards the door. Ftatateeta stops her ruthlessly.

FTATATEETA. You are my nursling. You have said " So be it " ; and if you die for it, you must make the Queen's word good. [*She hands Cleopatra to Cæsar, who takes her back, almost beside herself with apprehension, to the throne*].

CÆSAR. Now, if you quail— ! [*He seats himself on the throne*].

She stands on the step, all but unconscious, waiting for death. The Roman soldiers troop in tumultuously through the corridor, headed by their ensign with his eagle, and their bucinator, a burly fellow with his instrument coiled round his body, its brazen bell shaped like the head of a howling wolf. When they reach the transept, they stare in amazement at the throne ; dress into ordered rank opposite it ; draw their swords and lift them in the air with a shout of Hail, Cæsar. *Cleopatra turns and stares wildly at Cæsar ; grasps the situation ; and, with a great sob of relief, falls into his arms.*

ACT II

*Alexandria. A hall on the first floor of the Palace, ending
in a loggia approached by two steps. Through the arches of
the loggia the Mediterranean can be seen, bright in the
morning sun. The clean lofty walls, painted with a procession
of the Egyptian theocracy, presented in profile as flat ornament, and the absence of mirrors, sham perspectives, stuffy
upholstery and textiles, make the place handsome, wholesome,
simple and cool, or, as a rich English manufacturer would
express it, poor, bare, ridiculous and unhomely. For Tottenham Court Road civilization is to this Egyptian civilization as
glass bead and tattoo civilization is to Tottenham Court Road.*

*The young king Ptolemy Dionysus (aged ten) is at the top
of the steps, on his way in through the loggia, led by his
guardian Pothinus, who has him by the hand. The court is
assembled to receive him. It is made up of men and women
(some of the women being officials) of various complexions and
races, mostly Egyptian ; some of them, comparatively fair,
from lower Egypt, some, much darker, from upper Egypt ;
with a few Greeks and Jews. Prominent in a group on
Ptolemy's right hand is Theodotus, Ptolemy's tutor. Another
group, on Ptolemy's left, is headed by Achillas, the general
of Ptolemy's troops. Theodotus is a little old man, whose
features are as cramped and wizened as his limbs, except
his tall straight forehead, which occupies more space than all
the rest of his face. He maintains an air of magpie keenness
and profundity, listening to what the others say with the
sarcastic vigilance of a philosopher listening to the exercises
of his disciples. Achillas is a tall handsome man of thirty-five,
with a fine black beard curled like the coat of a poodle.
Apparently not a clever man, but distinguished and dignified.
Pothinus is a vigorous man of fifty, a eunuch, passionate,
energetic and quick witted, but of common mind and character;
impatient and unable to control his temper. He has fine
tawny hair, like fur. Ptolemy, the King, looks much older
than an English boy of ten ; but he has the childish air, the*

habit of being in leading strings, the mixture of impotence and petulance, the appearance of being excessively washed, combed and dressed by other hands, which is exhibited by court-bred princes of all ages.

All receive the King with reverences. He comes down the steps to a chair of state which stands a little to his right, the only seat in the hall. Taking his place before it, he looks nervously for instructions to Pothinus, who places himself at his left hand.

POTHINUS. The king of Egypt has a word to speak.

THEODOTUS [*in a squeak which he makes impressive by sheer self-opinionativeness*] Peace for the King's word !

PTOLEMY [*without any vocal inflexions : he is evidently repeating a lesson*] Take notice of this all of you. I am the first-born son of Auletes the Flute Blower who was your King. My sister Berenice drove him from his throne and reigned in his stead but—but— [*he hesitates*]—

POTHINUS [*stealthily prompting*]—but the gods would not suffer—

PTOLEMY. Yes—the gods would not suffer—not suffer – [*He stops ; then, crestfallen*] I forget what the gods would not suffer.

THEODOTUS. Let Pothinus, the King's guardian, speak for the King.

POTHINUS [*suppressing his impatience with difficulty*] The King wished to say that the gods would not suffer the impiety of his sister to go unpunished.

PTOLEMY [*hastily*] Yes : I remember the rest of it. [*He resumes his monotone*]. Therefore the gods sent a stranger one Mark Antony a Roman captain of horsemen across the sands of the desert and he set my father again upon the throne. And my father took Berenice my sister and struck her head off. And now that my father is dead yet another of his daughters my sister Cleopatra would snatch the kingdom from me and reign in my place. But the gods would not suffer— [*Pothinus coughs admonitorily*]—the gods—the gods would not suffer—

POTHINUS [*prompting*]—will not maintain—

PTOLEMY. Oh yes—will not maintain such iniquity they will give her head to the axe even as her sister's. But with the help of the witch Ftatateeta she hath cast a spell on the Roman Julius Cæsar to make him uphold her false pretence to rule in Egypt. Take notice then that I will not suffer—that I will not suffer—[*pettishly, to Pothinus*] What is it that I will not suffer?

POTHINUS [*suddenly exploding with all the force and emphasis of political passion*] The King will not suffer a foreigner to take from him the throne of our Egypt. [*A shout of applause*]. Tell the King, Achillas, how many soldiers and horsemen follow the Roman?

THEODOTUS. Let the King's general speak!

ACHILLAS. But two Roman legions, O King. Three thousand soldiers and scarce a thousand horsemen.

The court breaks into derisive laughter ; and a great chattering begins, amid which Rufio, a Roman officer, appears in the loggia. He is a burly, black-bearded man of middle age, very blunt, prompt and rough, with small clear eyes, and plump nose and cheeks, which, however, like the rest of his flesh, are in ironhard condition.

RUFIO [*from the steps*] Peace, ho! [*The laughter and chatter cease abruptly*]. Cæsar approaches.

THEODOTUS [*with much presence of mind*] The King permits the Roman commander to enter!

Cæsar, plainly dressed, but wearing an oak wreath to conceal his baldness, enters from the loggia, attended by Britannus, his secretary, a Briton, about forty, tall, solemn, and already slightly bald, with a heavy, drooping, hazel-colored moustache trained so as to lose its ends in a pair of trim whiskers. He is carefully dressed in blue, with portfolio, inkhorn, and reed pen at his girdle. His serious air and sense of the importance of the business in hand is in marked contrast to the kindly interest of Cæsar, who looks at the scene, which is new to him, with the frank curiosity of a child, and then turns to the king's chair : Britannus and Rufio posting themselves near the steps at the other side.

CÆSAR [*looking at Pothinus and Ptolemy*] Which is the King? the man or the boy?

POTHINUS. I am Pothinus, the guardian of my lord the King.

CÆSAR [*patting Ptolemy kindly on the shoulder*] So you are the King. Dull work at your age, eh? [*To Pothinus*] Your servant, Pothinus. [*He turns away unconcernedly and comes slowly along the middle of the hall, looking from side to side at the courtiers until he reaches Achillas*]. And this gentleman?

THEODOTUS. Achillas, the King's general.

CÆSAR [*to Achillas, very friendly*] A general, eh? I am a general myself. But I began too old, too old. Health and many victories, Achillas!

ACHILLAS. As the gods will, Cæsar.

CÆSAR [*turning to Theodotus*] And you, sir, are—?

THEODOTUS. Theodotus, the King's tutor.

CÆSAR. You teach men how to be kings, Theodotus. That is very clever of you. [*Looking at the gods on the walls as he turns away from Theodotus and goes up again to Pothinus*] And this place?

POTHINUS. The council chamber of the chancellors of the King's treasury, Cæsar.

CÆSAR. Ah! that reminds me. I want some money.

POTHINUS. The King's treasury is poor, Cæsar.

CÆSAR. Yes: I notice that there is but one chair in it.

RUFIO [*shouting gruffly*] Bring a chair there, some of you, for Cæsar.

PTOLEMY [*rising shyly to offer his chair*] Cæsar—

CÆSAR [*kindly*] No, no, my boy: that is your chair of state. Sit down.

He makes Ptolemy sit down again. Meanwhile Rufio, looking about him, sees in the nearest corner an image of the god Ra, represented as a seated man with the head of a hawk. Before the image is a bronze tripod, about as large as a three-legged stool, with a stick of incense burning on it. Rufio, with Roman resourcefulness and indifference to foreign superstitions, promptly seizes the tripod; shakes off the incense ; blows away the ash ; and dumps it down behind Cæsar, nearly in the middle of the hall.

RUFIO. Sit on that, Cæsar.

A shiver runs through the court, followed by a hissing whisper of Sacrilege !

CÆSAR [*seating himself*] Now, Pothinus, to business. I am badly in want of money.

BRITANNUS [*disapproving of these informal expressions*] My master would say that there is a lawful debt due to Rome by Egypt, contracted by the King's deceased father to the Triumvirate ; and that it is Cæsar's duty to his country to require immediate payment.

CÆSAR [*blandly*] Ah, I forgot. I have not made my companions known here. Pothinus : this is Britannus, my secretary. He is an islander from the western end of the world, a day's voyage from Gaul. [*Britannus bows stiffly*]. This gentleman is Rufio, my comrade in arms. [*Rufio nods*]. Pothinus : I want 1,600 talents.

The courtiers, appalled, murmur loudly, and Theodotus and Achillas appeal mutely to one another against so monstrous a demand.

POTHINUS [*aghast*] Forty million sesterces ! Impossible. There is not so much money in the King's treasury.

CÆSAR [*encouragingly*] Only sixteen hundred talents, Pothinus. Why count it in sesterces ? A sestertius is only worth a loaf of bread.

POTHINUS. And a talent is worth a racehorse. I say it is impossible. We have been at strife here, because the King's sister Cleopatra falsely claims his throne. The King's taxes have not been collected for a whole year.

CÆSAR. Yes they have, Pothinus. My officers have been collecting them all morning. [*Renewed whisper and sensation, not without some stifled laughter, among the courtiers*].

RUFIO [*bluntly*] You must pay, Pothinus. Why waste words ? You are getting off cheaply enough.

POTHINUS [*bitterly*] Is it possible that Cæsar, the conqueror of the world, has time to occupy himself with such a trifle as our taxes ?

CÆSAR. My friend : taxes are the chief business of a conqueror of the world.

POTHINUS. Then take warning, Cæsar. This day, the treasures of the temple and the gold of the King's treasury shall be sent to the mint to be melted down for our ransom in the sight of the people. They shall see us sitting under bare walls and drinking from wooden cups. And their wrath be on your head, Cæsar, if you force us to this sacrilege !

CÆSAR. Do not fear, Pothinus : the people know how well wine tastes in wooden cups. In return for your bounty, I will settle this dispute about the throne for you, if you will. What say you ?

POTHINUS. If I say no, will that hinder you ?

RUFIO [defiantly] No.

CÆSAR. You say the matter has been at issue for a year, Pothinus. May I have ten minutes at it ?

POTHINUS. You will do your pleasure, doubtless.

CÆSAR. Good ! But first, let us have Cleopatra here.

THEODOTUS. She is not in Alexandria : she is fled into Syria.

CÆSAR. I think not. [To Rufio] Call Totateeta.

RUFIO [calling] Ho there, Teetatota.

Ftatateeta enters the loggia, and stands arrogantly at the top of the steps.

FTATATEETA. Who pronounces the name of Ftatateeta, the Queen's chief nurse ?

CÆSAR. Nobody can pronounce it, Tota, except yourself. Where is your mistress ?

Cleopatra, who is hiding behind Ftatateeta, peeps out at them, laughing. Cæsar rises.

CÆSAR. Will the Queen favor us with her presence for a moment ?

CLEOPATRA [pushing Ftatateeta aside and standing haughtily on the brink of the steps] Am I to behave like a Queen ?

CÆSAR. Yes.

Cleopatra immediately comes down to the chair of state ; seizes Ptolemy ; drags him out of his seat ; then takes his *place in the chair. Ftatateeta seats herself on the step of the loggia, and sits there, watching the scene with sibylline intensity.*

PTOLEMY [*mortified, and struggling with his tears*] Cæsar : this is how she treats me always. If I am a king why is she allowed to take everything from me ?

CLEOPATRA. You are not to be King, you little cry-baby. You are to be eaten by the Romans.

CÆSAR [*touched by Ptolemy's distress*] Come here, my boy, and stand by me.

Ptolemy goes over to Cæsar, who, resuming his seat on the tripod, takes the boy's hand to encourage him. Cleopatra, furiously jealous, rises and glares at them.

CLEOPATRA [*with flaming cheeks*] Take your throne : I dont want it. [*She flings away from the chair, and approaches Ptolemy, who shrinks from her*]. Go this instant and sit down in your place.

CÆSAR. Go, Ptolemy. Always take a throne when it is offered to you.

RUFIO. I hope you will have the good sense to follow your own advice when we return to Rome, Cæsar.

Ptolemy slowly goes back to the throne, giving Cleopatra a wide berth, in evident fear of her hands. She takes his place beside Cæsar.

CÆSAR. Pothinus—

CLEOPATRA [*interrupting him*] Are you not going to speak to me ?

CÆSAR. Be quiet. Open your mouth again before I give you leave ; and you shall be eaten.

CLEOPATRA. I am not afraid. A queen must not be afraid. Eat my husband there, if you like : he is afraid.

CÆSAR [*starting*] Your husband ! What do you mean ?

CLEOPATRA [*pointing to Ptolemy*] That little thing.

The two Romans and the Briton stare at one another in amazement.

THEODOTUS. Cæsar : you are a stranger here, and not conversant with our laws. The kings and queens of Egypt may not marry except with their own royal blood. Ptolemy

and Cleopatra are born king and consort just as they are
born brother and sister.

BRITANNUS [*shocked*] Cæsar : this is not proper.

THEODOTUS [*outraged*] How !

CÆSAR [*recovering his self-possession*] Pardon him, Theodotus : he is a barbarian, and thinks that the customs of his
tribe and island are the laws of nature.

BRITANNUS. On the contrary, Cæsar, it is these Egyptians
who are barbarians ; and you do wrong to encourage them.
I say it is a scandal.

CÆSAR. Scandal or not, my friend, it opens the gate of
peace. [*He addresses Pothinus seriously*]. Pothinus : hear
what I propose.

RUFIO. Hear Cæsar there.

CÆSAR. Ptolemy and Cleopatra shall reign jointly in
Egypt.

ACHILLAS. What of the King's younger brother and
Cleopatra's younger sister ?

RUFIO [*explaining*] There is another little Ptolemy,
Cæsar : so they tell me.

CÆSAR. Well, the little Ptolemy can marry the other
sister ; and we will make them both a present of Cyprus.

POTHINUS [*impatiently*] Cyprus is of no use to anybody.

CÆSAR. No matter : you shall have it for the sake of
peace.

BRITANNUS [*unconsciously anticipating a later statesman*]
Peace with honor, Pothinus.

POTHINUS [*mutinously*] Cæsar : be honest. The money
you demand is the price of our freedom. Take it ; and leave
us to settle our own affairs.

THE BOLDER COURTIERS [*encouraged by Pothinus's tone
and Cæsar's quietness*] Yes, yes. Egypt for the Egyptians !

*The conference now becomes an altercation, the Egyptians
becoming more and more heated. Cæsar remains unruffled ;
but Rufio grows fiercer and doggeder, and Britannus haughtily
indignant.*

RUFIO [*contemptuously*] Egypt for the Egyptians ! Do
you forget that there is a Roman army of occupation here,

left by Aulus Gabinius when he set up your toy king for you?

ACHILLAS [*suddenly asserting himself*] And now under my command. *I* am the Roman general here, Cæsar.

CÆSAR [*tickled by the humor of the situation*] And also the Egyptian general, eh?

POTHINUS [*triumphantly*] That is so, Cæsar.

CÆSAR [*to Achillas*] So you can make war on the Egyptians in the name of Rome, and on the Romans—on me, if necessary—in the name of Egypt?

ACHILLAS. That is so, Cæsar.

CÆSAR. And which side are you on at present, if I may presume to ask, general?

ACHILLAS. On the side of the right and of the gods.

CÆSAR. Hm! How many men have you?

ACHILLAS. That will appear when I take the field.

RUFIO [*truculently*] Are your men Romans? If not, it matters not how many there are, provided you are no stronger than 500 to ten.

POTHINUS. It is useless to try to bluff us, Rufio. Cæsar has been defeated before and may be defeated again. A few weeks ago Cæsar was flying for his life before Pompey: a few months hence he may be flying for his life before Cato and Juba of Numidia, the African King.

ACHILLAS [*following up Pothinus's speech menacingly*] What can you do with 4,000 men?

THEODOTUS [*following up Achillas's speech with a raucous squeak*] And without money? Away with you.

ALL THE COURTIERS [*shouting fiercely and crowding towards Cæsar*] Away with you. Egypt for the Egyptians! Begone.

Rufio bites his beard, too angry to speak. Cæsar sits as comfortably as if he were at breakfast, and the cat were clamoring for a piece of Finnan-haddie.

CLEOPATRA. Why do you let them talk to you like that, Cæsar? Are you afraid?

CÆSAR. Why, my dear, what they say is quite true.

CLEOPATRA. But if you go away, I shall not be Queen.

CÆSAR. I shall not go away until you are Queen.

POTHINUS. Achillas : if you are not a fool, you will take that girl whilst she is under your hand.

RUFIO [*daring them*] Why not take Cæsar as well, Achillas?

POTHINUS [*retorting the defiance with interest*] Well said, Rufio. Why not ?

RUFIO. Try, Achillas. [*Calling*] Guard there.

The loggia immediately fills with Cæsar's soldiers, who stand, sword in hand, at the top of the steps, waiting the word to charge from their centurion, who carries a cudgel. For a moment the Egyptians face them proudly : then they retire sullenly to their former places.

BRITANNUS. You are Cæsar's prisoners, all of you.

CÆSAR [*benevolently*] Oh no, no, no. By no means. Cæsar's guests, gentlemen.

CLEOPATRA. Wont you cut their heads off ?

CÆSAR. What ! Cut off your brother's head ?

CLEOPATRA. Why not ? He would cut off mine, if he got the chance. Wouldnt you, Ptolemy ?

PTOLEMY [*pale and obstinate*] I would. I will, too, when I grow up.

Cleopatra is rent by a struggle between her newly-acquired dignity as a queen, and a strong impulse to put out her tongue at him. She takes no part in the scene which follows, but watches it with curiosity and wonder, fidgeting with the restlessness of a child, and sitting down on Cæsar's tripod when he rises.

POTHINUS. Cæsar : if you attempt to detain us—

RUFIO. He will succeed, Egyptian : make up your mind to that. We hold the palace, the beach, and the eastern harbor. The road to Rome is open ; and you shall travel it if Cæsar chooses.

CÆSAR [*courteously*] I could do no less, Pothinus, to secure the retreat of my own soldiers. I am accountable for every life among them. But you are free to go. So are all here, and in the palace.

RUFIO [*aghast at this clemency*] What ! Renegades and all ?

CÆSAR [*softening the expression*] Roman army of occupation and all, Rufio.

POTHINUS [*bewildered*] But—but—but—

CÆSAR. Well, my friend ?

POTHINUS. You are turning us out of our own palace into the streets ; and you tell us with a grand air that we are free to go ! It is for you to go.

CÆSAR. Your friends are in the street, Pothinus. You will be safer there.

POTHINUS. This is a trick. I am the king's guardian : I refuse to stir. I stand on my right here. Where is your right ?

CÆSAR. It is in Rufio's scabbard, Pothinus. I may not be able to keep it there if you wait too long.

Sensation.

POTHINUS [*bitterly*] And this is Roman justice !

THEODOTUS. But not Roman gratitude, I hope.

CÆSAR. Gratitude ! Am I in your debt for any service, gentlemen ?

THEODOTUS. Is Cæsar's life of so little account to him that he forgets that we have saved it ?

CÆSAR. My life ! Is that all ?

THEODOTUS. Your life. Your laurels. Your future.

POTHINUS. It is true. I can call a witness to prove that but for us, the Roman army of occupation, led by the greatest soldier in the world, would now have Cæsar at its mercy. [*Calling through the loggia*] Ho, there, Lucius Septimius [*Cæsar starts, deeply moved*] : if my voice can reach you, come forth and testify before Cæsar.

CÆSAR [*shrinking*] No, no.

THEODOTUS. Yes, I say. Let the military tribune bear witness.

Lucius Septimius, a clean shaven, trim athlete of about 40, *with symmetrical features, resolute mouth, and handsome, thin Roman nose, in the dress of a Roman officer, comes in through the loggia and confronts Cæsar, who hides his face with his robe for a moment ; then, mastering himself, drops it, and confronts the tribune with dignity.*

POTHINUS. Bear witness, Lucius Septimius. Cæsar came hither in pursuit of his foe. Did we shelter his foe ?

LUCIUS. As Pompey's foot touched the Egyptian shore, his head fell by the stroke of my sword.

THEODOTUS [*with viperish relish*] Under the eyes of his wife and child ! Remember that, Cæsar ! They saw it from the ship he had just left. We have given you a full and sweet measure of vengeance.

CÆSAR [*with horror*] Vengeance !

POTHINUS. Our first gift to you, as your galley came into the roadstead, was the head of your rival for the empire of the world. Bear witness, Lucius Septimius : is it not so ?

LUCIUS. It is so. With this hand, that slew Pompey, I placed his head at the feet of Cæsar.

CÆSAR. Murderer ! So would you have slain Cæsar, had Pompey been victorious at Pharsalia.

LUCIUS. Woe to the vanquished, Cæsar ! When I served Pompey, I slew as good men as he, only because he conquered them. His turn came at last.

THEODOTUS [*flatteringly*] The deed was not yours, Cæsar, but ours—nay, mine ; for it was done by my counsel. Thanks to us, you keep your reputation for clemency, and have your vengeance too.

CÆSAR. Vengeance ! Vengeance ! ! Oh, if I could stoop to vengeance, what would I not exact from you as the price of this murdered man's blood ? [*They shrink back, appalled and disconcerted*]. Was he not my son-in-law, my ancient friend, for 20 years the master of great Rome, for 30 years the compeller of victory ? Did not I, as a Roman, share his glory ? Was the Fate that forced us to fight for the mastery of the world, of our making ? Am I Julius Cæsar, or am I a wolf, that you fling to me the grey head of the old soldier, the laurelled conqueror, the mighty Roman, treacherously struck down by this callous ruffian, and then claim my gratitude for it ! [*To Lucius Septimius*] Begone : you fill me with horror.

LUCIUS [*cold and undaunted*] Pshaw ! You have seen severed heads before, Cæsar, and severed right hands too,

I think ; some thousands of them, in Gaul, after you vanquished Vercingetorix. Did you spare him, with all your clemency ? Was that vengeance ?

CÆSAR. No, by the gods ! would that it had been ! Vengeance at least is human. No, I say : those severed right hands, and the brave Vercingetorix basely strangled in a vault beneath the Capitol, were [*with shuddering satire*] a wise severity, a necessary protection to the commonwealth, a duty of statesmanship—follies and fictions ten times bloodier than honest vengeance ! What a fool was I then ! To think that men's lives should be at the mercy of such fools ! [*Humbly*] Lucius Septimius, pardon me : why should the slayer of Vercingetorix rebuke the slayer of Pompey ? You are free to go with the rest. Or stay if you will : I will find a place for you in my service.

LUCIUS. The odds are against you, Cæsar. I go. [*He turns to go out through the loggia*].

RUFIO [*full of wrath at seeing his prey escaping*] That means that he is a Republican.

LUCIUS [*turning defiantly on the loggia steps*] And what are you ?

RUFIO. A Cæsarian, like all Cæsar's soldiers.

CÆSAR [*courteously*] Lucius : believe me, Cæsar is no Cæsarian. Were Rome a true republic, then were Cæsar the first of Republicans. But you have made your choice. Farewell.

LUCIUS. Farewell. Come, Achillas, whilst there is yet time.

Cæsar, seeing that Rufio's temper threatens to get the worse of him, puts his hand on his shoulder and brings him down the hall out of harm's way, Britannus accompanying them and posting himself on Cæsar's right hand. This movement brings the three in a little group to the place occupied by Achillas, who moves haughtily away and joins Theodotus on the other side. Lucius Septimius goes out through the soldiers in the loggia. Pothinus, Theodotus and Achillas follow him with the courtiers, very mistrustful of the soldiers, who close up in their rear and go out after them, keeping them moving without much ceremony. The King is left in his chair, piteous, obstinate, with twitching face and fingers. During these movements Rufio maintains an energetic grumbling, as follows :—

RUFIO [*as Lucius departs*] Do you suppose he would let us go if he had our heads in his hands ?

CÆSAR. I have no right to suppose that his ways are any baser than mine.

RUFIO. Psha !

CÆSAR. Rufio : if I take Lucius Septimius for my model, and become exactly like him, ceasing to be Cæsar, will you serve me still ?

BRITANNUS. Cæsar : this is not good sense. Your duty to Rome demands that her enemies should be prevented from doing further mischief. [*Cæsar, whose delight in the moral eye-to-business of his British secretary is inexhaustible, smiles indulgently*].

RUFIO. It is no use talking to him, Britannus : you may save your breath to cool your porridge. But mark this, Cæsar. Clemency is very well for you ; but what is it for your soldiers, who have to fight tomorrow the men you spared yesterday ? You may give what orders you please ; but I tell you that your next victory will be a massacre, thanks to your clemency. *I*, for one, will take no prisoners. I will kill my enemies in the field ; and then you can preach as much clemency as you please : I shall never have to fight them again. And now, with your leave, I will see these gentry off the premises. [*He turns to go*].

CÆSAR [*turning also and seeing Ptolemy*] What ! have they left the boy alone ! Oh shame, shame !

RUFIO [*taking Ptolemy's hand and making him rise*] Come, your majesty !

PTOLEMY [*to Cæsar, drawing away his hand from Rufio*] Is he turning me out of my palace ?

RUFIO [*grimly*] You are welcome to stay if you wish.

CÆSAR [*kindly*] Go, my boy. I will not harm you ; but you will be safer away, among your friends. Here you are in the lion's mouth.

PTOLEMY [*turning to go*] It is not the lion I fear, but

[*looking at Rufio*] the jackal. [*He goes out through the loggia*].

CÆSAR [*laughing approvingly*] Brave boy !

CLEOPATRA [*jealous of Cæsar's approbation, calling after Ptolemy*] Little silly. You think that very clever.

CÆSAR. Britannus : attend the King. Give him in charge to that Pothinus fellow. [*Britannus goes out after Ptolemy*].

RUFIO [*pointing to Cleopatra*] And this piece of goods ? What is to be done with her? However, I suppose I may leave that to you. [*He goes out through the loggia*].

CLEOPATRA [*flushing suddenly and turning on Cæsar*] Did you mean me to go with the rest ?

CÆSAR [*a little preoccupied, goes with a sigh to Ptolemy's chair, whilst she waits for his answer with red cheeks and clenched fists*] You are free to do just as you please, Cleopatra.

CLEOPATRA. Then you do not care whether I stay or not ?

CÆSAR [*smiling*] Of course I had rather you stayed.

CLEOPATRA. Much, much rather ?

CÆSAR [*nodding*] Much, much rather.

CLEOPATRA. Then I consent to stay, because I am asked. But I do not want to, mind.

CÆSAR. That is quite understood. [*Calling*] Totateeta.

Ftatateeta, still seated, turns her eyes on him with a sinister expression, but does not move.

CLEOPATRA [*with a splutter of laughter*] Her name is not Totateeta : it is Ftatateeta. [*Calling*] Ftatateeta. [*Ftatateeta instantly rises and comes to Cleopatra*].

CÆSAR [*stumbling over the name*] Tfatafeeta will forgive the erring tongue of a Roman. Tota : the Queen will hold her state here in Alexandria. Engage women to attend upon her ; and do all that is needful.

FTATATEETA. Am I then the mistress of the Queen's household ?

CLEOPATRA [*sharply*] No : *I* am the mistress of the Queen's household. Go and do as you are told, or I will have you thrown into the Nile this very afternoon, to poison the poor crocodiles.

CÆSAR [shocked] Oh no, no.

CLEOPATRA. Oh yes, yes. You are very sentimental, Cæsar ; but you are clever ; and if you do as I tell you, you will soon learn to govern.

Cæsar, quite dumbfounded by this impertinence, turns in his chair and stares at her.

Ftatateeta, smiling grimly, and shewing a splendid set of teeth, goes, leaving them alone together.

CÆSAR. Cleopatra : I really think I must eat you, after all.

CLEOPATRA [kneeling beside him and looking at him with eager interest, half real, half affected to shew how intelligent she is] You must not talk to me now as if I were a child.

CÆSAR. You have been growing up since the sphinx introduced us the other night ; and you think you know more than I do already.

CLEOPATRA [taken down, and anxious to justify herself] No : that would be very silly of me : of course I know that. But— [suddenly] are you angry with me ?

CÆSAR. No.

CLEOPATRA [only half believing him] Then why are you so thoughtful ?

CÆSAR [rising] I have work to do, Cleopatra.

CLEOPATRA [drawing back] Work ! [Offended] You are tired of talking to me ; and that is your excuse to get away from me.

CÆSAR [sitting down again to appease her] Well, well : another minute. But then—work !

CLEOPATRA. Work ! what nonsense ! You must remember that you arc a king now : I have made you one. Kings dont work.

CÆSAR. Oh ! Who told you that, little kitten ? Eh ?

CLEOPATRA. My father was King of Egypt ; and he never worked. But he was a great king, and cut off my sister's head because she rebelled against him and took the throne from him.

CÆSAR. Well ; and how did he get his throne back again?

CLEOPATRA [eagerly, her eyes lighting up] I will tell you.

A beautiful young man, with strong round arms, came over the desert with many horsemen, and slew my sister's husband and gave my father back his throne. [*Wistfully*] I was only twelve then. Oh, I wish he would come again, now that I am queen. I would make him my husband.

CÆSAR. It might be managed, perhaps ; for it was I who sent that beautiful young man to help your father.

CLEOPATRA [*enraptured*] You know him !

CÆSAR [*nodding*] I do.

CLEOPATRA. Has he come with you ? [*Cæsar shakes his head : she is cruely disappointed*]. Oh, I wish he had, I wish he had. If only I were a little older ; so that he might not think me a mere kitten, as you do ! But perhaps that is because you are old. He is many many years younger than you, is he not ?

CÆSAR [*as if swallowing a pill*] He is somewhat younger.

CLEOPATRA. Would he be my husband, do you think, if I asked him ?

CÆSAR. Very likely.

CLEOPATRA. But I should not like to ask him. Could you not persuade him to ask me—without knowing that I wanted him to ?

CÆSAR [*touched by her innocence of the beautiful young man's character*] My poor child !

CLEOPATRA. Why do you say that as if you were sorry for me ? Does he love anyone else ?

CÆSAR. I am afraid so.

CLEOPATRA [*tearfully*] Then I shall not be his first love.

CÆSAR. Not quite the first. He is greatly admired by women.

CLEOPATRA. I wish I could be the first. But if he loves me, I will make him kill all the rest. Tell me : is he still beautiful ? Do his strong round arms shine in the sun like marble ?

CÆSAR. He is in excellent condition—considering how much he eats and drinks.

CLEOPATRA. Oh, you must not say common, earthly things about him ; for I love him. He is a god.

CÆSAR. He is a great captain of horsemen, and swifter of foot than any other Roman.

CLEOPATRA. What is his real name?

CÆSAR [*puzzled*] His real name?

CLEOPATRA. Yes. I always call him Horus, because Horus is the most beautiful of our gods. But I want to know his real name.

CÆSAR. His name is Mark Antony.

CLEOPATRA [*musically*] Mark Antony, Mark Antony, Mark Antony! What a beautiful name! [*She throws her arms round Cæsar's neck*]. Oh, how I love you for sending him to help my father! Did you love my father very much?

CÆSAR. No, my child; but your father, as you say, never worked. I always work. So when he lost his crown he had to promise me 16,000 talents to get it back for him.

CLEOPATRA. Did he ever pay you?

CÆSAR. Not in full.

CLEOPATRA. He was quite right: it was too dear. The whole world is not worth 16,000 talents.

CÆSAR. That is perhaps true, Cleopatra. Those Egyptians who work paid as much of it as he could drag from them. The rest is still due. But as I most likely shall not get it, I must go back to my work. So you must run away for a little and send my secretary to me.

CLEOPATRA [*coaxing*] No: I want to stay and hear you talk about Mark Antony.

CÆSAR. But if I do not get to work, Pothinus and the rest of them will cut us off from the harbor; and then the way from Rome will be blocked.

CLEOPATRA. No matter: I dont want you to go back to Rome.

CÆSAR. But you want Mark Antony to come from it.

CLEOPATRA [*springing up*] Oh yes, yes, yes: I forgot. Go quickly and work, Cæsar; and keep the way over the sea open for my Mark Antony. [*She runs out through the loggia, kissing her hand to Mark Antony across the sea*].

CÆSAR [*going briskly up the middle of the hall to the loggia steps*] Ho, Britannus. [*He is startled by the entry of a wounded Roman soldier, who confronts him from the upper step*]. What now ?

SOLDIER [*pointing to his bandaged head*] This, Cæsar ; and two of my comrades killed in the market place.

CÆSAR [*quiet, but attending*] Ay. Why ?

SOLDIER. There is an army come to Alexandria, calling itself the Roman army.

CÆSAR. The Roman army of occupation. Ay ?

SOLDIER. Commanded by one Achillas.

CÆSAR. Well ?

SOLDIER. The citizens rose against us when the army entered the gates. I was with two others in the market place when the news came. They set upon us. I cut my way out ; and here I am.

CÆSAR. Good. I am glad to see you alive. [*Rufio enters the loggia hastily, passing behind the soldier to look out through one of the arches at the quay beneath*]. Rufio : we are besieged.

RUFIO. What ! Already ?

CÆSAR. Now or tomorrow : what does it matter ? We shall be besieged.

Britannus runs in.

BRITANNUS. Cæsar—

CÆSAR [*anticipating him*] Yes : I know. [*Rufio and Britannus come down the hall from the loggia at opposite sides, past Cæsar, who waits for a moment near the step to say to the soldier*] Comrade : give the word to turn out on the beach and stand by the boats. Get your wound attended to. Go. [*The soldier hurries out. Cæsar comes down the hall between Rufio and Britannus*] Rufio : we have some ships in the west harbor. Burn them.

RUFIO [*staring*] Burn them ! !

CÆSAR. Take every boat we have in the east harbor, and seize the Pharos—that island with the lighthouse. Leave half our men behind to hold the beach and the quay outside this palace : that is the way home.

RUFIO [*disapproving strongly*] Are we to give up the city ?

CÆSAR. We have not got it, Rufio. This palace we have ;

and—what is that building next door ?

RUFIO. The theatre.

CÆSAR. We will have that too : it commands the strand. For the rest, Egypt for the Egyptians !

RUFIO. Well, you know best, I suppose. Is that all ?

CÆSAR. That is all. Are those ships burnt yet ?

RUFIO. Be easy : I shall waste no more time. [*He runs out*].

BRITANNUS. Cæsar : Pothinus demands speech of you. In my opinion he needs a lesson. His manner is most insolent.

CÆSAR. Where is he ?

BRITANNUS. He waits without.

CÆSAR. Ho there ! admit Pothinus.

Pothinus appears in the loggia, and comes down the hall very haughtily to Cæsar's left hand.

CÆSAR. Well, Pothinus ?

POTHINUS. I have brought you our ultimatum, Cæsar.

CÆSAR. Ultimatum ! The door was open : you should have gone out through it before you declared war. You are my prisoner now. [*He goes to the chair and loosens his toga*].

POTHINUS [*scornfully*] I your prisoner ! Do you know that you are in Alexandria, and that King Ptolemy, with an army outnumbering your little troop a hundred to one, is in possession of Alexandria ?

CÆSAR [*unconcernedly taking off his toga and throwing it on the chair*] Well, my friend, get out if you can. And tell your friends not to kill any more Romans in the market place. Otherwise my soldiers, who do not share my celebrated clemency, will probably kill you. Britannus : pass the word to the guard ; and fetch my armor. [*Britannus runs out. Rufio returns*]. Well ?

RUFIO [*pointing from the loggia to a cloud of smoke drifting over the harbor*] See there ! [*Pothinus runs eagerly up the steps to look out*].

CÆSAR. What, ablaze already ! Impossible !

RUFIO. Yes, five good ships, and a barge laden with oil grappled to each. But it is not my doing : the Egyptians have saved me the trouble. They have captured the west harbor.

CÆSAR [*anxiously*] And the east harbor ? The lighthouse, Rufio ?

RUFIO [*with a sudden splutter of raging ill usage, coming down to Cæsar and scolding him*] Can I embark a legion in five minutes ? The first cohort is already on the beach. We can do no more. If you want faster work, come and do it yourself.

CÆSAR [*soothing him*] Good, good. Patience, Rufio, patience.

RUFIO. Patience ! Who is impatient here, you or I ? Would I be here, if I could not oversee them from that balcony ?

CÆSAR. Forgive me, Rufio ; and [*anxiously*] hurry them as much as—

He is interrupted by an outcry as of an old man in the extremity of misfortune. It draws near rapidly ; and Theodotus rushes in, tearing his hair, and squeaking the most lamentable exclamations. Rufio steps back to stare at him, amazed at his frantic condition. Pothinus turns to listen.

THEODOTUS [*on the steps, with uplifted arms*] Horror unspeakable ! Woe, alas ! Help !

RUFIO. What now ?

CÆSAR [*frowning*] Who is slain ?

THEODOTUS. Slain ! Oh, worse than the death of ten thousand men ! Loss irreparable to mankind !

RUFIO. What has happened, man ?

THEODOTUS [*rushing down the hall between them*] The fire has spread from your ships. The first of the seven wonders of the world perishes. The library of Alexandria is in flames.

RUFIO. Psha ! [*Quite relieved, he goes up to the loggia and watches the preparations of the troops on the beach*].

CÆSAR. Is that all ?

THEODOTUS [*unable to believe his senses*] All ! Cæsar : will you go down to posterity as a barbarous soldier too ignorant to know the value of books ?

CÆSAR. Theodotus : I am an author myself ; and I tell you it is better that the Egyptians should live their lives than dream them away with the help of books.

THEODOTUS [*kneeling, with genuine literary emotion : the passion of the pedant*] Cæsar : once in ten generations of men, the world gains an immortal book.

CÆSAR [*inflexible*] If it did not flatter mankind, the common executioner would burn it.

THEODOTUS. Without history, death will lay you beside your meanest soldier.

CÆSAR. Death will do that in any case. I ask no better grave.

THEODOTUS. What is burning there is the memory of mankind.

CÆSAR. A shameful memory. Let it burn.

THEODOTUS [*wildly*] Will you destroy the past ?

CÆSAR. Ay, and build the future with its ruins. [*Theodotus, in despair, strikes himself on the temples with his fists*]. But harken, Theodotus, teacher of kings : you who valued Pompey's head no more than a shepherd values an onion, and who now kneel to me, with tears in your old eyes, to plead for a few sheepskins scrawled with errors. I cannot spare you a man or a bucket of water just now ; but you shall pass freely out of the palace. Now, away with you to Achillas ; and borrow his legions to put out the fire. [*He hurries him to the steps*].

POTHINUS [*significantly*] You understand, Theodotus : I remain a prisoner.

THEODOTUS. A prisoner !

CÆSAR. Will you stay to talk whilst the memory of mankind is burning ? [*Calling through the loggia*] Ho there ! Pass Theodotus out. [*To Theodotus*] Away with you.

THEODOTUS [*To Pothinus*] I must go to save the library. [*He hurries out*].

CÆSAR. Follow him to the gate, Pothinus. Bid him urge your people to kill no more of my soldiers, for your sake.

POTHINUS. My life will cost you dear if you take it, Cæsar. [*He goes out after Theodotus*].

Rufio, absorbed in watching the embarkation, does not notice the departure of the two Egyptians.

RUFIO [*shouting from the loggia to the beach*] All ready, there ?

A CENTURION [*from below*] All ready. We wait for Cæsar.

CÆSAR. Tell them Cæsar is coming—the rogues ! [*Calling*] Britannicus. [*This magniloquent version of his secretary's name is one of Cæsar's jokes. In later years it would have meant, quite seriously and officially, Conqueror of Britain*].

RUFIO [*calling down*] Push off, all except the longboat. Stand by it to embark, Cæsar's guard there. [*He leaves the balcony and comes down into the hall*]. Where are those Egyptians ? Is this more clemency ? Have you let them go ?

CÆSAR [*chuckling*] I have let Theodotus go to save the library. We must respect literature, Rufio.

RUFIO [*raging*] Folly on folly's head ! I believe if you could bring back all the dead of Spain, Gaul, and Thessaly to life, you would do it that we might have the trouble of fighting them over again.

CÆSAR. Might not the gods destroy the world if their only thought were to be at peace next year ? [*Rufio, out of all patience, turns away in anger. Cæsar suddenly grips his sleeve, and adds slyly in his ear*] Besides, my friend : every Egyptian we imprison means imprisoning two Roman soldiers to guard him. Eh ?

RUFIO. Agh ! I might have known there was some fox's trick behind your fine talking. [*He gets away from Cæsar with an ill-humored shrug, and goes to the balcony for another look at the preparations ; finally goes out*].

CÆSAR. Is Britannus asleep ? I sent him for my armor an hour ago. [*Calling*] Britannicus, thou British islander. Britannicus !

Cleopatra runs in through the loggia with Cæsar's helmet and sword, snatched from Britannus, who follows her with a cuirass and greaves. They come down to Cæsar, she to his left hand, Britannus to his right.

CLEOPATRA. I am going to dress you, Cæsar. Sit down.

[*He obeys*]. These Roman helmets are so becoming!
[*She takes off his wreath*]. Oh! [*She bursts out laughing
at him*].

CÆSAR. What are you laughing at?

CLEOPATRA. Youre bald [*beginning with a big B, and
ending with a splutter*].

CÆSAR [*almost annoyed*] Cleopatra! [*He rises, for the
convenience of Britannus, who puts the cuirass on him*].

CLEOPATRA. So that is why you wear the wreath—to
hide it.

BRITANNUS. Peace, Egyptian: they are the bays of the
conqueror. [*He buckles the cuirass*].

CLEOPATRA. Peace, thou: islander! [*To Cæsar*] You
should rub your head with strong spirits of sugar, Cæsar.
That will make it grow.

CÆSAR [*with a wry face*] Cleopatra: do you like to be
reminded that you are very young?

CLEOPATRA [*pouting*] No.

CÆSAR [*sitting down again, and setting out his leg for
Britannus, who kneels to put on his greaves*] Neither do I like
to be reminded that I am—middle aged. Let me give you
ten of my superfluous years. That will make you 26, and
leave me only—no matter. Is it a bargain?

CLEOPATRA. Agreed. 26, mind. [*She puts the helmet on
him*]. Oh! How nice! You look only about 50 in it!

BRITANNUS [*looking up severely at Cleopatra*] You must
not speak in this manner to Cæsar.

CLEOPATRA. Is it true that when Cæsar caught you on
that island, you were painted all over blue?

BRITANNUS. Blue is the color worn by all Britons of good
standing. In war we stain our bodies blue; so that though
our enemies may strip us of our clothes and our lives, they
cannot strip us of our respectability. [*He rises*].

CLEOPATRA [*with Cæsar's sword*] Let me hang this on.
Now you look splendid. Have they made any statues of
you in Rome?

CÆSAR. Yes, many statues.

CLEOPATRA. You must send for one and give it to me.

RUFIO [*coming back into the loggia, more impatient than ever*] Now Cæsar : have you done talking ? The moment your foot is aboard there will be no holding our men back : the boats will race one another for the lighthouse.

CÆSAR [*drawing his sword and trying the edge*] Is this well set today, Britannicus ? At Pharsalia it was as blunt as a barrel-hoop.

BRITANNUS. It will split one of the Egyptian's hairs today, Cæsar. I have set it myself.

CLEOPATRA [*suddenly throwing her arms in terror round Cæsar*] Oh, you are not really going into battle to be killed ?

CÆSAR. No, Cleopatra. No man goes to battle to be killed.

CLEOPATRA. But they do get killed. My sister's husband was killed in battle. You must not go. Let him go [*pointing to Rufio. They all laugh at her*]. Oh please, please dont go. What will happen to me if you never come back ?

CÆSAR [*gravely*] Are you afraid ?

CLEOPATRA [*shrinking*] No.

CÆSAR [*with quiet authority*] Go to the balcony ; and you shall see us take the Pharos. You must learn to look on battles. Go. [*She goes, downcast, and looks out from the balcony*]. That is well. Now, Rufio. March.

CLEOPATRA [*suddenly clapping her hands*] Oh, you will not be able to go !

CÆSAR. Why ? What now ?

CLEOPATRA. They are drying up the harbor with buckets —a multitude of soldiers—over there [*pointing out across the sea to her left*]—they are dipping up the water.

RUFIO [*hastening to look*] It is true. The Egyptian army ! Crawling over the edge of the west harbor like locusts. [*With sudden anger he strides down to Cæsar*]. This is your accursed clemency, Cæsar. Theodotus has brought them.

CÆSAR [*delighted at his own cleverness*] I meant him to, Rufio. They have come to put out the fire. The library will keep them busy whilst we seize the lighthouse. Eh ? [*He rushes out buoyantly through the loggia, followed by Britannus*].

RUFIO [*disgustedly*] More foxing ! Agh ! [*He rushes off. A shout from the soldiers announces the appearance of Cæsar below*].

CENTURION [*below*] All aboard.   Give   way   there. [*Another shout*].

CLEOPATRA [*waving her scarf through the loggia arch*] Goodbye, goodbye, dear Cæsar.   Come back safe.   Goodbye !

ACT III

The edge of the quay in front of the palace, looking out west over the east harbor of Alexandria to Pharos island, just off the end of which, and connected with it by a narrow mole, is the famous lighthouse, a gigantic square tower of white marble diminishing in size storey by storey to the top, on which stands a cresset beacon. The island is joined to the main land by the Heptastadium, a great mole or causeway five miles long bounding the harbor on the south.

In the middle of the quay a Roman sentinel stands on guard, pilum in hand, looking out to the lighthouse with strained attention, his left hand shading his eyes. The pilum is a stout wooden shaft 4½ feet long, with an iron spit about three feet long fixed in it. The sentinel is so absorbed that he does not notice the approach from the north end of the quay of four Egyptian market porters carrying rolls of carpet, preceded by Ftatateeta and Apollodorus the Sicilian. Apollodorus is a dashing young man of about 24, handsome and debonair, dressed with deliberate æstheticism in the most delicate purples and dove greys, with ornaments of bronze, oxydized silver, and stones of jade and agate. His sword, designed as carefully as a medieval cross, has a blued blade shewing through an openwork scabbard of purple leather and filagree. The porters, conducted by Ftatateeta, pass along the quay behind the sentinel to the steps of the palace, where they put down their bales and squat on the ground. Apollodorus does not pass along with them : he halts, amused by the preoccupation of the sentinel.

APOLLODORUS [calling to the sentinel] Who goes there, eh ?

SENTINEL [starting violently and turning with his pilum at the charge, revealing himself as a small, wiry, sandy-haired, conscientious young man with an elderly face] Whats this ? Stand. Who are you ?

APOLLODORUS. I am Apollodorus the Sicilian. Why,

man, what are you dreaming of ? Since I came through the lines beyond the theatre there, I have brought my caravan past three sentinels, all so busy staring at the lighthouse that not one of them challenged me. Is this Roman discipline ?

SENTINEL. We are not here to watch the land but the sea. Cæsar has just landed on the Pharos. [*Looking at Ftatateeta*] What have you here ? Who is this piece of Egyptian crockery ?

FTATATEETA. Apollodorus : rebuke this Roman dog ; and bid him bridle his tongue in the presence of Ftatateeta, the mistress of the Queen's household.

APOLLODORUS. My friend : this is a great lady, who stands high with Cæsar.

SENTINEL [*not at all impressed, pointing to the carpets*] And what is all this truck ?

APOLLODORUS. Carpets for the furnishing of the Queen's apartments in the palace. I have picked them from the best carpets in the world ; and the Queen shall choose the best of my choosing.

SENTINEL. So you are the carpet merchant ?

APOLLODORUS [*hurt*] My friend : I am a patrician.

SENTINEL. A patrician ! A patrician keeping a shop instead of following arms !

APOLLODORUS. I do not keep a shop. Mine is a temple of the arts. I am a worshipper of beauty. My calling is to choose beautiful things for beautiful queens. My motto is Art for Art's sake.

SENTINEL. That is not the password.

APOLLODORUS. It is a universal password.

SENTINEL. I know nothing about universal passwords. Either give me the password for the day or get back to your shop.

Ftatateeta, roused by his hostile tone, steals towards the edge of the quay with the step of a panther, and gets behind him.

APOLLODORUS. How if I do neither ?

SENTINEL. Then I will drive this pilum through you.

APOLLODORUS. At your service, my friend. [*He draws his sword, and springs to his guard with unruffled grace*].

FTATATEETA [*suddenly seizing the sentinel's arms from behind*] Thrust your knife into the dog's throat, Apollodorus. [*The chivalrous Apollodorus laughingly shakes his head ; breaks ground away from the sentinel towards the palace ; and lowers his point*].

SENTINEL [*struggling vainly*] Curse on you ! Let me go. Help ho !

FTATATEETA [*lifting him from the ground*] Stab the little Roman reptile. Spit him on your sword.

A couple of Roman soldiers, with a centurion, come running along the edge of the quay from the north end. They rescue their comrade, and throw off Ftatateeta, who is sent reeling away on the left hand of the sentinel.

CENTURION [*an unattractive man of fifty, short in his speech and manners, with a vinewood cudgel in his hand*] How now ? What is all this ?

FTATATEETA [*to Apollodorus*] Why did you not stab him ? There was time !

APOLLODORUS. Centurion : I am here by order of the Queen to—

CENTURION [*interrupting him*] The Queen ! Yes, yes : [*to the sentinel*] pass him in. Pass all these bazaar people in to the Queen, with their goods. But mind you pass no one out that you have not passed in—not even the Queen herself.

SENTINEL. This old woman is dangerous : she is as strong as three men. She wanted the merchant to stab me.

APOLLODORUS. Centurion : I am not a merchant. I am a patrician and a votary of art.

CENTURION. Is the woman your wife ?

APOLLODORUS [*horrified*] No, no ! [*Correcting himself politely*] Not that the lady is not a striking figure in her own way. But [*emphatically*] she is not my wife.

FTATATEETA [*to the centurion*] Roman : I am Ftatateeta, the mistress of the Queen's household.

CENTURION. Keep your hands off our men, mistress ; or I will have you pitched into the harbor, though you were as strong as ten men. [*To his men*] To your posts : march ! [*He returns with his men the way they came*].

FTATATEETA [*looking malignantly after him*] We shall see whom Isis loves best : her servant Ftatateeta or a dog of a Roman.

SENTINEL [*to Apollodorus, with a wave of his pilum towards the palace*] Pass in there ; and keep your distance. [*Turning to Ftatateeta*] Come within a yard of me, you old crocodile ; and I will give you this [*the pilum*] in your jaws.

CLEOPATRA [*calling from the palace*] Ftatateeta, Ftatateeta.

FTATATEETA [*looking up, scandalized*] Go from the window, go from the window. There are men here.

CLEOPATRA. I am coming down.

FTATATEETA [*distracted*] No, no. What are you dreaming of ? O ye gods, ye gods ! Apollodorus : bid your men pick up your bales ; and in with me quickly.

APOLLODORUS. Obey the mistress of the Queen's household.

FTATATEETA [*impatiently, as the porters stoop to lift the bales*] Quick, quick : she will be out upon us. [*Cleopatra comes from the palace and runs across the quay to Ftatateeta*]. Oh that ever I was born !

CLEOPATRA [*eagerly*] Ftatateeta : I have thought of something. I want a boat—at once.

FTATATEETA. A boat ! No, no : you cannot, Apollodorus : speak to the Queen.

APOLLODORUS [*gallantly*] Beautiful queen : I am Apollodorus the Sicilian, your servant, from the bazaar. I have brought you the three most beautiful Persian carpets in the world to choose from.

CLEOPATRA. I have no time for carpets today. Get me a boat.

FTATATEETA. What whim is this ? You cannot go on the water except in the royal barge.

APOLLODORUS. Royalty, Ftatateeta, lies not in the barge but in the Queen. [*To Cleopatra*] The touch of your majesty's foot on the gunwale of the meanest boat in the harbor will make it royal. [*He turns to the harbor and calls seaward*] Ho there, boatman ! Pull in to the steps.

CLEOPATRA. Apollodorus : you are my perfect knight ; and I will always buy my carpets through you. [*Apollodorus bows joyously. An oar appears above the quay ; and the boatman, a bullet-headed, vivacious, grinning fellow, burnt almost black by the sun, comes up a flight of steps from the water on the sentinel's right, oar in hand, and waits at the top*]. Can you row, Apollodorus ?

APOLLODORUS. My oars shall be your majesty's wings. Whither shall I row my Queen ?

CLEOPATRA. To the lighthouse. Come. [*She makes for the steps*].

SENTINEL [*opposing her with his pilum at the charge*] Stand. You cannot pass.

CLEOPATRA [*flushing angrily*] How dare you ? Do you know that I am the Queen ?

SENTINEL. I have my orders. You cannot pass.

CLEOPATRA. I will make Cæsar have you killed if you do not obey me.

SENTINEL. He will do worse to me if I disobey my officer. Stand back.

CLEOPATRA. Ftatateeta : strangle him.

SENTINEL [*alarmed—looking apprehensively at Ftatateeta, and brandishing his pilum*] Keep off, there.

CLEOPATRA [*running to Apollodorus*] Apollodorus : make your slaves help us.

APOLLODORUS. I shall not need their help, lady. [*He draws his sword*]. Now, soldier : choose which weapon you will defend yourself with. Shall it be sword against pilum, or sword against sword ?

SENTINEL. Roman against Sicilian, curse you. Take that. [*He hurls his pilum at Apollodorus, who drops expertly on one knee. The pilum passes whizzing over his head and falls harmless. Apollodorus, with a cry of triumph, springs up and attacks the sentinel, who draws his sword and defends himself, crying*] Ho there, guard. Help !

Cleopatra, half frightened, half delighted, takes refuge near the palace, where the porters are squatting among the bales. The boatman, alarmed, hurries down the steps out of

*harm's way, but stops, with his head just visible above the edge
of the quay, to watch the fight. The sentinel is handicapped
by his fear of an attack in the rear from Ftatateeta. His
swordsmanship, which is of a rough and ready sort, is heavily
taxed, as he has occasionally to strike at her to keep her off
between a blow and a guard with Apollodorus. The centurion
returns with several soldiers. Apollodorus springs back
towards Cleopatra as this reinforcement confronts him.*

CENTURION [*coming to the sentinel's right hand*] What is
this ? What now ?

SENTINEL [*panting*] I could do well enough by myself if
it werent for the old woman. Keep her off me : that is all
the help I need.

CENTURION. Make your report, soldier. What has
happened ?

FTATATEETA. Centurion : he would have slain the Queen.

SENTINEL [*bluntly*] I would, sooner than let her pass. She
wanted to take boat, and go—so she said—to the lighthouse.
I stopped her, as I was ordered to ; and she set this fellow
on me. [*He goes to pick up his pilum and returns to his
place with it*].

CENTURION [*turning to Cleopatra*] Cleopatra : I am loth
to offend you ; but without Cæsar's express order we dare
not let you pass beyond the Roman lines.

APOLLODORUS. Well, Centurion ; and has not the lighthouse been within the Roman lines since Cæsar landed there?

CLEOPATRA. Yes, yes. Answer that, if you can.

CENTURION [*to Apollodorus*] As for you, Apollodorus,
you may thank the gods that you are not nailed to the palace
door with a pilum for your meddling.

APOLLODORUS [*urbanely*] My military friend, I was not
born to be slain by so ugly a weapon. When I fall, it will
be [*holding up his sword*] by this white queen of arms, the
only weapon fit for an artist. And now that you are convinced that we do not want to go beyond the lines, let me
finish killing your sentinel and depart with the Queen.

CENTURION [*as the sentinel makes an angry demonstration*]
Peace there, Cleopatra : I must abide by my orders, and

not by the subtleties of this Sicilian. You must withdraw into the palace and examine your carpets there.

CLEOPATRA [*pouting*] I will not : I am the Queen. Cæsar does not speak to me as you do. Have Cæsar's centurions changed manners with his scullions ?

CENTURION [*sulkily*] I do my duty. That is enough for me.

APOLLODORUS. Majesty : when a stupid man is doing something he is ashamed of, he always declares that it is his duty.

CENTURION [*angry*] Apollodorus—

APOLLODORUS [*interrupting him with defiant elegance*] I will make amends for that insult with my sword at fitting time and place. Who says artist, says duellist. [*To Cleopatra*] Hear my counsel, star of the east. Until word comes to these soldiers from Cæsar himself, you are a prisoner. Let me go to him with a message from you, and a present ; and before the sun has stooped half way to the arms of the sea, I will bring you back Cæsar's order of release.

CENTURION [*sneering at him*] And you will sell the Queen the present, no doubt.

APOLLODORUS. Centurion : the Queen shall have from me, without payment, as the unforced tribute of Sicilian taste to Egyptian beauty, the richest of these carpets for her present to Cæsar.

CLEOPATRA [*exultantly, to the centurion*] Now you see what an ignorant common creature you are !

CENTURION [*curtly*] Well, a fool and his wares are soon parted. [*He turns to his men*]. Two more men to this post here ? and see that no one leaves the palace but this man and his merchandize. If he draws his sword again inside the lines, kill him. To your posts. March.

He goes out, leaving two auxiliary sentinels with the other.

APOLLODORUS [*with polite goodfellowship*] My friends : will you not enter the palace and bury our quarrel in a bowl of wine ? [*He takes out his purse, jingling the coins in it*]. The Queen has presents for you all.

SENTINEL [*very sulky*] You heard our orders.   Get about your business.

FIRST AUXILIARY. Yes : you ought to know better.   Off with you.

SECOND AUXILIARY [*looking longingly at the purse—this sentinel is a hooknosed man, unlike his comrade, who is squab faced*] Do not tantalize a poor man.

APOLLODORUS [*to Cleopatra*] Pearl of Queens :   the centurion is at hand ; and the Roman soldier is incorrupt- ible when his officer is looking.   I must carry your word to Cæsar.

CLEOPATRA [*who has been meditating among the carpets*] Are these carpets very heavy ?

APOLLODORUS. It matters not how heavy.   There are plenty of porters.

CLEOPATRA. How do they put the carpets into boats ? Do they throw them down ?

APOLLODORUS. Not into small boats, majesty.   It would sink them.

CLEOPATRA. Not into that man's boat, for instance ? [*pointing to the boatman*].

APOLLODORUS. No.   Too small.

CLEOPATRA. But you can take a carpet to Cæsar in it if I send one ?

APOLLODORUS. Assuredly.

CLEOPATRA. And you will have it carried gently down the steps and take great care of it ?

APOLLODORUS. Depend on me.

CLEOPATRA. Great, great care ?

APOLLODORUS. More than of my own body.

CLEOPATRA. You will promise me not to let the porters drop it or throw it about ?

APOLLODORUS. Place the most delicate glass goblet in the palace in the heart of the roll, Queen ; and if it be broken, my head shall pay for it.

CLEOPATRA. Good.   Come, Ftatateeta. [*Ftatateeta comes to her.   Apollodorus offers to squire them into the palace*]. No, Apollodorus, you must not come.   I will choose a carpet for myself. You must wait here. [*She runs into the palace*].

APOLLODORUS [*to the porters*] Follow this lady [*indicating Ftatateeta*] and obey her.

The porters rise and take up their bales.

FTATATEETA [*addressing the porters as if they were vermin*] This way. And take your shoes off before you put your feet on those stairs.

She goes in, followed by the porters with the carpets. Meanwhile Apollodorus goes to the edge of the quay and looks out over the harbor. The sentinels keep their eyes on him malignantly.

APOLLODORUS [*addressing the sentinel*] My friend—

SENTINEL [*rudely*] Silence there.

FIRST AUXILIARY. Shut your muzzle, you.

SECOND AUXILIARY [*in a half whisper, glancing apprehensively towards the north end of the quay*] Cant you wait a bit ?

APOLLODORUS. Patience, worthy three-headed donkey. [*They mutter ferociously ; but he is not at all intimidated*]. Listen : were you set here to watch me, or to watch the Egyptians ?

SENTINEL. We know our duty.

APOLLODORUS. Then why dont you do it ? There is something going on over there [*pointing southwestward to the mole*].

SENTINEL [*sulkily*] I do not need to be told what to do by the like of you.

APOLLODORUS. Blockhead. [*He begins shouting*] Ho there, Centurion. Hoiho !

SENTINEL. Curse your meddling. [*Shouting*] Hoiho ! Alarm ! Alarm !

FIRST AND SECOND AUXILIARIES. Alarm ! alarm ! Hoiho !

The Centurion comes running in with his guard.

CENTURION. What now ? Has the old woman attacked you again ? [*Seeing Apollodorus*] Are you here still ?

APOLLODORUS [*pointing as before*] See there. The Egyptians are moving. They are going to recapture the

Pharos. They will attack by sea and land : by land along the great mole ; by sea from the west harbor. Stir yourselves, my military friends : the hunt is up. [*A clangor of trumpets from several points along the quay*]. Aha ! I told you so.

CENTURION [*quickly*] The two extra men pass the alarm to the south posts. One man keep guard here. The rest with me—quick.

The two auxiliary sentinels run off to the south. The centurion and his guard run off northward ; and immediately afterwards the bucina sounds. The four porters come from the palace carrying a carpet, followed by Ftatateeta.

SENTINEL [*handling his pilum apprehensively*] You again ! [*The porters stop*].

FTATATEETA. Peace, Roman fellow : you are now singlehanded. Apollodorus : this carpet is Cleopatra's present to Cæsar. It has rolled up in it ten precious goblets of the thinnest Iberian crystal, and a hundred eggs of the sacred blue pigeon. On your honor, let not one of them be broken.

APOLLODORUS. On my head be it ! [*To the porters*] Into the boat with them carefully.

The porters carry the carpet to the steps.

FIRST PORTER [*looking down at the boat*] Beware what you do, sir. Those eggs of which the lady speaks must weigh more than a pound apiece. This boat is too small for such a load.

BOATMAN [*excitedly rushing up the steps*] Oh thou injurious porter ! Oh thou unnatural son of a she-camel ! [*To Apollodorus*] My boat, sir, hath often carried five men. Shall it not carry your lordship and a bale of pigeon's eggs ? [*To the porter*] Thou mangey dromedary, the gods shall punish thee for this envious wickedness.

FIRST PORTER [*stolidly*] I cannot quit this bale now to beat thee ; but another day I will lie in wait for thee.

APOLLODORUS [*going between them*] Peace there. If the boat were but a single plank, I would get to Cæsar on it.

FTATATEETA [*anxiously*] In the name of the gods, Apollodorus, run no risks with that bale.

T.P.—7

APOLLODORUS. Fear not, thou venerable grotesque : I guess its great worth. [*To the porters*] Down with it, I say ; and gently ; or ye shall eat nothing but stick for ten days.

The boatman goes down the steps, followed by the porters with the bale : Ftatateeta and Apollodorus watching from the edge.

APOLLODORUS. Gently, my sons, my children—[*with sudden alarm*] gently, ye dogs. Lay it level in the stern—so —tis well.

FTATATEETA [*screaming down at one of the porters*] Do not step on it, do not step on it. Oh thou brute beast !

FIRST PORTER [*ascending*] Be not excited, mistress : all is well.

FTATATEETA [*panting*] All well ! Oh, thou hast given my heart a turn ! [*She clutches her side, gasping*].

The four porters have now come up and are waiting at the stairhead to be paid.

APOLLODORUS. Here, ye hungry ones. [*He gives money to the first porter, who holds it in his hand to shew to the others. They crowd greedily to see how much it is, quite prepared, after the Eastern fashion, to protest to heaven against their patron's stinginess. But his liberality overpowers them*].

FIRST PORTER. O bounteous prince !

SECOND PORTER. O lord of the bazaar !

THIRD PORTER. O favored of the gods !

FOURTH PORTER. O father to all the porters of the market !

SENTINEL [*enviously, threatening them fiercely with his pilum*] Hence, dogs : off. Out of this. [*They fly before him northward along the quay*].

APOLLODORUS. Farewell, Ftatateeta. I shall be at the lighthouse before the Egyptians. [*He descends the steps*].

FTATATEETA. The gods speed thee and protect my nursling !

The sentry returns from chasing the porters and looks down at the boat, standing near the stairhead lest Ftatateeta should attempt to escape.

APOLLODORUS [*from beneath, as the boat moves off*] Farewell, valiant pilum pitcher.

SENTINEL. Farewell, shopkeeper.

APOLLODORUS. Ha, ha ! Pull, thou brave boatman, pull. Soho-o-o-o-o ! [*He begins to sing in barcarolle measure to the rhythm of the oars*]

> My heart, my heart, spread out thy wings :
> Shake off thy heavy load of love—

Give me the oars, O son of a snail.

SENTINEL [*threatening Ftatateeta*] Now mistress : back to your henhouse. In with you.

FTATATEETA [*falling on her knees and stretching her hands over the waters*] Gods of the seas, bear her safely to the shore !

SENTINEL. Bear who safely ? What do you mean ?

FTATATEETA [*looking darkly at him*] Gods of Egypt and of Vengeance, let this Roman fool be beaten like a dog by his captain for suffering her to be taken over the waters.

SENTINEL. Accursed one : is she then in the boat ? [*He calls over the sea*] Hoiho, there, boatman ! Hoiho !

APOLLODORUS [*singing in the distance*]

> My heart, my heart, be whole and free :
> Love is thine only enemy.

Meanwhile Rufio, the morning's fighting done, sits munching dates on a faggot of brushwood outside the door of the lighthouse, which towers gigantic to the clouds on his left. His helmet, full of dates, is between his knees ; and a leathern bottle of wine is by his side. Behind him the great stone pedestal of the lighthouse is shut in from the open sea by a low stone parapet, with a couple of steps in the middle to the broad coping. A huge chain with a hook hangs down from the lighthouse crane above his head. Faggots like the one he sits on lie beneath it ready to be drawn up to feed the beacon.

Cæsar is standing on the step at the parapet looking out anxiously, evidently ill at ease. Britannus comes out of the lighthouse door.

RUFIO. Well, my British islander. Have you been up to the top ?

BRITANNUS. I have. I reckon it at 200 feet high.

RUFIO. Anybody up there ?

BRITANNUS. One elderly Tyrian to work the crane ; and his son, a well conducted youth of 14.

RUFIO [*looking at the chain*] What ! An old man and a boy work that ! Twenty men, you mean.

BRITANNUS. Two only, I assure you. They have counterweights, and a machine with boiling water in it which I do not understand : it is not of British design. They use it to haul up barrels of oil and faggots to burn in the brazier on the roof.

RUFIO. But—

BRITANNUS. Excuse me : I came down because there are messengers coming along the mole to us from the island. I must see what their business is. [*He hurries out past the lighthouse*].

CÆSAR [*coming away from the parapet, shivering and out of sorts*] Rufio : this has been a mad expedition. We shall be beaten. I wish I knew how our men are getting on with that barricade across the great mole.

RUFIO [*angrily*] Must I leave my food and go starving to bring you a report ?

CÆSAR [*soothing him nervously*] No, Rufio, no. Eat, my son, eat. [*He takes another turn, Rufio chewing dates meanwhile*]. The Egyptians cannot be such fools as not to storm the barricade and swoop down on us here before it is finished. It is the first time I have ever run an avoidable risk. I should not have come to Egypt.

RUFIO. An hour ago you were all for victory.

CÆSAR [*apologetically*] Yes : I was a fool—rash, Rufio— boyish.

RUFIO. Boyish ! Not a bit of it. Here [*offering him a handful of dates*].

CÆSAR. What are these for ?

RUFIO. To eat. Thats whats the matter with you. When a man comes to your age, he runs down before his midday meal. Eat and drink ; and then have another look at our chances.

CÆSAR [*taking the dates*] My age ! [*He shakes his head and bites a date*]. Yes, Rufio : I am an old man—worn out now—true, quite true. [*He gives way to melancholy contemplation, and eats another date*]. Achillas is still in his prime : Ptolemy is a boy. [*He eats another date, and plucks up a little*]. Well, every dog has his day ; and I have had mine : I cannot complain. [*With sudden cheerfulness*] These dates are not bad, Rufio. [*Britannus returns, greatly excited, with a leathern bag. Cæsar is himself again in a moment*]. What now ?

BRITANNUS [*triumphantly*] Our brave Rhodian mariners have captured a treasure. There ! [*He throws the bag down at Cæsar's feet*]. Our enemies are delivered into our hands.

CÆSAR. In that bag ?

BRITANNUS. Wait till you hear, Cæsar. This bag contains all the letters which have passed between Pompey's party and the army of occupation here.

CÆSAR. Well ?

BRITANNUS [*impatient of Cæsar's slowness to grasp the situation*] Well, we shall now know who your foes are. The name of every man who has plotted against you since you crossed the Rubicon may be in these papers, for all we know.

CÆSAR. Put them in the fire.

BRITANNUS. Put them—[*he gasps*] ! ! ! !

CÆSAR. In the fire. Would you have me waste the next three years of my life in proscribing and condemning men who will be my friends when I have proved that my friendship is worth more than Pompey's was—than Cato's is. O incorrigible British islander : am I a bull dog, to seek quarrels merely to shew how stubborn my jaws are ?

BRITANNUS. But your honor—the honor of Rome—

CÆSAR. I do not make human sacrifices to my honor, as your Druids do. Since you will not burn these, at least I can drown them. [*He picks up the bag and throws it over the parapet into the sea*].

BRITANNUS. Cæsar : this is mere eccentricity. Are

traitors to be allowed to go free for the sake of a paradox?

RUFIO [*rising*] Cæsar : when the islander has finished preaching, call me again. I am going to have a look at the boiling water machine. [*He goes into the lighthouse*].

BRITANNUS [*with genuine feeling*] O Cæsar, my great master, if I could but persuade you to regard life seriously, as men do in my country!

CÆSAR. Do they truly do so, Britannus?

BRITANNUS. Have you not been there? Have you not seen them? What Briton speaks as you do in your moments of levity? What Briton neglects to attend the services at the sacred grove? What Briton wears clothes of many colors as you do, instead of plain blue, as all solid, well esteemed men should? These are moral questions with us.

CÆSAR. Well, well, my friend : some day I shall settle down and have a blue toga, perhaps. Meanwhile, I must get on as best I can in my flippant Roman way. [*Apollodorus comes past the lighthouse*]. What now?

BRITANNUS [*turning quickly, and challenging the stranger with official haughtiness*] What is this? Who are you? How did you come here?

APOLLODORUS. Calm yourself, my friend : I am not going to eat you. I have come by boat, from Alexandria, with precious gifts for Cæsar.

CÆSAR. From Alexandria!

BRITANNUS [*severely*] That is Cæsar, sir.

RUFIO [*appearing at the lighthouse door*] Whats the matter now?

APOLLODORUS. Hail, great Cæsar! I am Apollodorus the Sicilian, an artist.

BRITANNUS. An artist! Why have they admitted this vagabond?

CÆSAR. Peace, man. Apollodorus is a famous patrician amateur.

BRITANNUS [*disconcerted*] I crave the gentleman's pardon. [*To Cæsar*] I understood him to say that he was a professional. [*Somewhat out of countenance, he allows Apollodorus to approach Cæsar, changing places with him. Rufio, after looking Apollodorus up and down with marked disparagement, goes to the other side of the platform*].

CÆSAR. You are welcome, Apollodorus. What is your business ?

APOLLODORUS. First, to deliver to you a present from the Queen of Queens.

CÆSAR. Who is that ?

APOLLODORUS. Cleopatra of Egypt.

CÆSAR [*taking him into his confidence in his most winning manner*] Apollodorus : this is no time for playing with presents. Pray you, go back to the Queen, and tell her that if all goes well I shall return to the palace this evening.

APOLLODORUS. Cæsar : I cannot return. As I approached the lighthouse, some fool threw a great leathern bag into the sea. It broke the nose of my boat ; and I had hardly time to get myself and my charge to the shore before the poor little cockleshell sank.

CÆSAR. I am sorry, Apollodorus. The fool shall be rebuked. Well, well : what have you brought me ? The Queen will be hurt if I do not look at it.

RUFIO. Have we time to waste on this trumpery ? The Queen is only a child.

CÆSAR. Just so : that is why we must not disappoint her. What is the present, Apollodorus ?

APOLLODORUS. Cæsar : it is a Persian carpet—a beauty ! And in it are—so I am told—pigeons' eggs and crystal goblets and fragile precious things. I dare not for my head have it carried up that narrow ladder from the causeway.

RUFIO. Swing it up by the crane, then. We will send the eggs to the cook ; drink our wine from the goblets ; and the carpet will make a bed for Cæsar.

APOLLODORUS. The crane ! Cæsar : I have sworn to tender this bale of carpet as I tender my own life.

CÆSAR [*cheerfully*] Then let them swing you up at the same time ; and if the chain breaks, you and the pigeons' eggs will perish together. [*He goes to the chain and looks up along it, examining it curiously*].

APOLLODORUS [*to Britannus*] Is Cæsar serious ?

BRITANNUS. His manner is frivolous because he is an Italian ; but he means what he says.

APOLLODORUS. Serious or not, he spake well. Give me a squad of soldiers to work the crane.

BRITANNUS. Leave the crane to me. Go and await the descent of the chain.

APOLLODORUS. Good. You will presently see me there [*turning to them all and pointing with an eloquent gesture to the sky above the parapet*] rising like the sun with my treasure.

He goes back the way he came. Britannus goes into the lighthouse.

RUFIO [*ill-humoredly*] Are you really going to wait here for this foolery, Cæsar ?

CÆSAR [*backing away from the crane as it gives signs of working*] Why not ?

RUFIO. The Egyptians will let you know why not if they have the sense to make a rush from the shore end of the mole before our barricade is finished. And here we are waiting like children to see a carpet full of pigeons' eggs.

The chain rattles, and is drawn up high enough to clear the parapet. It then swings round out of sight behind the lighthouse.

CÆSAR. Fear not, my son Rufio. When the first Egyptian takes his first step along the mole, the alarm will sound ; and we two will reach the barricade from our end before the Egyptians reach it from their end—we two, Rufio : I, the old man, and you, his biggest boy. And the old man will be there first. So peace ; and give me some more dates.

APOLLODORUS [*from the causeway below*] Soho, haul away. So-ho-o-o-o ! [*The chain is drawn up and comes round again from behind the lighthouse. Apollodorus is swinging in the air with his bale of carpet at the end of it. He breaks into song as he soars above the parapet*]

> Aloft, aloft, behold the blue
> That never shone in woman's eyes—

Easy there : stop her. [*He ceases to rise*]. Further round ! [*The chain comes forward above the platform*].

RUFIO [*calling up*] Lower away there. [*The chain and its load begin to descend*].

APOLLODORUS [*calling up*] Gently—slowly—mind the eggs.

RUFIO [*calling up*] Easy there—slowly—slowly.

Apollodorus and the bale are deposited safely on the flags in the middle of the platform. Rufio and Cæsar help Apollodorus to cast off the chain from the bale.

RUFIO. Haul up.

The chain rises clear of their heads with a rattle. Britannus comes from the lighthouse and helps them to uncord the carpet.

APOLLODORUS [*when the cords are loose*] Stand off, my friends : let Cæsar see. [*He throws the carpet open*].

RUFIO. Nothing but a heap of shawls. Where are the pigeons' eggs ?

APOLLODORUS. Approach, Cæsar ; and search for them among the shawls.

RUFIO [*drawing his sword*] Ha, treachery ! Keep back, Cæsar : I saw the shawl move : there is something alive there.

BRITANNUS [*drawing his sword*] It is a serpent.

APOLLODORUS. Dares Cæsar thrust his hand into the sack where the serpent moves ?

RUFIO [*turning on him*] Treacherous dog—

CÆSAR. Peace. Put up your swords. Apollodorus : your serpent seems to breathe very regularly. [*He thrusts his hand under the shawls and draws out a bare arm*]. This is a pretty little snake.

RUFIO [*drawing out the other arm*] Let us have the rest of you.

They pull Cleopatra up by the wrists into a sitting position. Britannus, scandalized, sheathes his sword with a drive of protest.

CLEOPATRA [*gasping*] Oh, I'm smothered. Oh, Cæsar, a man stood on me in the boat ; and a great sack of something fell upon me out of the sky ; and then the boat sank ; and then I was swung up into the air and bumped down.

CÆSAR [*petting her as she rises and takes refuge on his breast*] Well, never mind : here you are safe and sound at last.

RUFIO. Ay ; and now that she is here, what are we to do with her ?

BRITANNUS. She cannot stay here, Cæsar, without the companionship of some matron.

CLEOPATRA [*jealously, to Cæsar, who is obviously perplexed*] Arnt you glad to see me ?

CÆSAR. Yes, yes ; *I* am very glad. But Rufio is very angry ; and Britannus is shocked.

CLEOPATRA [*contemptuously*] You can have their heads cut off, can you not ?

CÆSAR. They would not be so useful with their heads cut off as they are now, my sea bird.

RUFIO [*to Cleopatra*] We shall have to go away presently and cut some of your Egyptians' heads off. How will you like being left here with the chance of being captured by that little brother of yours if we are beaten ?

CLEOPATRA. But you mustnt leave me alone. Cæsar : you will not leave me alone, will you ?

RUFIO. What ! not when the trumpet sounds and all our lives depend on Cæsar's being at the barricade before the Egyptians reach it ? Eh ?

CLEOPATRA. Let them lose their lives : they are only soldiers.

CÆSAR [*gravely*] Cleopatra : when that trumpet sounds, we must take every man his life in his hand, and throw it in the face of Death. And of my soldiers who have trusted me there is not one whose hand I shall not hold more sacred than your head. [*Cleopatra is overwhelmed. Her eyes fill with tears*]. Apollodorus : you must take her back to the palace.

APOLLODORUS. Am I a dolphin, Cæsar, to cross the seas with young ladies on my back ? My boat is sunk : all yours are either at the barricade or have returned to the city. I will hail one if I can : that is all I can do. [*He goes back to the causeway*].

CLEOPATRA [*struggling with her tears*] It does not matter. I will not go back. Nobody cares for me.

CÆSAR. Cleopatra—

CLEOPATRA. You want me to be killed.

CÆSAR [*still more gravely*] My poor child : your life matters little here to anyone but yourself. [*She gives way altogether at this, casting herself down on the faggots weeping. Suddenly a great tumult is heard in the distance, bucinas and trumpets sounding through a storm of shouting. Britannus rushes to the parapet and looks along the mole. Cæsar and Rufio turn to one another with quick intelligence*].

CÆSAR. Come, Rufio.

CLEOPATRA [*scrambling to her knees and clinging to him*] No no. Do not leave me, Cæsar. [*He snatches his skirt from her clutch*]. Oh !

BRITANNUS [*from the parapet*] Cæsar : we are cut off. The Egyptians have landed from the west harbor between us and the barricade ! ! !

RUFIO [*running to see*] Curses ! It is true. We are caught like rats in a trap.

CÆSAR [*ruthfully*] Rufio, Rufio : my men at the barricade are between the sea party and the shore party. I have murdered them.

RUFIO [*coming back from the parapet to Cæsar's right hand*] Ay : that comes of fooling with this girl here.

APOLLODORUS [*coming up quickly from the causeway*] Look over the parapet, Cæsar.

CÆSAR. We have looked, my friend. We must defend ourselves here.

APOLLODORUS. I have thrown the ladder into the sea. They cannot get in without it.

RUFIO. Ay ; and we cannot get out. Have you thought of that ?

APOLLODORUS. Not get out ! Why not ? You have ships in the east harbor.

BRITANNUS [*hopefully, at the parapet*] The Rhodian galleys are standing in towards us already. [*Cæsar quickly joins Britannus at the parapet*].

RUFIO [*to Apollodorus, impatiently*] And by what road are we to walk to the galleys, pray ?

APOLLODORUS [*with gay, defiant rhetoric*] By the road that leads everywhere—the diamond path of the sun and moon. Have you never seen the child's shadow play of The Broken Bridge ? " Ducks and geese with ease get over "—eh ? [*He throws away his cloak and cap, and binds his sword on his back*].

RUFIO. What are you talking about ?

APOLLODORUS. I will shew you. [*Calling to Britannus*] How far off is the nearest galley ?

BRITANNUS. Fifty fathom.

CÆSAR. No, no : they are further off than they seem in this clear air to your British eyes. Nearly quarter of a mile, Apollodorus.

APOLLODORUS. Good. Defend yourselves here until I send you a boat from that galley.

RUFIO. Have you wings, perhaps ?

APOLLODORUS. Water wings, soldier. Behold !

He runs up the steps between Cæsar and Britannus to the coping of the parapet ; springs into the air ; and plunges head foremost into the sea.

CÆSAR [*like a schoolboy—wildly excited*] Bravo, bravo ! [*Throwing off his cloak*] By Jupiter, I will do that too.

RUFIO [*seizing him*] You are mad. You shall not.

CÆSAR. Why not ? Can I not swim as well as he ?

RUFIO [*frantic*] Can an old fool dive and swim like a young one ? He is twenty-five and you are fifty.

CÆSAR [*breaking loose from Rufio*] Old ! ! !

BRITANNUS [*shocked*] Rufio : you forget yourself.

CÆSAR. I will race you to the galley for a week's pay, father Rufio.

CLEOPATRA. But me ! me ! ! me ! ! ! what is to become of me ?

CÆSAR. I will carry you on my back to the galley like a dolphin. Rufio : when you see me rise to the surface, throw her in : I will answer for her. And then in with you after her, both of you.

CLEOPATRA. No, no, NO. I shall be drowned.

BRITANNUS. Cæsar : I am a man and a Briton, not a fish. I must have a boat. I cannot swim.

CLEOPATRA. Neither can I.

CÆSAR [to Britannus] Stay here, then, alone, until I recapture the lighthouse : I will not forget you. Now, Rufio.

RUFIO. You have made up your mind to this folly ?

CÆSAR. The Egyptians have made it up for me. What else is there to do ? And mind where you jump : I do not want to get your fourteen stone in the small of my back as I come up. [He runs up the steps and stands on the coping].

BRITANNUS [anxiously] One last word, Cæsar. Do not let yourself be seen in the fashionable part of Alexandria until you have changed your clothes.

CÆSAR [calling over the sea] Ho, Apollodorus : [he points skyward and quotes the barcarolle]

The white upon the blue above—

APOLLODORUS [swimming in the distance]

Is purple on the green below—

CÆSAR [exultantly] Aha ! [He plunges into the sea].

CLEOPATRA [running excitedly to the steps] Oh, let me see. He will be drowned [Rufio seizes her]—Ah—ah—ah—ah ! [He pitches her screaming into the sea. Rufio and Britannus roar with laughter].

RUFIO [looking down after her] He has got her. [To Britannus] Hold the fort, Briton. Cæsar will not forget you. [He springs off].

BRITANNUS [running to the steps to watch them as they swim] All safe, Rufio ?

RUFIO [swimming] All safe.

CÆSAR [swimming further off] Take refuge up there by the beacon ; and pile the fuel on the trap door, Britannus.

BRITANNUS [*calling in reply*] I will first do so, and then commend myself to my country's gods. [*A sound of cheering from the sea. Britannus gives full vent to his excitement*]. The boat has reached him : Hip, hip, hip, hurrah !

Cleopatra's sousing in the east harbor of Alexandria was in October 48 B.C. In March 47 she is passing the afternoon in her boudoir in the palace, among a bevy of her ladies, listening to a slave girl who is playing the harp in the middle of the room. The harpist's master, an old musician, with a lined face, prominent brows, white beard, moustache and eyebrows twisted and horned at the ends, and a consciously keen and pretentious expression, is squatting on the floor close to her on her right, watching her performance. Ftatateeta is in attendance near the door, in front of a group of female slaves. Except the harp player all are seated : Cleopatra in a chair opposite the door on the other side of the room ; the rest on the ground. Cleopatra's ladies are all young, the most conspicuous being Charmian and Iras, her favorites. Charmian is a hatchet faced, terra cotta colored little goblin, swift in her movements, and neatly finished at the hands and feet. Iras is a plump, goodnatured creature, rather fatuous, with a profusion of red hair, and a tendency to giggle on the slightest provocation.

CLEOPATRA. Can I—

FTATATEETA [*insolently, to the player*] Peace, thou ! The Queen speaks. [*The player stops*].

CLEOPATRA [*to the old musician*] I want to learn to play the harp with my own hands. Cæsar loves music. Can you teach me ?

MUSICIAN. Assuredly I and no one else can teach the queen. Have I not discovered the lost method of the ancient Egyptians, who could make a pyramid tremble by touching a bass string ? All the other teachers are quacks : I have exposed them repeatedly.

CLEOPATRA. Good : you shall teach me. How long will it take ?

MUSICIAN. Not very long: only four years. Your Majesty must first become proficient in the philosophy of Pythagoras.

CLEOPATRA. Has she [*indicating the slave*] become proficient in the philosophy of Pythagoras ?

MUSICIAN. Oh, she is but a slave. She learns as a dog learns.

CLEOPATRA. Well, then, I will learn as a dog learns ; for she plays better than you. You shall give me a lesson every day for a fortnight. [*The musician hastily scrambles to his feet and bows profoundly*]. After that, whenever I strike a false note you shall be flogged ; and if I strike so many that there is not time to flog you, you shall be thrown into the Nile to feed the crocodiles. Give the girl a piece of gold ; and send them away.

MUSICIAN [*much taken aback*] But true art will not be thus forced.

FTATATEETA [*pushing him out*] What is this ? Answering the Queen, forsooth. Out with you.

He is pushed out by Ftatateeta, the girl following with her harp, amid the laughter of the ladies and slaves.

CLEOPATRA. Now, can any of you amuse me ? Have you any stories or any news ?

IRAS. Ftatateeta—

CLEOPATRA. Oh, Ftatateeta, Ftatateeta, always Ftatateeta. Some new tale to set me against her.

IRAS. No : this time Ftatateeta has been virtuous. [*All the ladies laugh—not the slaves*]. Pothinus has been trying to bribe her to let him speak with you.

CLEOPATRA [*wrathfully*] Ha ! you all sell audiences with me, as if I saw whom you please, and not whom I please. I should like to know how much of her gold piece that harp girl will have to give up before she leaves the palace.

IRAS. We can easily find out that for you.

The ladies laugh.

CLEOPATRA [*frowning*] You laugh ; but take care, take care. I will find out some day how to make myself served as Cæsar is served.

CHARMIAN. Old hooknose ! [*They laugh again*].

CLEOPATRA [*revolted*] Silence. Charmian : do not you be a silly little Egyptian fool. Do you know why I allow you all to chatter impertinently just as you please, instead of treating you as Ftatateeta would treat you if she were Queen ?

CHARMIAN. Because you try to imitate Cæsar in everything ; and he lets everybody say what they please to him.

CLEOPATRA. No ; but because I asked him one day why he did so ; and he said " Let your women talk ; and you will learn something from them." What have I to learn from them ? I said. " What they are " said he ; and oh ! you should have seen his eye as he said it. You would have curled up, you shallow things. [*They laugh. She turns fiercely on Iras*]. At whom are you laughing—at me or at Cæsar ?

IRAS. At Cæsar.

CLEOPATRA. If you were not a fool, you would laugh at me ; and if you were not a coward you would not be afraid to tell me so. [*Ftatateeta returns*]. Ftatateeta : they tell me that Pothinus has offered you a bribe to admit him to my presence.

FTATATEETA [*protesting*] Now by my father's gods—

CLEOPATRA [*cutting her short despotically*] Have I not told you not to deny things ? You would spend the day calling your father's gods to witness to your virtues if I let you. Go take the bribe ; and bring in Pothinus. [*Ftatateeta is about to reply*]. Dont answer me. Go.

Ftatateeta goes out ; and Cleopatra rises and begins to prowl to and fro between her chair and the door, meditating. All rise and stand.

IRAS [*as she reluctantly rises*] Hcigho ! I wish Cæsar were back in Rome.

CLEOPATRA [*threateningly*] It will be a bad day for you all when he goes. Oh, if I were not ashamed to let him see that I am as cruel at heart as my father, I would make you repent that speech ! Why do you wish him away ?

CHARMIAN. He makes you so terribly prosy and serious and learned and philosophical. It is worse than being religious, at our ages. [*The ladies laugh*].

CLEOPATRA. Cease that endless cackling, will you. Hold your tongues.

CHARMIAN [*with mock resignation*] Well, well : we must try to live up to Cæsar.

They laugh again. Cleopatra rages silently as she continues to prowl to and fro. Ftatateeta comes back with Pothinus, who halts on the threshold.

FTATATEETA [*at the door*] Pothinus craves the ear of the—

CLEOPATRA. There, there : that will do : let him come in. [*She resumes her seat. All sit down except Pothinus, who advances to the middle of the room. Ftatateeta takes her former place*]. Well, Pothinus : what is the latest news from your rebel friends ?

POTHINUS [*haughtily*] I am no friend of rebellion. And a prisoner does not receive news.

CLEOPATRA. You are no more a prisoner than I am— than Cæsar is. These six months we have been besieged in this palace by my subjects. You are allowed to walk on the beach among the soldiers. Can I go further myself, or can Cæsar ?

POTHINUS. You are but a child, Cleopatra, and do not understand these matters.

The ladies laugh. Cleopatra looks inscrutably at him.

CHARMIAN. I see you do not know the latest news, Pothinus.

POTHINUS. What is that ?

CHARMIAN. That Cleopatra is no longer a child. Shall I tell you how to grow much older, and much, much wiser in one day ?

POTHINUS. I should prefer to grow wiser without growing older.

CHARMIAN. Well, go up to the top of the lighthouse ; and get somebody to take you by the hair and throw you into the sea. [*The ladies laugh*].

CLEOPATRA. She is right, Pothinus : you will come to the shore with much conceit washed out of you. [*The ladies laugh. Cleopatra rises impatiently*]. Begone, all of you. I will speak with Pothinus alone. Drive them out, Ftatateeta. [*They run out laughing. Ftatateeta shuts the door on them*]. What are you waiting for ?

FTATATEETA. It is not meet that the Queen remain alone with—

CLEOPATRA [*interrupting her*] Ftatateeta : must I sacrifice you to your father's gods to teach you that *I* am Queen of Egypt, and not you ?

FTATATEETA [*indignantly*] You are like the rest of them. You want to be what these Romans call a New Woman. [*She goes out, banging the door*].

CLEOPATRA [*sitting down again*] Now, Pothinus : why did you bribe Ftatateeta to bring you hither ?

POTHINUS [*studying her gravely*] Cleopatra : what they tell me is true. You are changed.

CLEOPATRA. Do you speak with Cæsar every day for six months : and you will be changed.

POTHINUS. It is the common talk that you are infatuated with this old man ?

CLEOPATRA. Infatuated ? What does that mean ? Made foolish, is it not ? Oh no : I wish I were.

POTHINUS. You wish you were made foolish ! How so ?

CLEOPATRA. When I was foolish, I did what I liked, except when Ftatateeta beat me ; and even then I cheated her and did it by stealth. Now that Cæsar has made me wise, it is no use my liking or disliking : I do what must be done, and have no time to attend to myself. That is not happiness ; but it is greatness. If Cæsar were gone, I think I could govern the Egyptians ; for what Cæsar is to me, I am to the fools around me.

POTHINUS [*looking hard at her*] Cleopatra : this may be the vanity of youth.

CLEOPATRA. No, no : it is not that I am so clever, but that the others are so stupid.

POTHINUS [*musingly*] Truly, that is the great secret.

CLEOPATRA. Well, now tell me what you came to say ?

POTHINUS [*embarrassed*] I ! Nothing.

CLEOPATRA. Nothing !

POTHINUS. At least—to beg for my liberty : that is all.

CLEOPATRA. For that you would have knelt to Cæsar. No, Pothinus : you came with some plan that depended on Cleopatra being a little nursery kitten. Now that Cleopatra is a Queen, the plan is upset.

POTHINUS [*bowing his head submissively*] It is so.

CLEOPATRA [*exultant*] Aha !

POTHINUS [*raising his eyes keenly to hers*] Is Cleopatra then indeed a Queen, and no longer Cæsar's prisoner and slave ?

CLEOPATRA. Pothinus : we are all Cæsar's slaves—all we in this land of Egypt—whether we will or no. And she who is wise enough to know this will reign when Cæsar departs.

POTHINUS. You harp on Cæsar's departure.

CLEOPATRA. What if I do ?

POTHINUS. Does he not love you ?

CLEOPATRA. Love me ! Pothinus : Cæsar loves no one. Who are those we love. Only those whom we do not hate : all people are strangers and enemies to us except those we love. But it is not so with Cæsar. He has no hatred in him : he makes friends with everyone as he does with dogs and children. His kindness to me is a wonder : neither mother, father, nor nurse have ever taken so much care for me, or thrown open their thoughts to me so freely.

POTHINUS. Well : is not this love ?

CLEOPATRA. What ! when he will do as much for the first girl he meets on his way back to Rome ? Ask his slave, Britannus : he has been just as good to him. Nay, ask his very horse ! His kindness is not for anything in me : it is in his own nature.

POTHINUS. But how can you be sure that he does not love you as men love women ?

CLEOPATRA. Because I cannot make him jealous. I have tried.

POTHINUS. Hm ! Perhaps I should have asked, then, do you love him ?

CLEOPATRA. Can one love a god? Besides, I love another Roman : one whom I saw long before Cæsar—no god, but a man—one who can love and hate—one whom I can hurt and who would hurt me.

POTHINUS. Does Cæsar know this ?

CLEOPATRA. Yes.

POTHINUS. And he is not angry ?

CLEOPATRA. He promises to send him to Egypt to please me!

POTHINUS. I do not understand this man.

CLEOPATRA [with superb contempt] You understand Cæsar ! How could you ? [Proudly] I do—by instinct.

POTHINUS [deferentially, after a moment's thought] Your Majesty caused me to be admitted today. What message has the Queen for me ?

CLEOPATRA. This. You think that by making my brother king, you will rule in Egypt, because you are his guardian and he is a little silly.

POTHINUS. The Queen is pleased to say so.

CLEOPATRA. The Queen is pleased to say this also. That Cæsar will eat up you, and Achillas, and my brother, as a cat eats up mice ; and that he will put on this land of Egypt as a shepherd puts on his garment. And when he has done that, he will return to Rome, and leave Cleopatra here as his viceroy.

POTHINUS [breaking out wrathfully] That he shall never do. We have a thousand men to his ten ; and we will drive him and his beggarly legions into the sea.

CLEOPATRA [with scorn, getting up to go] You rant like any common fellow. Go, then, and marshal your thousands ; and make haste ; for Mithridates of Pergamos is at hand with reinforcements for Cæsar. Cæsar has held you at bay with two legions : we shall see what he will do with twenty.

POTHINUS. Cleopatra—

CLEOPATRA. Enough, enough : Cæsar has spoiled me for talking to weak things like you. [She goes out. Pothinus, with a gesture of rage, is following, when Ftatateeta enters and stops him.]

POTHINUS. Let me go forth from this hateful place.

FTATATEETA. What angers you ?

POTHINUS. The curse of all the gods of Egypt be upon her ! She has sold her country to the Roman, that she may buy it back from him with her kisses.

FTATATEETA. Fool : did she not tell you that she would have Cæsar gone ?

POTHINUS. You listened ?

FTATATEETA. I took care that some honest woman should be at hand whilst you were with her.

POTHINUS. Now by the gods—

FTATATEETA. Enough of your gods ! Cæsar's gods are all powerful here. It is no use you coming to Cleopatra : you are only an Egyptian. She will not listen to any of her own race : she treats us all as children.

POTHINUS. May she perish for it !

FTATATEETA [*balefully*] May your tongue wither for that wish! Go! send for Lucius Septimius, the slayer of Pompey. He is a Roman : may be she will listen to him. Begone !

POTHINUS [*darkly*] I know to whom I must go now.

FTATATEETA [*suspiciously*] To whom, then ?

POTHINUS. To a greater Roman than Lucius. And mark this, mistress. You thought, before Cæsar came, that Egypt should presently be ruled by you and your crew in the name of Cleopatra. I set myself against it—

FTATATEETA [*interrupting him—wrangling*] Ay ; that it might be ruled by you and your crew in the name of Ptolemy.

POTHINUS. Better me, or even you, than a woman with a Roman heart ; and that is what Cleopatra is now become. Whilst I live, she shall never rule. So guide yourself accordingly. [*He goes out*].

It is by this time drawing on to dinner time. The table is laid on the roof of the palace ; and thither Rufio is now climbing, ushered by a majestic palace official, wand of office in hand, and followed by a slave carrying an inlaid stool. After many stairs they emerge at last into a massive colonnade on the roof. Light curtains are drawn between the columns on the north and east to soften the westering sun. The official leads Rufio to one of these shaded sections. A cord for pulling the curtains apart hangs down between the pillars.

THE OFFICIAL [*bowing*] The Roman commander will await Cæsar here.

The slave sets down the stool near the southernmost column, and slips out through the curtains.

RUFIO [*sitting down, a little blown*] Pouf ! That was a climb. How high have we come ?

THE OFFICIAL. We are on the palace roof, O Beloved of Victory !

RUFIO. Good ! the Beloved of Victory has no more stairs to get up.

A second official enters from the opposite end, walking backwards.

THE SECOND OFFICIAL. Cæsar approaches.

Cæsar, fresh from the bath, clad in a new tunic of purple silk, comes in, beaming and festive, followed by two slaves carrying a light couch, which is hardly more than an elaborately designed bench. They place it near the northmost of the two curtained columns. When this is done they slip out through the curtains ; and the two officials, formally bowing, follow them. Rufio rises to receive Cæsar.

CÆSAR [*coming over to him*] Why, Rufio ! [*Surveying his dress with an air of admiring astonishment*] A new baldrick ! A new golden pommel to your sword ! And you have had your hair cut ! But not your beard—? impossible ! [*He sniffs at Rufio's beard*]. Yes, perfumed, by Jupiter Olympus !

RUFIO [*growling*] Well : is it to please myself ?

CÆSAR [*affectionately*] No, my son Rufio, but to please me—to celebrate my birthday.

RUFIO [*contemptuously*] Your birthday ! You always have a birthday when there is a pretty girl to be flattered or an ambassador to be conciliated. We had seven of them in ten months last year.

CÆSAR [*contritely*] It is true, Rufio ! I shall never break myself of these petty deceits.

RUFIO. Who is to dine with us—besides Cleopatra ?

CÆSAR. Apollodorus the Sicilian.

RUFIO. That popinjay !

CÆSAR. Come ! the popinjay is an amusing dog—tells a story ; sings a song ; and saves us the trouble of flattering the Queen. What does she care for old politicians and camp-fed bears like us ? No : Apollodorus is good company, Rufio, good company.

RUFIO. Well, he can swim a bit and fence a bit : he might be worse, if he only knew how to hold his tongue.

CÆSAR. The gods forbid he should ever learn ! Oh, this military life ! this tedious, brutal life of action ! That is the worst of us Romans : we are mere doers and drudgers : a swarm of bees turned into men. Give me a good talker —one with wit and imagination enough to live without continually doing something !

RUFIO. Ay ! a nice time he would have of it with you when dinner was over ! Have you noticed that I am before my time ?

CÆSAR. Aha ! I thought that meant something. What is it ?

RUFIO. Can we be overheard here ?

CÆSAR. Our privacy invites eavesdropping. I can remedy that. [*He claps his hands twice. The curtains are drawn, revealing the roof garden with a banqueting table set across in the middle for four persons, one at each end, and two side by side. The side next Cæsar and Rufio is blocked with golden wine vessels and basins. A gorgeous major-domo is superintending the laying of the table by a staff of slaves. The colonnade goes round the garden at both sides to the further end, where a gap in it, like a great gateway, leaves the view open to the sky beyond the western edge of the roof, except in the middle, where a life size image of Ra, seated on a huge plinth, towers up, with hawk head and crown of asp and disk. His altar, which stands at his feet, is a single white stone.*] Now everybody can see us, nobody will think of listening to us. [*He sits down on the bench left by the two slaves*].

RUFIO [*sitting down on his stool*] Pothinus wants to speak to you. I advise you to see him : there is some plotting going on here among the women.

CÆSAR. Who is Pothinus ?

RUFIO. The fellow with hair like squirrel's fur—the little King's bear leader, whom you kept prisoner.

CÆSAR [*annoyed*] And has he not escaped ?

RUFIO. No.

CÆSAR [*rising imperiously*] Why not ? You have been guarding this man instead of watching the enemy. Have I not told you always to let prisoners escape unless there are special orders to the contrary ? Are there not enough mouths to be fed without him ?

RUFIO. Yes ; and if you would have a little sense and let me cut his throat, you would save his rations. Anyhow, he wont escape. Three sentries have told him they would put a pilum through him if they saw him again. What more can they do ? He prefers to stay and spy on us. So would I if I had to do with generals subject to fits of clemency.

CÆSAR [*resuming his seat, argued down*] Hm ! And so he wants to see me.

RUFIO. Ay. I have brought him with me. He is waiting there [*jerking his thumb over his shoulder*] under guard.

CÆSAR. And you want me to see him ?

RUFIO [*obstinately*] I dont want anything. I daresay you will do what you like. Dont put it on to me.

CÆSAR [*with an air of doing it expressly to indulge Rufio*] Well, well : let us have him.

RUFIO [*calling*] Ho there, guard ! Release your man and send him up. [*Beckoning*]. Come along !

Pothinus enters and stops mistrustfully between the two, looking from one to the other.

CÆSAR [*graciously*] Ah, Pothinus ! You are welcome. And what is the news this afternoon ?

POTHINUS. Cæsar : I come to warn you of a danger, and to make you an offer.

CÆSAR. Never mind the danger. Make the offer.

RUFIO. Never mind the offer. Whats the danger ?

POTHINUS. Cæsar : you think that Cleopatra is devoted to you.

CÆSAR [*gravely*] My friend : I already know what I think. Come to your offer.

POTHINUS. I will deal plainly. I know not by what strange gods you have been enabled to defend a palace and a few yards of beach against a city and an army. Since we cut you off from Lake Mareotis, and you dug wells in the salt sea sand and brought up buckets of fresh water from them, we have known that your gods are irresistible, and that you are a worker of miracles. I no longer threaten you—

RUFIO [*sarcastically*] Very handsome of you, indeed.

POTHINUS. So be it : you are the master. Our gods sent the north west winds to keep you in our hands ; but you have been too strong for them.

CÆSAR [*gently urging him to come to the point*] Yes, yes, my friend. But what then ?

RUFIO. Spit it out, man. What have you to say ?

POTHINUS. I have to say that you have a traitress in your camp. Cleopatra—

THE MAJOR-DOMO [*at the table, announcing*] The Queen ! [*Cæsar and Rufio rise*].

RUFIO [*aside to Pothinus*] You should have spat it out sooner, you fool. Now it is too late.

Cleopatra, in gorgeous raiment, enters in state through the gap in the colonnade, and comes down past the image of Ra and past the table to Cæsar. Her retinue, headed by Ftatateeta, joins the staff at the table. Cæsar gives Cleopatra his seat, which she takes.

CLEOPATRA [*quickly, seeing Pothinus*] What is he doing here ?

CÆSAR [*seating himself beside her, in the most amiable of tempers*] Just going to tell me something about you. You shall hear it. Proceed, Pothinus.

POTHINUS [*disconcerted*] Cæsar—[*he stammers*].

CÆSAR. Well, out with it.

POTHINUS. What I have to say is for your ear, not for the Queen's.

CLEOPATRA [*with subdued ferocity*] There are means of making you speak. Take care.

POTHINUS [*defiantly*] Cæsar does not employ those means.

CÆSAR. My friend : when a man has anything to tell in this world, the difficulty is not to make him tell it, but to prevent him from telling it too often. Let me celebrate my birthday by setting you free. Farewell : we shall not meet again.

CLEOPATRA [*angrily*] Cæsar : this mercy is foolish.

POTHINUS [*to Cæsar*] Will you not give me a private audience ? Your life may depend on it. [*Cæsar rises loftily*].

RUFIO [*aside to Pothinus*] Ass ! Now we shall have some heroics.

CÆSAR [*oratorically*] Pothinus—

RUFIO [*interrupting him*] Cæsar : the dinner will spoil if you begin preaching your favorite sermon about life and death.

CLEOPATRA [*priggishly*] Peace, Rufio. I desire to hear Cæsar.

RUFIO [*bluntly*] Your Majesty has heard it before. You repeated it to Apollodorus last week ; and he thought it was all your own. [*Cæsar's dignity collapses. Much tickled, he sits down again and looks roguishly at Cleopatra, who is furious. Rufio calls as before*] Ho there, guard ! Pass the prisoner out. He is released. [*To Pothinus*] Now off with you. You have lost your chance.

POTHINUS [*his temper overcoming his prudence*] I will speak.

CÆSAR [*to Cleopatra*] You see. Torture would not have wrung a word from him.

POTHINUS. Cæsar : you have taught Cleopatra the arts by which the Romans govern the world.

CÆSAR. Alas ! they cannot even govern themselves. What then ?

POTHINUS. What then ? Are you so besotted with her beauty that you do not see that she is impatient to reign in Egypt alone, and that her heart is set on your departure ?

CLEOPATRA [*rising*] Liar !

CÆSAR [*shocked*] What ! Protestations ! Contradictions !

CLEOPATRA [*ashamed, but trembling with suppressed rage*] No. I do not deign to contradict. Let him talk. [*She sits down again*].

POTHINUS. From her own lips I have heard it. You are to be her catspaw : you are to tear the crown from her brother's head and set it on her own, delivering us all into her hand—delivering yourself also. And then Cæsar can return to Rome, or depart through the gate of death, which is nearer and surer.

CÆSAR [*calmly*] Well, my friend ; and is not this very natural ?

POTHINUS [*astonished*] Natural ! Then you do not resent treachery ?

CÆSAR. Resent ! O thou foolish Egyptian, what have I to do with resentment ? Do I resent the wind when it chills me, or the night when it makes me stumble in the darkness ? Shall I resent youth when it turns from age, and ambition when it turns from servitude ? To tell me such a story as this is but to tell me that the sun will rise tomorrow.

CLEOPATRA [*unable to contain herself*] But it is false— false. I swear it.

CÆSAR. It is true, though you swore it a thousand times, and believed all you swore. [*She is convulsed with emotion. To screen her, he rises and takes Pothinus to Rufio, saying*] Come, Rufio : let us see Pothinus past the guard. I have a word to say to him. [*Aside to them*] We must give the Queen a moment to recover herself. [*Aloud*] Come. [*He takes Pothinus and Rufio out with him, conversing with them meanwhile*]. Tell your friends, Pothinus, that they must not think I am opposed to a reasonable settlement of the country's affairs—[*They pass out of hearing*].

CLEOPATRA [*in a stifled whisper*] Ftatateeta, Ftatateeta.

FTATATEETA [*hurrying to her from the table and petting her*] Peace, child : be comforted—

CLEOPATRA [*interrupting her*] Can they hear us ?

FTATATEETA. No, dear heart, no.

CLEOPATRA. Listen to me. If he leaves the Palace alive, never see my face again.

FTATATEETA. He ? Poth—

CLEOPATRA [*striking her on the mouth*] Strike his life out as I strike his name from your lips. Dash him down from the wall. Break him on the stones. Kill, kill, kill him.

FTATATEETA [*shewing all her teeth*] The dog shall perish.

CLEOPATRA. Fail in this, and you go out from before me for ever.

FTATATEETA [*resolutely*] So be it. You shall not see my face until his eyes are darkened.

Cæsar comes back, with Apollodorus, exquisitely dressed, and Rufio.

CLEOPATRA [*to Ftatateeta*] Come soon—soon. [*Ftatateeta turns her meaning eyes for a moment on her mistress ; then goes grimly away past Ra and out. Cleopatra runs like a gazelle to Cæsar*] So you have come back to me, Cæsar. [*Caressingly*] I thought you were angry. Welcome, Apollodorus. [*She gives him her hand to kiss, with her other arm about Cæsar*].

APOLLODORUS. Cleopatra grows more womanly beautiful from week to week.

CLEOPATRA. Truth, Apollodorus ?

APOLLODORUS. Far, far short of the truth ! Friend Rufio threw a pearl into the sea : Cæsar fished up a diamond.

CÆSAR. Cæsar fished up a touch of rheumatism, my friend. Come : to dinner ! to dinner ! [*They move towards the table*].

CLEOPATRA [*skipping like a young fawn*] Yes, to dinner. I have ordered such a dinner for you, Cæsar !

CÆSAR. Ay ? What are we to have ?

CLEOPATRA. Peacocks' brains.

CÆSAR [*as if his mouth watered*] Peacocks' brains, Apollodorus !

APOLLODORUS. Not for me. I prefer nightingales' tongues. [*He goes to one of the two covers set side by side*].

CLEOPATRA. Roast boar, Rufio !

RUFIO [*gluttonously*] Good ! [*He goes to the seat next Apollodorus, on his left*].

CÆSAR [*looking at his seat, which is at the end of the table, to Ra's left hand*] What has become of my leathern cushion ?

CLEOPATRA [*at the opposite end*] I have got new ones for you.

THE MAJOR-DOMO. These cushions, Cæsar, are of Maltese gauze, stuffed with rose leaves.

CÆSAR. Rose leaves ! Am I a caterpillar ? [*He throws the cushions away and seats himself on the leather mattress underneath*].

CLEOPATRA. What a shame ! My new cushions !

THE MAJOR-DOMO [*at Cæsar's elbow*] What shall we serve to whet Cæsar's appetite ?

CÆSAR. What have you got ?

THE MAJOR-DOMO. Sea hedgehogs, black and white sea acorns, sea nettles, beccaficoes, purple shellfish—

CÆSAR. Any oysters ?

THE MAJOR-DOMO. Assuredly.

CÆSAR. British oysters ?

THE MAJOR-DOMO [*assenting*] British oysters, Cæsar.

CÆSAR. Oysters, then. [*The Major-Domo signs to a slave at each order ; and the slave goes out to execute it*]. I have been in Britain—that western land of romance—the last piece of earth on the edge of the ocean that surrounds the world. I went there in search of its famous pearls. The British pearl was a fable ; but in searching for it I found the British oyster.

APOLLODORUS. All posterity will bless you for it. [*To the Major-Domo*] Sea hedgehogs for me.

RUFIO. Is there nothing solid to begin with ?

THE MAJOR-DOMO. Fieldfares with asparagus—

CLEOPATRA [*interrupting*] Fattened fowls ! have some fattened fowls, Rufio.

RUFIO. Ay, that will do.

CLEOPATRA [*greedily*] Fieldfares for me.

THE MAJOR-DOMO. Cæsar will deign to choose his wine ? Sicilian Lesbian, Chian—

RUFIO [*contemptuously*] All Greek.

APOLLODORUS. Who would drink Roman wine when he could get Greek. Try the Lesbian, Cæsar.

CÆSAR. Bring me my barley water.

RUFIO [*with intense disgust*] Ugh ! Bring me my Falernian. [*The Falernian is presently brought to him*].

CLEOPATRA [*pouting*] It is waste of time giving you dinners, Cæsar. My scullions would not condescend to your diet.

CÆSAR [*relenting*] Well, well : let us try the Lesbian. [*The Major-Domo fills Cæsar's goblet ; then Cleopatra's and Apollodorus's*]. But when I return to Rome, I will make laws against these extravagances. I will even get the laws carried out.

CLEOPATRA [*coaxingly*] Never mind. Today you are to be like other people : idle, luxurious, and kind. [*She stretches her hand to him along the table*].

CÆSAR. Well, for once I will sacrifice my comfort— [*kissing her hand*] there ! [*He takes a draught of wine*]. Now are you satisfied ?

CLEOPATRA. And you no longer believe that I long for your departure for Rome ?

CÆSAR. I no longer believe anything. My brains are asleep. Besides, who knows whether I shall return to Rome ?

RUFIO [*alarmed*] How ? Eh ? What ?

CÆSAR. What has Rome to shew me that I have not seen already ? One year of Rome is like another, except that I grow older, whilst the crowd in the Appian Way is always the same age.

APOLLODORUS. It is no better here in Egypt. The old men, when they are tired of life, say " We have seen everything except the source of the Nile."

CÆSAR [*his imagination catching fire*] And why not see that ? Cleopatra : will you come with me and track the flood to its cradle in the heart of the regions of mystery ?

Shall we leave Rome behind us—Rome, that has achieved greatness only to learn how greatness destroys nations of men who are not great ! Shall I make you a new kingdom, and build you a holy city there in the great unknown ?

CLEOPATRA [*rapturously*] Yes, yes. You shall.

RUFIO. Ay : now he will conquer Africa with two legions before we come to the roast boar.

APOLLODORUS. Come : no scoffing. This is a noble scheme : in it Cæsar is no longer merely the conquering soldier, but the creative poet-artist. Let us name the holy city, and consecrate it with Lesbian wine.

CÆSAR. Cleopatra shall name it herself.

CLEOPATRA. It shall be called Cæsar's Gift to his Beloved.

APOLLODORUS. No, no. Something vaster than that— something universal, like the starry firmament.

CÆSAR [*prosaically*] Why not simply The Cradle of the Nile ?

CLEOPATRA. No : the Nile is my ancestor ; and he is a god. Oh ! I have thought of something. The Nile shall name it himself. Let us call upon him. [*To the Major-Domo*] Send for him. [*The three men stare at one another; but the Major-Domo goes out as if he had received the most matter-of-fact order*]. And [*to the retinue*] away with you all.

The retinue withdraws, making obeisance.

A priest enters, carrying a miniature sphinx with a tiny tripod before it. A morsel of incense is smoking in the tripod. The priest comes to the table and places the image in the middle of it. The light begins to change to the magenta purple of the Egyptian sunset, as if the god had brought a strange colored shadow with him. The three men are determined not to be impressed ; but they feel curious in spite of themselves.

CÆSAR. What hocus-pocus is this ?

CLEOPATRA. You shall see. And it is n o t hocus-pocus. To do it properly, we should kill something to please him ; but perhaps he will answer Cæsar without that if we spill some wine to him.

APOLLODORUS [*turning his head to look up over his shoulder at Ra*] Why not appeal to our hawkheaded friend here ?

CLEOPATRA [*nervously*] Sh! He will hear you and be angry.

RUFIO [*phlegmatically*] The source of the Nile is out of his district, I expect.

CLEOPATRA. No : I will have my city named by nobody but my dear little sphinx, because it was in its arms that Cæsar found me asleep. [*She languishes at Cæsar then turns curtly to the priest*]. Go. I am a priestess, and have power to take your charge from you. [*The priest makes a reverence and goes out*]. Now let us call on the Nile all together. Perhaps he will rap on the table.

CÆSAR. What! table rapping! Are such superstitions still believed in this year 707 of the Republic?

CLEOPATRA. It is no superstition : our priests learn lots of things from the tables. Is it not so, Apollodorus?

APOLLODORUS. Yes : I profess myself a converted man. When Cleopatra is priestess, Apollodorus is devotee. Propose the conjuration.

CLEOPATRA. You must say with me " Send us thy voice, Father Nile."

ALL FOUR [*holding their glasses together before the idol*] Send us thy voice, Father Nile.

The death cry of a man in mortal terror and agony answers them. Appalled, the men set down their glasses, and listen. Silence. The purple deepens in the sky. Cæsar, glancing at Cleopatra, catches her pouring out her wine before the god, with gleaming eyes, and mute assurances of gratitude and worship. Apollodorus springs up and runs to the edge of the roof to peer down and listen.

CÆSAR [*looking piercingly at Cleopatra*] What was that?

CLEOPATRA [*petulantly*] Nothing. They are beating some slave.

CÆSAR. Nothing.

RUFIO. A man with a knife in him, I'll swear.

CÆSAR [*rising*] A murder!

APOLLODORUS [*at the back, waving his hand for silence*] S-sh! Silence. Did you hear that?

CÆSAR. Another cry?

T.P.—8

APOLLODORUS [*returning to the table*] No, a thud. Something fell on the beach, I think.

RUFIO [*grimly, as he rises*] Something with bones in it, eh?

CÆSAR [*shuddering*] Hush, hush, Rufio. [*He leaves the table and returns to the colonnade : Rufio following at his left elbow, and Apollodorus at the other side*].

CLEOPATRA [*still in her place at the table*] Will you leave me, Cæsar ? Apollodorus : are you going ?

APOLLODORUS. Faith, dearest Queen, my appetite is gone.

CÆSAR. Go down to the courtyard, Apollodorus ; and find out what has happened.

Apollodorus nods and goes out, making for the staircase by which Rufio ascended.

CLEOPATRA. Your soldiers have killed somebody, perhaps. What does it matter ?

The murmur of a crowd rises from the beach below. Cæsar and Rufio look at one another.

CÆSAR. This must be seen to. [*He is about to follow Apollodorus when Rufio stops him with a hand on his arm as Ftatateeta comes back by the far end of the roof, with dragging steps, a drowsy satiety in her eyes and in the corners of the bloodhound lips. For a moment Cæsar suspects that she is drunk with wine. Not so Rufio : he knows well the red vintage that has inebriated her*].

RUFIO [*in a low tone*] There is some mischief between those two.

FTATATEETA. The Queen looks again on the face of her servant.

Cleopatra looks at her for a moment with an exultant reflection of her murderous expression. Then she flings her arms round her ; kisses her repeatedly and savagely ; and tears off her jewels and heaps them on her. The two men turn from the spectacle to look at one another. Ftatateeta drags herself sleepily to the altar ; kneels before Ra ; and remains there in prayer. Cæsar goes to Cleopatra, leaving Rufio in the colonnade.

CÆSAR [*with searching earnestness*] Cleopatra : what has happened ?

CLEOPATRA [*in mortal dread of him, but with her utmost cajolery*] Nothing, dearest Cæsar. [*With sickly sweetness, her voice almost failing*] Nothing. I am innocent. [*She approaches him affectionately*] Dear Cæsar : are you angry with me ? Why do you look at me so ? I have been here with you all the time. How can I know what has happened ?

CÆSAR [*reflectively*] That is true.

CLEOPATRA [*greatly relieved, trying to caress him*] Of course it is true. [*He does not respond to the caress*] You know it is true, Rufio.

The murmur without suddenly swells to a roar and subsides.

RUFIO. I shall know presently. [*He makes for the altar in the burly trot that serves him for a stride, and touches Ftatateeta on the shoulder*]. Now, mistress : I shall want you. [*He orders her, with a gesture, to go before him*].

FTATATEETA [*rising and glowering at him*] My place is with the Queen.

CLEOPATRA. She has done no harm, Rufio.

CÆSAR [*to Rufio*] Let her stay.

RUFIO [*sitting down on the altar*] Very well. Then my place is here too ; and you can see what is the matter for yourself. The city is in a pretty uproar, it seems.

CÆSAR [*with grave displeasure*] Rufio : there is a time for obedience.

RUFIO. And there is a time for obstinacy. [*He folds his arms doggedly*].

CÆSAR [*to Cleopatra*] Send her away.

CLEOPATRA [*whining in her eagerness to propitiate him*] Yes, I will. I will do whatever you ask me, Cæsar, always, because I love you. Ftatateeta : go away.

FTATATEETA. The Queen's word is my will. I shall be at hand for the Queen's call. [*She goes out past Ra, as she came*].

RUFIO [*following her*] Remember, Cæsar, your bodyguard also is within call. [*He follows her out*].

Cleopatra, presuming upon Cæsar's submission to Rufio, leaves the table and sits down on the bench in the colonnade.

CLEOPATRA. Why do you allow Rufio to treat you so? You should teach him his place.

CÆSAR. Teach him to be my enemy, and to hide his thoughts from me as you are now hiding yours.

CLEOPATRA [*her fears returning*] Why do you say that, Cæsar? Indeed, indeed, I am not hiding anything. You are wrong to treat me like this. [*She stifles a sob*]. I am only a child; and you turn into stone because you think some one has been killed. I cannot bear it. [*She purposely breaks down and weeps. He looks at her with profound sadness and complete coldness. She looks up to see what effect she is producing. Seeing that he is unmoved, she sits up, pretending to struggle with her emotion and to put it bravely away*]. But there: I know you hate tears: you shall not be troubled with them. I know you are not angry, but only sad; only I am so silly, I cannot help being hurt when you speak coldly. Of course you are quite right: it is dreadful to think of anyone being killed or even hurt; and I hope nothing really serious has—[*her voice dies away under his contemptuous penetration*].

CÆSAR. What has frightened you into this? What have you done? [*A trumpet sounds on the beach below*]. Aha! that sounds like the answer.

CLEOPATRA [*sinking back trembling on the bench and covering her face with her hands*] I have not betrayed you, Cæsar: I swear it.

CÆSAR. I know that. I have not trusted you. [*He turns from her, and is about to go out when Apollodorus and Britannus drag in Lucius Septimius to him. Rufio follows. Cæsar shudders*]. Again, Pompey's murderer!

RUFIO. The town has gone mad, I think. They are for tearing the palace down and driving us into the sea straight away. We laid hold of this renegade in clearing them out of the courtyard.

CÆSAR. Release him. [*They let go his arms*]. What has offended the citizens, Lucius Septimius?

LUCIUS. What did you expect, Cæsar? Pothinus was a favorite of theirs.

CÆSAR. What has happened to Pothinus? I set him free, here, not half an hour ago. Did they not pass him out?

LUCIUS. Ay, through the gallery arch sixty feet above ground, with three inches of steel in his ribs. He is as dead as Pompey. We are quits now, as to killing—you and I.

CÆSAR [*shocked*] Assassinated!—our prisoner, our guest! [*He turns reproachfully on Rufio*] Rufio—

RUFIO [*emphatically—anticipating the question*] Whoever did it was a wise man and a friend of yours [*Cleopatra is greatly emboldened*]; but none of us had a hand in it. So it is no use to frown at me. [*Cæsar turns and looks at Cleopatra*].

CLEOPATRA [*violently—rising*] He was slain by order of the Queen of Egypt. I am not Julius Cæsar the dreamer, who allows every slave to insult him. Rufio has said I did well: now the others shall judge me too. [*She turns to the others*]. This Pothinus sought to make me conspire with him to betray Cæsar to Achillas and Ptolemy. I refused; and he cursed me and came privily to Cæsar to accuse me of his own treachery. I caught him in the act; and he insulted me—me, the Queen! to my face. Cæsar would not avenge me: he spoke him fair and set him free. Was I right to avenge myself? Speak, Lucius.

LUCIUS. I do not gainsay it. But you will get little thanks from Cæsar for it.

CLEOPATRA. Speak, Apollodorus. Was I wrong?

APOLLODORUS. I have only one word of blame, most beautiful. You should have called upon me, your knight; and in fair duel I should have slain the slanderer.

CLEOPATRA [*passionately*] I will be judged by your very slave, Cæsar. Britannus: speak. Was I wrong?

BRITANNUS. Were treachery, falsehood, and disloyalty left unpunished, society must become like an arena full of wild beasts, tearing one another to pieces. Cæsar is in the wrong.

CÆSAR [*with quiet bitterness*] And so the verdict is against me, it seems.

CLEOPATRA [*vehemently*] Listen to me, Cæsar. If one man in all Alexandria can be found to say that I did wrong, I swear to have myself crucified on the door of the palace by my own slaves.

CÆSAR. If one man in all the world can be found, now or forever, to know that you did wrong, that man will have either to conquer the world as I have, or be crucified by it. [*The uproar in the streets again reaches them*]. Do you hear? These knockers at your gate are also believers in vengeance and in stabbing. You have slain their leader: it is right that they shall slay you. If you doubt it, ask your four counsellors here. And then in the name of that right [*he emphasizes the word with great scorn*] shall I not slay them for murdering their Queen, and be slain in my turn by their countrymen as the invader of their fatherland? Can Rome do less then than slay these slayers, too, to shew the world how Rome avenges her sons and her honor. And so, to the end of history, murder shall breed murder, always in the name of right and honor and peace, until the gods are tired of blood and create a race that can understand. [*Fierce uproar. Cleopatra becomes white with terror*]. Hearken, you who must not be insulted. Go near enough to catch their words: you will find them bitterer than the tongue of Pothinus. [*Loftily, wrapping himself up in an impenetrable dignity*] Let the Queen of Egypt now give her orders for vengeance, and take her measures for defence; for she has renounced Cæsar. [*He turns to go*].

CLEOPATRA [*terrified, running to him and falling on her knees*] You will not desert me, Cæsar. You will defend the palace.

CÆSAR. You have taken the powers of life and death upon you. I am only a dreamer.

CLEOPATRA. But they will kill me.

CÆSAR. And why not?

CLEOPATRA. In pity—

CÆSAR. Pity! What! has it come to this so suddenly, that nothing can save you now but pity? Did it save Pothinus?

She rises, wringing her hands, and goes back to the bench in despair. Apollodorus shews his sympathy with her by quietly posting himself behind the bench. The sky has by this time become the most vivid purple, and soon begins to change to a glowing pale orange, against which the colonnade and the great image shew darklier and darklier.

RUFIO. Cæsar : enough of preaching. The enemy is at the gate.

CÆSAR [*turning on him and giving way to his wrath*] Ay; and what has held him baffled at the gate all these months ? Was it my folly, as you deem it, or your wisdom ? In this Egyptian Red Sea of blood, whose hand has held all your heads above the waves? [*Turning on Cleopatra*] And yet, when Cæsar says to such an one, " Friend, go free," you, clinging for your little life to my sword, dare steal out and stab him in the back ? And you, soldiers and gentlemen, and honest servants as you forget that you are, applaud this assassination, and say " Cæsar is in the wrong." By the gods, I am tempted to open my hand and let you all sink into the flood.

CLEOPATRA [*with a ray of cunning hope*] But, Cæsar, if you do, you will perish yourself.

Cæsar's eyes blaze.

RUFIO [*greatly alarmed*] Now, by great Jove, you filthy little Egyptian rat, that is the very word to make him walk out alone into the city and leave us here to be cut to pieces. [*Desperately, to Cæsar*] Will you desert us because we are a parcel of fools ? I mean no harm by killing : I do it as a dog kills a cat, by instinct. We are all dogs at your heels ; but we have served you faithfully.

CÆSAR [*relenting*] Alas, Rufio, my son, my son : as dogs we are like to perish now in the streets.

APOLLODORUS [*at his post behind Cleopatra's seat*] Cæsar : what you say has an Olympian ring in it : it must be right ; for it is fine art. But I am still on the side of Cleopatra. If we must die, she shall not want the devotion of a man's heart nor the strength of a man's arm.

CLEOPATRA [*sobbing*] But I dont want to die.

CÆSAR [*sadly*] Oh, ignoble, ignoble !

LUCIUS [*coming forward between Cæsar and Cleopatra*] Hearken to me, Cæsar. It may be ignoble ; but I also mean to live as long as I can.

CÆSAR. Well, my friend, you are likely to outlive Cæsar. Is it any magic of mine, think you, that has kept your army and this whole city at bay for so long ? Yesterday, what quarrel had they with me that they should risk their lives against me ? But today we have flung them down their hero, murdered ; and now every man of them is set upon clearing out this nest of assassins—for such we are and no more. Take courage then ; and sharpen your sword. Pompey's head has fallen ; and Cæsar's head is ripe.

APOLLODORUS Does Cæsar despair ?

CÆSAR [*with infinite pride*] He who has never hoped can never despair. Cæsar, in good or bad fortune, looks his fate in the face.

LUCIUS. Look it in the face, then ; and it will smile as it always has on Cæsar.

CÆSAR [*with involuntary haughtiness*] Do you presume to encourage me ?

LUCIUS. I offer you my services. I will change sides if you will have me.

CÆSAR [*suddenly coming down to earth again, and looking sharply at him, divining that there is something behind the offer*] What ! At this point ?

LUCIUS [*firmly*] At this point.

RUFIO. Do you suppose Cæsar is mad, to trust you ?

LUCIUS. I do not ask him to trust me until he is victorious. I ask for my life, and for a command in Cæsar's army. And since Cæsar is a fair dealer, I will pay in advance.

CÆSAR. Pay ! How ?

LUCIUS. With a piece of good news for you.

Cæsar divines the news in a flash.

RUFIO. What news ?

CÆSAR [*with an elate and buoyant energy which makes Cleopatra sit up and stare*] What news ! What news, did you say, my son Rufio ? The relief has arrived : what other

news remains for us ? Is it not so, Lucius Septimius ?
Mithridates of Pergamos is on the march.

LUCIUS. He has taken Pelusium.

CÆSAR [*delighted*] Lucius Septimius : you are henceforth
my officer. Rufio : the Egyptians must have sent every
soldier from the city to prevent Mithridates crossing the
Nile. There is nothing in the streets now but mob—mob !

LUCIUS. It is so. Mithridates is marching by the great
road to Memphis to cross above the Delta. Achillas will
fight him there.

CÆSAR [*all audacity*] Achillas shall fight Cæsar there.
See, Rufio. [*He runs to the table; snatches a napkin; and
draws a plan on it with his finger dipped in wine, whilst Rufio
and Lucius Septimius crowd about him to watch, all looking
closely, for the light is now almost gone*]. Here is the palace
[*pointing to his plan*] : here is the theatre. You [*to Rufio*]
take twenty men and pretend to go by that street [*pointing
it out*] ; and whilst they are stoning you, out go the cohorts
by this and this. My streets are right, are they, Lucius ?

LUCIUS. Ay, that is the fig market—

CÆSAR [*too much excited to listen to him*] I saw them the
day we arrived. Good ! [*He throws the napkin on the table,
and comes down again into the colonnade*]. Away, Britannus:
tell Petronius that within an hour half our forces must take
ship for the western lake. See to my horse and armor.
[*Britannus runs out*]. With the rest, *I* shall march round the
lake and up the Nile to meet Mithridates. Away, Lucius ;
and give the word. [*Lucius hurries out after Britannus*].
Apollodorus : lend me your sword and your right arm for
this campaign.

APOLLODORUS. Ay, and my heart and life to boot.

CÆSAR [*grasping his hand*] I accept both. [*Mighty hand-
shake*]. Are you ready for work ?

APOLLODORUS. Ready for Art—the Art of War [*he rushes
out after Lucius, totally forgetting Cleopatra*].

RUFIO. Come ! this is something like business.

CÆSAR [*buoyantly*] Is it not, my only son ? [*He claps his
hands. The slaves hurry in to the table*]. No more of this

mawkish revelling : away with all this stuff : shut it out of my sight and be off with you. [*The slaves begin to remove the table; and the curtains are drawn, shutting in the colonnade*]. You understand about the streets, Rufio ?

RUFIO. Ay, I think I do. I will get through them, at all events.

The bucina sounds busily in the courtyard beneath.

CÆSAR. Come, then : we must talk to the troops and hearten them. You down to the beach : I to the courtyard. [*He makes for the staircase*].

CLEOPATRA [*rising from her seat, where she has been quite neglected all this time, and stretching out her hands timidly to him*] Cæsar.

CÆSAR [*turning*] Eh ?

CLEOPATRA. Have you forgotten me ?

CÆSAR [*indulgently*] I am busy now, my child, busy. When I return your affairs shall be settled. Farewell ; and be good and patient.

He goes, preoccupied and quite indifferent. She stands with clenched fists, in speechless rage and humiliation.

RUFIO. That game is played and lost, Cleopatra. The woman always gets the worst of it.

CLEOPATRA [*haughtily*] Go. Follow your master.

RUFIO [*in her ear, with rough familiarity*] A word first. Tell your executioner that if Pothinus had been properly killed—in the throat—he would not have called out. Your man bungled his work.

CLEOPATRA [*enigmatically*] How do you know it was a man ?

RUFIO [*startled, and puzzled*] It was not you : you were with us when it happened. [*She turns her back scornfully on him. He shakes his head, and draws the curtains to go out. It is now a magnificent moonlit night. The table has been removed. Ftatateeta is seen in the light of the moon and stars, again in prayer before the white altar-stone of Ra. Rufio starts; closes the curtains again softly; and says in a low voice to Cleopatra*] Was it she ? with her own hand ?

CLEOPATRA [*threateningly*] Whoever it was, let my enemies

beware of her. Look to it, Rufio, you who dare make the Queen of Egypt a fool before Cæsar.

RUFIO [*looking grimly at her*] I will look to it, Cleopatra. [*He nods in confirmation of the promise, and slips out through the curtains, loosening his sword in its sheath as he goes*].

ROMAN SOLDIERS [*in the courtyard below*] Hail, Cæsar ! Hail, hail !

Cleopatra listens. The bucina sounds again, followed by several trumpets.

CLEOPATRA [*wringing her hands and calling*] Ftatateeta. Ftatateeta. It is dark ; and I am alone. Come to me. [*Silence*] Ftatateeta. [*Louder*] Ftatateeta. [*Silence. In a panic she snatches the cord and pulls the curtains apart*].

Ftatateeta is lying dead on the altar of Ra, with her throat cut. Her blood deluges the white stone.

High noon. Festival and military pageant on the esplanade before the palace. In the east harbor Cæsar's galley, so gorgeously decorated that it seems to be rigged with flowers, is alongside the quay, close to the steps Apollodorus descended when he embarked with the carpet. A Roman guard is posted there in charge of a gangway, whence a red floorcloth is laid down the middle of the esplanade, turning off to the north opposite the central gate in the palace front, which shuts in the esplanade on the south side. The broad steps of the gate, crowded with Cleopatra's ladies, all in their gayest attire, are like a flower garden. The façade is lined by her guard, officered by the same gallants to whom Bel Affris announced the coming of Cæsar six months before in the old palace on the Syrian border. The north side is lined by Roman soldiers, with the townsfolk on tiptoe behind them, peering over their heads at the cleared esplanade, in which the officers stroll about, chatting. Among these are Belzanor and the Persian; also the centurion, vinewood cudgel in hand, battle worn, thick-booted, and much outshone, both socially and decoratively, by the Egyptian officers.

Apollodorus makes his way through the townsfolk and calls to the officers from behind the Roman line.

APOLLODORUS. Hullo! May I pass?

CENTURION. Pass Apollodorus the Sicilian there! [*The soldiers let him through*].

BELZANOR. Is Cæsar at hand?

APOLLODORUS. Not yet. He is still in the market place. I could not stand any more of the roaring of the soldiers! After half an hour of the enthusiasm of an army, one feels the need of a little sea air.

PERSIAN. Tell us the news. Hath he slain the priests?

APOLLODORUS. Not he. They met him in the market place with ashes on their heads and their gods in their hands. They placed the gods at his feet. The only one that was worth looking at was Apis : a miracle of gold and ivory work. By my advice he offered the chief priest two talents for it.

BELZANOR [*appalled*] Apis the all-knowing for two talents! What said the chief Priest ?

APOLLODORUS. He invoked the mercy of Apis, and asked for five.

BELZANOR. There will be famine and tempest in the land for this.

PERSIAN. Pooh ! Why did not Apis cause Cæsar to be vanquished by Achillas ? Any fresh news from the war, Apollodorus ?

APOLLODORUS. The little King Ptolemy was drowned.

BELZANOR. Drowned ! How ?

APOLLODORUS. With the rest of them. Cæsar attacked them from three sides at once and swept them into the Nile. Ptolemy's barge sank.

BELZANOR. A marvellous man, this Cæsar ! Will he come soon, think you ?

APOLLODORUS. He was settling the Jewish question when I left.

A flourish of trumpets from the north, and commotion among the townsfolk, announces the approach of Cæsar.

PERSIAN. He has made short work of them. Here he comes. [*He hurries to his post in front of the Egyptian lines*].

BELZANOR [*following him*] Ho there ! Cæsar comes.

The soldiers stand at attention, and dress their lines. Apollodorus goes to the Egyptian line.

CENTURION [*hurrying to the gangway guard*] Attention there ! Cæsar comes.

Cæsar arrives in state with Rufio : Britannus following. The soldiers receive him with enthusiastic shouting.

CÆSAR. I see my ship awaits me. The hour of Cæsar's farewell to Egypt has arrived. And now, Rufio, what remains to be done before I go ?

RUFIO [*at his left hand*] You have not yet appointed a Roman governor for this province.

CÆSAR [*looking whimsically at him, but speaking with*

perfect gravity] What say you to Mithridates of Pergamos, my reliever and rescuer, the great son of Eupator ?

RUFIO. Why, that you will want him elsewhere. Do you forget that you have some three or four armies to conquer on your way home ?

CÆSAR. Indeed ! Well, what say you to yourself ?

RUFIO [*incredulously*] I ! I a governor ! What are you dreaming of ? Do you not know that I am only the son of a freedman ?

CÆSAR [*affectionately*] Has not Cæsar called you his son ? [*Calling to the whole assembly*] Peace awhile there ; and hear me.

THE ROMAN SOLDIERS. Hear Cæsar.

CÆSAR. Hear the service, quality, rank and name of the Roman governor. By service, Cæsar's shield ; by quality, Cæsar's friend ; by rank, a Roman soldier. [*The Roman soldiers give a triumphant shout*]. By name, Rufio. [*They shout again*].

RUFIO [*kissing Cæsar's hand*] Ay : I am Cæsar's shield ; but of what use shall I be when I am no longer on Cæsar's arm ? Well, no matter—[*He becomes husky, and turns away to recover himself*].

CÆSAR. Where is that British Islander of mine ?

BRITANNUS [*coming forward on Cæsar's right hand*] Here, Cæsar.

CÆSAR. Who bade you, pray, thrust yourself into the battle of the Delta, uttering the barbarous cries of your native land, and affirming yourself a match for any four of the Egyptians, to whom you applied unseemly epithets ?

BRITANNUS. Cæsar : I ask you to excuse the language that escaped me in the heat of the moment.

CÆSAR. And how did you, who cannot swim, cross the canal with us when we stormed the camp ?

BRITANNUS. Cæsar : I clung to the tail of your horse.

CÆSAR. These are not the deeds of a slave, Britannicus, but of a free man.

BRITANNUS. Cæsar : I was born free.

CÆSAR. But they call you Cæsar's slave.

BRITANNUS. Only as Cæsar's slave have I found real freedom.

CÆSAR [*moved*] Well said. Ungrateful that I am, I was about to set you free ; but now I will not part from you for a million talents. [*He claps him friendly on the shoulder. Britannus, gratified, but a trifle shamefaced, takes his hand and kisses it sheepishly*].

BELZANOR [*to the Persian*] This Roman knows how to make men serve him.

PERSIAN. Ay : men too humble to become dangerous rivals to him.

BELZANOR. O subtle one ! O cynic !

CÆSAR [*seeing Apollodorus in the Egyptian corner, and calling to him*] Apollodorus : I leave the art of Egypt in your charge. Remember : Rome loves art and will encourage it ungrudgingly.

APOLLODORUS. I understand, Cæsar. Rome will produce no art itself ; but it will buy up and take away whatever the other nations produce.

CÆSAR. What ! Rome produce no art ! Is peace not an art ? is war not an art ? is government not an art ? is civilization not an art ? All these we give you in exchange for a few ornaments. You will have the best of the bargain. [*Turning to Rufio*] And now, what else have I to do before I embark ? [*Trying to recollect*] There is something I cannot remember : what can it be ? Well, well : it must remain undone : we must not waste this favorable wind. Farewell, Rufio.

RUFIO. Cæsar : I am loth to let you go to Rome without your shield. There are too many daggers there.

CÆSAR. It matters not : I shall finish my life's work on my way back ; and then I shall have lived long enough. Besides : I have always disliked the idea of dying : I had rather be killed. Farewell.

RUFIO [*with a sigh, raising his hands and giving Cæsar up as incorrigible*] Farewell. [*They shake hands*].

CÆSAR [*waving his hand to Apollodorus*] Farewell, Apollodorus, and my friends, all of you. Aboard !

The gangway is run out from the quay to the ship. As Cæsar moves towards it, Cleopatra, cold and tragic, cunningly dressed in black, without ornaments or decoration of any kind, and thus making a striking figure among the brilliantly dressed bevy of ladies as she passes through it, comes from the palace and stands on the steps. Cæsar does not see her until she speaks.

CLEOPATRA. Has Cleopatra no part in this leavetaking?

CÆSAR [*enlightened*] Ah, I knew there was something. [*To Rufio*] How could you let me forget her, Rufio? [*Hastening to her*] Had I gone without seeing you, I should never have forgiven myself. [*He takes her hands, and brings her into the middle of the esplanade. She submits stonily*]. Is this mourning for me?

CLEOPATRA. No.

CÆSAR [*remorsefully*] Ah, that was thoughtless of me! It is for your brother.

CLEOPATRA. No.

CÆSAR. For whom, then?

CLEOPATRA. Ask the Roman governor whom you have left us.

CÆSAR. Rufio?

CLEOPATRA. Yes: Rufio. [*She points at him with deadly scorn*]. He who is to rule here in Cæsar's name, in Cæsar's way, according to Cæsar's boasted laws of life.

CÆSAR [*dubiously*] He is to rule as he can, Cleopatra. He has taken the work upon him, and will do it in his own way.

CLEOPATRA. Not in your way, then?

CÆSAR [*puzzled*] What do you mean by my way?

CLEOPATRA. Without punishment. Without revenge. Without judgment.

CÆSAR [*approvingly*] Ay: that is the right way, the great way, the only possible way in the end. [*To Rufio*] Believe it, Rufio, if you can.

RUFIO. Why, I believe it, Cæsar. You have convinced me of it long ago. But look you. You are sailing for Numidia today. Now tell me: if you meet a hungry lion there, you will not punish it for wanting to eat you?

CÆSAR [*wondering what he is driving at*] No.

RUFIO. Nor revenge upon it the blood of those it has already eaten.

CÆSAR. No.

RUFIO. Nor judge it for its guiltiness.

CÆSAR. No.

RUFIO. What, then, will you do to save your life from it ?

CÆSAR [*promptly*] Kill it, man, without malice, just as it would kill me. What does this parable of the lion mean ?

RUFIO. Why, Cleopatra had a tigress that killed men at her bidding. I thought she might bid it kill you some day. Well, had I not been Cæsar's pupil, what pious things might I not have done to that tigress ! I might have punished it. I might have revenged Pothinus on it.

CÆSAR [*interjects*] Pothinus !

RUFIO [*continuing*] I might have judged it. But I put all these follies behind me ; and, without malice, only cut its throat. And that is why Cleopatra comes to you in mourning.

CLEOPATRA [*vehemently*] He has shed the blood of my servant Ftatateeta. On your head be it as upon his, Cæsar, if you hold him free of it.

CÆSAR [*energetically*] On my head be it, then ; for it was well done. Rufio : had you set yourself in the seat of the judge, and with hateful ceremonies and appeals to the gods handed that woman over to some hired executioner to be slain before the people in the name of justice, never again would I have touched your hand without a shudder. But this was natural slaying : I feel no horror at it.

Rufio, satisfied, nods at Cleopatra, mutely inviting her to mark that.

CLEOPATRA [*pettish and childish in her impotence*] No : not when a Roman slays an Egyptian. All the world will now see how unjust and corrupt Cæsar is.

CÆSAR [*taking her hands coaxingly*] Come : do not be angry with me. I am sorry for that poor Totateeta. [*She laughs in spite of herself*]. Aha ! you are laughing. Does that mean reconciliation ?

CLEOPATRA [*angry with herself for laughing*] No, no, NO!! But it is so ridiculous to hear you call her Totateeta.

CÆSAR. What! As much a child as ever, Cleopatra! Have I not made a woman of you after all?

CLEOPATRA. Oh, it is you who are a great baby: you make me seem silly because you will not behave seriously. But you have treated me badly; and I do not forgive you.

CÆSAR. Bid me farewell.

CLEOPATRA. I will not.

CÆSAR [*coaxing*] I will send you a beautiful present from Rome.

CLEOPATRA [*proudly*] Beauty from Rome to Egypt indeed! What can Rome give me that Egypt cannot give me?

APOLLODORUS. That is true, Cæsar. If the present is to be really beautiful, I shall have to buy it for you in Alexandria.

CÆSAR. You are forgetting the treasures for which Rome is most famous, my friend. You cannot buy them in Alexandria.

APOLLODORUS. What are they, Cæsar?

CÆSAR. Her sons. Come, Cleopatra: forgive me and bid me farewell; and I will send you a man, Roman from head to heel and Roman of the noblest; not old and ripe for the knife; not lean in the arms and cold in the heart; not hiding a bald head under his conqueror's laurels; not stooped with the weight of the world on his shoulders; but brisk and fresh, strong and young, hoping in the morning, fighting in the day, and revelling in the evening. Will you take such an one in exchange for Cæsar?

CLEOPATRA [*palpitating*] His name, his name?

CÆSAR. Shall it be Mark Antony? [*She throws herself into his arms*].

RUFIO. You are a bad hand at a bargain, mistress, if you will swop Cæsar for Antony.

CÆSAR. So now you are satisfied.

CLEOPATRA. You will not forget.

CÆSAR. I will not forget. Farewell: I do not think we

shall meet again. Farewell. [*He kisses her on the forehead. She is much affected and begins to sniff. He embarks*].

THE ROMAN SOLDIERS [*as he sets his foot on the gangway*] Hail, Cæsar ; and farewell !

He reaches the ship and returns Rufio's wave of the hand.

APOLLODORUS [*to Cleopatra*] No tears, dearest Queen : they stab your servant to the heart. He will return some day.

CLEOPATRA. I hope not. But I cant help crying, all the same. [*She waves her handkerchief to Cæsar ; and the ship begins to move*].

THE ROMAN SOLDIERS [*drawing their swords and raising them in the air*] Hail, Cæsar !

NOTES TO CÆSAR AND CLEOPATRA

CLEOPATRA'S CURE FOR BALDNESS

FOR the sake of conciseness in a hurried situation I have made Cleopatra recommend rum. This, I am afraid, is an anachronism : the only real one in the play. To balance it, I give a couple of the remedies she actually believed in. They are quoted by Galen from Cleopatra's book on Cosmetic.

"For bald patches, powder red sulphuret of arsenic and take it up with oak gum, as much as it will bear. Put on a rag and apply, having soaped the place well first. I have mixed the above with a foam of nitre, and it worked well."

Several other receipts follow, ending with : " The following is the best of all, acting for fallen hairs, when applied with oil or pomatum ; acts for falling off of eye-lashes or for people getting bald all over. It is wonderful. Of domestic mice burnt, one part ; of vine rag burnt, one part ; of horse's teeth burnt, one part ; of bear's grease one ; of deer's marrow one ; of reed bark one. To be pounded when dry, and mixed with plenty of honey til it gets the consistency of honey ; then the bear's grease and marrow to be mixed (when melted), the medicine to be put in a brass flask, and the bald part rubbed til it sprouts."

Concerning these ingredients, my fellow-dramatist Gilbert Murray, who, as a Professor of Greek, has applied to classical antiquity the methods of high scholarship (my own method is pure divination), writes to me as follows : " Some of this I dont understand, and possibly Galen did not, as he quotes your heroine's own language. Foam of nitre is, I think, something like soapsuds. Reed bark is an odd expression. It might mean the outside membrane of a reed : I do not know what it ought to be called. In the burnt mice receipt I take it that you first mixed the solid powders with honey, and then added the grease. I expect Cleopatra preferred it because in most of the others you have to lacerate the skin, prick it, or rub it till it bleeds. I do not know what vine rag is. I translate literally."

APPARENT ANACHRONISMS

The only way to write a play which shall convey to the general public an impression of antiquity is to make the characters speak blank verse and abstain from reference to steam, telegraphy, or any of the material conditions of their existence. The more ignorant men are, the more convinced are they that their little parish and their little chapel is an apex to which civilization and philosophy has painfully struggled up the pyramid of time from a desert of savagery. Savagery, they think, became barbarism ; barbarism became ancient civilization ; ancient civilization became Pauline Christianity ; Pauline Christianity became Roman Catholicism ; Roman Catholicism became the Dark Ages ; and the Dark Ages were finally enlightened by the Protestant instincts of the English race. The whole process is summed up as Progress with a capital P. And any elderly gentleman of Progressive temperament will testify that the improvement since he was a boy is enormous.

Now if we count the generations of Progressive elderly gentlemen since, say, Plato, and add together the successive enormous improvements to which each of them has testified, it will strike us at once as an unaccountable fact that the world, instead of having been improved in 67 generations out of all recognition, presents, on the whole, a rather less dignified appearance in Ibsen's Enemy of the People than in Plato's Republic. And in truth, the period of time covered by history is far too short to allow of any perceptible progress in the popular sense of Evolution of the Human Species. The notion that there has been any such Progress since Cæsar's time (less than 20 centuries) is too absurd for discussion. All the savagery, barbarism, dark ages and the rest of it of which we have any record as existing in the past, exists at the present moment. A British carpenter or stone-mason may point out that he gets twice as much money for his labor as his father did in the same trade, and that his suburban house, with its bath, its cottage piano, its drawing room suite, and its album of photographs, would have shamed the plainness of his grandmother's. But the descendants of feudal barons, living in squalid lodgings on a salary of fifteen shillings a week instead of in castles on princely revenues, do not congratulate the world on the change. Such changes, in fact, are not to the point. It has been known, as far back as our records go, that man running wild in the woods is different from man kennelled in a city slum ; that a dog seems to understand a shepherd better than a hewer of wood and drawer of water can understand an astronomer ; and that breeding, gentle nurture, and luxurious food and shelter will produce a kind of man with whom the common laborer is socially incompatible. The same thing is true of horses and dogs. Now there is clearly room for great changes in the world by increasing the percentage of individuals who are carefully bred and gently nurtured, even to finally making the most of every man and woman born. But that possibility existed in the days of the Hittites as much as it does today. It does not give the slightest real support to the common assumption that the civilized contemporaries of the Hittites were unlike their civilized descendants today.

This would appear the tritest commonplace if it were not that the ordinary citizen's ignorance of the past combines with his idealization of the present to mislead and flatter him. Our latest book on the new railway across Asia describes the dulness of the Siberian farmer and the vulgar pursepride of the Siberian man of business without the least consciousness that the string of contemptuous instances given might have been saved by writing simply " Farmers and provincial plutocrats in Siberia are exactly what they are in England." The latest professor descanting on the civilization of the Western Empire in the fifth century feels bound to assume, in the teeth of his own researches, that the Christian was one sort of animal and the Pagan another. It might as well be assumed as indeed it generally is assumed by implication, that a murder committed with a poisoned arrow is different from a murder committed with a Mauser rifle. All such notions are illusions. Go back to the first syllable of recorded time, and there you will find your Christian and your Pagan, your yokel and your poet, helot and hero, Don Quixote and Sancho, Tamino and Papageno, Newton and bushman unable to count eleven, all alive and contemporaneous, and all convinced that they are the heirs of all the ages and the privileged recipients of THE truth (all others damnable heresies), just as you have them today, flourishing in countries each of which is the bravest and best that ever sprang at Heaven's command from out the azure main.

Again, there is the illusion of " increased command over Nature," meaning that cotton is cheap and that ten miles of country road on a bicycle have replaced four on foot. But even if man's increased command over Nature included any increased command over himself (the only sort of command relevant to his evolution into a higher being), the fact remains that it is only by running away from the increased command over Nature to country places where Nature is still in primitive command over Man that he can recover from the effects of the smoke, the stench, the foul air, the overcrowding, the racket, the ugliness, the dirt which the cheap cotton costs us. If manufacturing activity means Progress, the town must be more advanced than the country ; and the field laborers and village artisans of today must be much less changed from the servants of Job than the proletariat of modern London from the proletariat of Cæsar's Rome. Yet the cockney proletarian is so inferior to the village laborer that it is only by steady recruiting from the country that London is kept alive. This does not seem as if the change since Job's time were Progress in the popular sense : quite the reverse. The common stock of discoveries in physics has accumulated a little : that is all.

One more illustration. Is the Englishman prepared to admit that the American is his superior as a human being ? I ask this question because the scarcity of labor in America relatively to the demand for it has led to a development of machinery there, and a consequent " increase of command over Nature " which makes many of our English methods appear almost medieval to the up-to-date Chicagoan. This means that the American has an advantage over the Englishman of exactly the same nature that the Englishman has over the contemporaries of Cicero. Is the Englishman prepared to draw the same conclusion in both cases ? I think not. The American, of course, will draw it cheerfully ; but I must then ask him whether, since a modern negro has a greater " command over Nature " than Washington had, we are also to accept the conclusion, involved in his former one, that humanity has progressed from Washington to the *fin de siècle* negro.

Finally, I would point out that if life is crowned by its success and devotion in industrial organization and ingenuity, we had better worship the ant and the bee (as moralists urge us to do in our childhood), and humble ourselves before the arrogance of the birds of Aristophanes.

My reason then for ignoring the popular conception of Progress in Cæsar and Cleopatra is that there is no reason to suppose that any Progress has taken place since their time. But even if I shared the popular delusion, I do not see that I could have made any essential difference in the play. I can only imitate humanity as I know it. Nobody knows whether Shakespear thought that ancient Athenian joiners, weavers, or bellows menders were any different from Elizabethan ones ; but it is quite certain that he could not have made them so, unless, indeed, he had played the literary man and made Quince say, not " Is all our company here ? " but " Bottom : was not that Socrates that passed us at the Piræus with Glaucon and Polemarchus on his way to the house of Kephalus ? " And so on.

CLEOPATRA

Cleopatra was only sixteen when Cæsar went to Egypt ; but in Egypt sixteen is a riper age than it is in England.

The childishness I have ascribed to her, as far as it is childishness of character and not lack of experience, is not a matter of years. It may be observed in our own climate at the present day in many women of fifty. It is a mistake to suppose that the difference between wisdom and folly has anything to do with the difference between physical age and physical youth. Some women are younger at seventy than most women at seventeen.

It must be borne in mind, too, that Cleopatra was a queen, and was therefore not the typical Greek-cultured, educated Egyptian lady of her time. To represent her by any such type would be as absurd as to represent George IV by a type founded on the attainments of Sir Isaac Newton. It is true that an ordinarily well educated Alexandrian girl of her time would no more have believed bogey stories about the Romans than the daughter of a modern Oxford professor would believe them about the Germans (though, by the way, it is possible to talk great nonsense at Oxford about foreigners when we are at war with them). But I do not feel bound to believe that Cleopatra was well educated. Her father, the illustrious Flute Blower, was not at all a parent of the Oxford professor type. And Cleopatra was a chip of the old block.

BRITANNUS

I find among those who have read this play in manuscript a strong conviction that an ancient Briton could not possibly have been like a modern one. I see no reason to adopt this curious view. It is true that the Roman and Norman conquests must have for a time disturbed the normal British type produced by the climate. But Britannus, born before these events, represents the unadulterated Briton who fought Cæsar and impressed Roman observers much as we should expect the ancestors of Mr Podsnap to impress the cultivated Italians of their time.

I am told that it is not scientific to treat national character as a product of climate. This only shews the wide difference between common knowledge and the intellectual game called science. We have men of exactly the same stock, and speaking the same language, growing in Great Britain, in Ireland, and in America. The result is three of the most distinctly marked nationalities under the sun. Racial characteristics are quite another matter. The difference between a Jew and a Gentile has nothing to do with the difference between an Englishman and a German. The characteristics of Britannus are local characteristics, not race characteristics. In an ancient Briton they would, I take it, be exaggerated, since modern Britain, disforested, drained, urbanified and consequently cosmopolized, is presumably less characteristically British than Cæsar's Britain.

And again I ask does anyone who, in the light of a competent knowledge of his own age, has studied history from contemporary documents, believe that 67 generations of promiscuous marriage have made any appreciable difference in the human fauna of these isles ? Certainly I do not.

JULIUS CÆSAR

As to Cæsar himself, I have purposely avoided the usual anachronism of going to Cæsar's books, and concluding that the style is the man. That is only true of authors who have the specific literary genius, and have practised long enough to attain complete self-expression in letters. It is not true even on these conditions in an age when literature is conceived as a game of style, and not as a vehicle of self-expression by the author. Now Cæsar was an amateur stylist writing books of travel and campaign histories in a style so impersonal that the authenticity of the later volumes is disputed. They reveal some of his qualities just as the Voyage of a Naturalist Round the World reveals some of Darwin's, without expressing his private personality. An Englishman reading them would say that Cæsar was a man of great common sense and good taste, meaning thereby a man without originality or moral courage.

In exhibiting Cæsar as a much more various person than the historian of the Gallic wars, I hope I have not been too much imposed on by the dramatic illusion to which all great men owe part of their reputation and some the whole of it. I admit that reputations gained in war are specially questionable. Able civilians taking up the profession of arms, like Cæsar and Cromwell, in middle age, have snatched all its laurels from opponent commanders bred to it, apparently because capable persons engaged in military pursuits are so scarce that the existence of two of them at the same time in the same hemisphere is extremely rare. The capacity of any conqueror is therefore more likely than not to be an illusion produced by the incapacity of his adversary. At all events, Cæsar might have won his battles without being wiser than Charles XII or Nelson or Joan of Arc, who were, like most modern " self-made " millionaires, half-witted geniuses, enjoying the worship accorded by all races to certain forms of insanity. But Cæsar's victories were only advertisements for an eminence that would never have become popular without them. Cæsar is greater off the battle field than on it. Nelson off his quarterdeck was so quaintly out of the question that when his head was injured at the battle of the Nile, and his conduct became for some years openly scandalous, the difference was not important enough to be noticed. It may, however, be said that peace hath her illusory reputations no less than war. And it is certainly true that in civil life mere capacity for work—the power of killing a dozen secretaries under you, so to speak, as a life-or-death courier kills horses—enables men with common ideas and superstitions to distance all competitors in the strife of political ambition. It was this power of work that astonished Cicero as the most prodigious of Cæsar's gifts, as it astonished later observers in Napoleon before it wore him out. How if Cæsar were nothing but a Nelson and a Gladstone combined ! a prodigy of vitality without any special quality of mind ! nay, with ideas that were worn out before he was born, as Nelson's and Gladstone's were ! I have considered that possibility too, and rejected it. I cannot cite all the stories about Cæsar which seem to me to shew that he was genuinely original ; but let me at least point out that I have been careful to attribute nothing but originality to him. Originality gives a man an air of frankness, generosity, and magnanimity by enabling him to estimate the value of truth, money, or success in any particular instance quite independently of convention and moral generalization. He therefore will not, in the ordinary Treasury bench fashion, tell a lie which everybody knows to be a lie (and consequently expects him as a matter of good taste to tell). His lies are not found out : they pass for candors. He understands the paradox of money, and gives it away when he can get most for it : in other words, when its value is least, which is just when a common man tries hardest to get it. He knows that the real moment of success is not the moment apparent to the crowd. Hence, in order to produce an impression of complete disinterestedness and magnanimity, he has only to act with entire selfishness ; and this is perhaps the only sense in which a man can be said to be *naturally* great. It is in this sense that I have represented Cæsar as great. Having virtue, he has no need of goodness. He is neither forgiving, frank, nor generous, because a man who is too great to resent has nothing to forgive ; a man who says things that other people are afraid to say need be no more frank than Bismarck was ; and there is no generosity in giving things you do not want to people of whom you intend to make use. This distinction between virtue and goodness is not understood in England : hence the poverty of our drama in heroes. Our stage attempts at them are mere goody-goodies. Goodness, in its popular British sense of self-denial, implies that man is vicious by nature, and that supreme goodness is supreme martyrdom. Not sharing that pious opinion, I have not given countenance to it in any of my plays. In this I follow the precedent of the ancient myths, which represent the hero as vanquishing his enemies, not in fair fight, but with enchanted sword, super-equine horse and magical invulnerability, the possession of which, from the vulgar moralistic point of view, robs his exploits of any merit whatever.

As to Cæsar's sense of humor, there is no more reason to assume that he lacked it than to assume that he was deaf or blind. It is said that on the occasion of his assassination by a conspiracy of moralists (it is always your moralist who makes assassination a duty, on the scaffold or off it), he defended himself until the good Brutus struck him, when he exclaimed " What! you too, Brutus! " and disdained further fight. If this be true, he must have been an incorrigible comedian. But even if we waive this story, or accept the traditional sentimental interpretation of it, there is still abundant evidence of his lightheartedness and adventurousness. Indeed it is clear from his whole history that what has been called his ambition was an instinct for exploration. He had much more of Columbus and Franklin in him than of Henry V.

However, nobody need deny Cæsar a share, at least, of the qualities I have attributed to him. All men, much more Julius Cæsars, possess all qualities in some degree. The really interesting question is whether I am right in assuming that the way to produce an impression of greatness is by exhibiting a man, not as mortifying his nature by doing his duty, in the manner which our system of putting little men into great positions (not having enough great men in our influential families to go round) forces us to inculcate, but as simply doing what he naturally wants to do. For this raises the question whether our world has not been wrong in its moral theory for the last 2,500 years or so. It must be a constant puzzle to many of us that the Christian era, so excellent in its intentions, should have been practically such a very discreditable episode in the history of the race. I doubt if this is altogether due to the vulgar and sanguinary sensationalism of our religious legends, with their substitution of gross physical torments and public executions for the passion of humanity. Islam, substituting voluptuousness for torment (a merely superficial difference, it is true) has done no better. It may have been the failure of

Christianity to emancipate itself from expiatory theories of
moral responsibility, guilt, innocence, reward, punishment,
and the rest of it, that baffled its intention of changing the
world.   But these are bound up in all philosophies of
creation as opposed to cosmism.   They may therefore be
regarded as the price we pay for popular religion.

CAPTAIN BRASSBOUND'S CONVERSION

AN ADVENTURE

1899

CAPTAIN BRASSBOUND'S CONVERSION

ACT I

On the heights overlooking the harbor of Mogador, a seaport on the west coast of Morocco, the missionary, in the coolness of the late afternoon, is following the precept of Voltaire by cultivating his garden. He is an elderly Scotchman, spiritually a little weatherbeaten, as having to navigate his creed in strange waters, crowded with other craft, but still a convinced son of the Free Church and the North African Mission, with a faithful brown eye, and a peaceful soul. Physically a wiry small-knit man, well tanned, clean shaven, with delicate resolute features and a twinkle of mild humor. He wears the sun helmet and pagri, the neutral-tinted spectacles, and the white canvas Spanish sand shoes of the modern Scotch missionary ; but instead of a cheap tourist's suit from Glasgow, a grey flannel shirt with white collar, a green sailor knot tie with a cheap pin in it, he wears a suit of clean white linen, acceptable in color, if not in cut, to the Moorish mind.

The view from the garden includes much Atlantic Ocean and a long stretch of sandy coast to the south, swept by the north east trade wind, and scantily nourishing a few stunted pepper trees, mangy palms, and tamarisks. The prospect ends, as far as the land is concerned, in little hills that come nearly to the sea ; rudiments, these, of the Atlas Mountains. The missionary, having had daily opportunities of looking at this seascape for thirty years or so, pays no heed to it, being absorbed in trimming a huge red geranium bush, to English eyes unnaturally big, which, with a dusty smilax or two, is the sole product of his pet flower-bed. He is sitting to his work on a Moorish stool. In the middle of the garden there is a pleasant seat in the shade of a tamarisk tree. The house is in the south west corner of the garden, and the geranium bush in the north east corner.

*At the garden-door of the house there appears presently a
man who is clearly no barbarian, being in fact a less agreeable
product peculiar to modern commercial civilization.   His
frame and flesh are those of an ill-nourished lad of seventeen;
but his age is inscrutable; only the absence of any sign of
grey in his mud colored hair suggests that he is at all events
probably under forty, without prejudice to the possibility of
his being under twenty.   A Londoner would recognize him at
once as an extreme but hardy specimen of the abortion produced by nurture in a city slum.   His utterance, affectedly
pumped and hearty, and naturally vulgar and nasal, is ready
and fluent: nature, a Board School education, and some kerb-
stone practice having made him a bit of an orator.   His dialect,
apart from its base nasal delivery, is not unlike that of smart
London society in its tendency to replace diphthongs by vowels
(sometimes rather prettily) and to shuffle all the traditional
vowel pronunciations.   He pronounces ow as ah, and i as aw,
using the ordinary ow for o, i for ā, ă for ŭ, and ĕ for ă, with
this reservation, that when any vowel is followed by an r, he
signifies its presence, not by pronouncing the r, which he never
does under these circumstances, but by prolonging and
modifying the vowel, sometimes even to the extreme degree of
pronouncing it properly.   As to his yol for l (a compendious
delivery of the provincial eh-al), and other metropolitan
refinements, amazing to all but cockneys, they cannot be
indicated, save in the above imperfect manner, without the aid
of a phonetic alphabet.   He is dressed in somebody else's
very second best as a coastguardsman, and gives himself the
airs of a stage tar with sufficient success to pass as a possible
fish porter of bad character in casual employment during busy
times at Billingsgate.   His manner shews an earnest disposition
to ingratiate himself with the missionary, probably for some
dishonest purpose.*

THE MAN. Awtenoon, Mr Renkin. [*The missionary sits
up quickly, and turns, resigning himself dutifully to the inter-
ruption*].   Yr honor's eolth.

RANKIN [*reservedly*] Good afternoon, Mr Drinkwotter.

DRINKWATER. Youre not best pleased to be hinterrapted in yr bit o gawdnin baw the lawk o me, gavner.

RANKIN. A missionary knows nothing of leks of that soart, or of disleks either, Mr Drinkwotter. What can I do for ye?

DRINKWATER [*heartily*] Nathink, gavner. Awve bror noos fer yer.

RANKIN. Well, sit ye doon.

DRINKWATER. Aw thenk yr honor. [*He sits down on the seat under the tree and composes himself for conversation*]. Hever ear o Jadge Ellam?

RANKIN. Sir Howrrd Hallam?

DRINKWATER. Thets im—enginest jadge in Hingland!—awlus gives the ket wen its robbry with voylence, bless is awt. Aw sy nathink agin im: awm all fer lor mawseolf, aw em.

RANKIN. Well?

DRINKWATER. Hever ear of is sist-in-lor: Lidy Sisly Winefleet?

RANKIN. Do ye mean the celebrated leddy—the traveller?

DRINKWATER. Yuss: should think aw doo. Walked acrost Harfricar with nathink but a little dawg, and wrowt abaht it in the Dily Mile [*the Daily Mail, a popular London newspaper*], she did.

RANKIN. Is she Sir Howrrd Hallam's sister-in-law?

DRINKWATER. Deceased wawfe's sister: yuss: thets wot she is.

RANKIN. Well, what about them?

DRINKWATER. Wot abaht them! Waw, theyre eah. Lannid aht of a steam yacht in Mogador awber not twenty minnits agow. Gorn to the British cornsl's. E'll send em orn to you: e ynt got naowheres to put em. Sor em awr (*hire*) a Harab an two Krooboys to kerry their laggige. Thort awd cam an teoll yer.

RANKIN. Thank you. Its verra kind of you, Mr Drink-wotter.

DRINKWATER. Downt mention it, gavner. Lor bless yer, wawnt it you as converted me? Wot was aw wen aw cam eah but a pore lorst sinner ? Downt aw ow y'a turn fer thet ? Besawds, gavner, this Lidy Sisly Winefleet mawt wornt to tike a walk crost Morocker—a rawd inter the mahntns or sech lawk. Weoll, as you knaow, gavner, thet cawnt be done eah withaht a hescort.

RANKIN. It's impoassible : th' would oall b' murrdered. Morocco is not lek the rest of Africa.

DRINKWATER. No, gavner : these eah Moors ez their religion ; an it mikes em dinegerous. Hever convert a Moor, gavner ?

RANKIN [*with a rueful smile*] No.

DRINKWATER [*solemnly*] Nor hever will, gavner.

RANKIN. I have been at work here for twenty-five years, Mr Drinkwotter ; and you are my first and only convert.

DRINKWATER. Downt seem naow good, do it, gavner ?

RANKIN. I dont say that. I hope I have done some good. They come to me for medicine when they are ill ; and they call me the Christian who is not a thief. That is something.

DRINKWATER. Their mawnds kennot rawse to Christiennity lawk hahrs ken, gavner : thets ah it is. Weoll, ez haw was syin, if a hescort is wornted, there's maw friend and commawnder Kepn Brarsbahnd of the schooner Thenksgivin, an is crew, incloodin mawseolf, will see the lidy an Jadge Ellam through henny little excursion in reason. Yr honor mawt mention it.

RANKIN. I will certainly not propose anything so dangerous as an excursion.

DRINKWATER [*virtuously*] Naow, gavner, nor would I awst you to. [*Shaking his head*] Naow, naow : it is dinegerous. But hall the more call for a hescort if they should ev it hin their mawnds to gow.

RANKIN. I hope they wont.

DRINKWATER. An sow aw do too, gavner.

RANKIN [*pondering*] Tis strange that they should come to Mogador, of all places ; and to my house ! I once met Sir Howrrd Hallam, years ago.

DRINKWATER [*amazed*] Naow ! didger ? Think o thet, gavner ! Waw, sow aw did too. But it were a misunnerstendin, thet wors. Lef the court withaht a stine on maw kerrickter, aw did.

RANKIN [*with some indignation*] I hope you dont think I met Sir Howrrd in that way.

DRINKWATER. Mawt yeppn to the honestest, best meanin pusson, aw do assure yer, gavner.

RANKIN. I would have you to know that I met him privately, Mr Drinkwotter. His brother was a dear friend of mine. Years ago. He went out to the West Indies.

DRINKWATER. The Wust Hindies ! Jist acrost there, tather sawd thet howcean [*pointing seaward*] ! Dear me ! We cams hin with vennity, and we deepawts in dawkness. Downt we, gavner ?

RANKIN [*pricking up his ears*] Eh ? Have you been reading that little book I gave you ?

DRINKWATER. Aw hcv, et odd tawms. Very camfitn, gavner. [*He rises, apprehensive lest further catechism should find him unprepared*]. Awll sy good awtenoon, gavner : youre busy hexpectin o Sr Ahrd an Lidy Sisly, ynt yet ? [*About to go*].

RANKIN [*stopping him*] No, stop : we're oalways ready for travellers here. I have something else to say—a question to ask you.

DRINKWATER [*with misgiving, which he masks by exaggerating his hearty sailor manner*] An weollcome, yr honor.

RANKIN. Who is this Captain Brassbound ?

DRINKWATER [*guiltily*] Kepn Brarsbahnd ! E's—weoll, e's maw Kepn, gavner.

RANKIN. Yes. Well ?

DRINKWATER [*feebly*] Kepn of the schooner Thenksgivin, gavner.

RANKIN [*searchingly*] Have ye ever haird of a bad character in these seas called Black Paquito ?

DRINKWATER [*with a sudden radiance of complete enlightenment*] Aoh, nar aw tikes yer wiv me, yr honor. Nah sammun es bin a teolln you thet Kepn Brarsbahnd an Bleck Pakeetow is hawdentically the sime pussn. Ynt thet sow ?

RANKIN. That is so. [*Drinkwater slaps his knee trium-*

phantly.   The missionary proceeds determinedly] And the
someone was a verra honest, straightforward man, as far
as I could judge.

DRINKWATER [*embracing the implication*] Course e wors,
gavner. Ev aw said a word agin him ? Ev aw nah ?

RANKIN. But is Captain Brassbound Black Paquito then?

DRINKWATER. Waw, its the nime is blessed mather give
im at er knee, bless is little awt ! Ther ynt naow awm in it.
She were a Wust Hinjin—howver there agin, yer see [*pointing
seaward*]—leastwaws, naow she wornt : she were a Brazilian,
aw think ; an Pakeetow's Brazilian for a bloomin little
perrit—awskin yr pawdn for the word. [*Sentimentally*]
Lawk as a Hinglish lidy mawt call er little boy Birdie.

RANKIN [*not quite convinced*] But why Black Paquito ?

DRINKWATER [*artlessly*] Waw, the bird in its netral stite
bein green, an e evin bleck air, y' knaow—

RANKIN [*cutting him short*] I see. And now I will put
ye another question. What is Captain Brassbound, or
Paquito, or whatever he calls himself ?

DRINKWATER [*officiously*] Brarsbahnd, gavner. Awlus
calls isseolf Brarsbahnd.

RANKIN. Well, Brassbound then. What is he ?

DRINKWATER [*fervently*] You awsks me wot e is, gavner ?

RANKIN [*firmly*] I do.

DRINKWATER [*with rising enthusiasm*] An shll aw teoll
yer wot e is, yr honor ?

RANKIN [*not at all impressed*] If ye will be so good, Mr
Drinkwotter.

DRINKWATER [*with overwhelming conviction*] Then awll
teoll you, gavner, wot he is. Ee's a Paffick Genlmn : thets
wot e is.

RANKIN [*gravely*] Mr Drinkwotter : pairfection is an
attribute, not of West Coast captains, but of thr Maaker.
And there are gentlemen and gentlemen in the world,
espaecially in these latitudes. Which sort of gentleman is he?

DRINKWATER. Hinglish   genlmn,   gavner.   Hinglish
speakin ; Hinglish fawther ; West Hinjin plawnter ;
Hinglish true blue breed. [*Reflectively*] Tech o brahn from

the mather, preps, she bein Brazilian.

RANKIN. Now on your faith as a Christian, Felix Drink-wotter, is Captain Brassbound a slaver or not?

DRINKWATER [*surprised into his natural cockney pertness*] Naow e ynt.

RANKIN. Are ye sure?

DRINKWATER. Waw, a sliver is abaht the wanne thing in the wy of a genlmn o fortn thet e ynt.

RANKIN. Ive haird that expression "gentleman of fortune" before, Mr Drinkwotter. It means pirate. Do ye know that?

DRINKWATER. Bless yr awt, y' cawnt be a pawrit naradys. Waw, the aw seas is wuss pleest nor Piccadilly Suckus. If aw was to do orn thet there Hetlentic Howcean the things aw did as a bwoy in the Worterleoo Rowd, awd cv maw air cat afore aw could turn maw ed. Pawrit be blaowed!— awskink yr pawdn, gavner. Nah, jest to shaow you ah little thet there striteforard man y' mide mention on knaowed wot e was atorkin abaht : oo would you spowse was the marster to wich Kepn Brarsbahnd served apprentice, as yr mawt sy?

RANKIN. I dont know.

DRINKWATER. Gawdn, gavner, Gawdn. Gawdn o Kaw-toom— stetcher stends in Trifawlgr Square to this dy. Trined Bleck Pakeetow in smawshin hap the slive riders, e did. Promist Gawdn e wouldnt never smaggle slives nor gin, an [*with suppressed aggravation*] wownt, gavner, not if we gows dahn on ahr bloomin bended knees to im to do it.

RANKIN [*drily*] And do ye go down on your bended knees to him to do it?

DRINKWATER [*somewhat abashed*] Some of huz is han-converted men, gavner ; an thcy sy : You smaggles wanne thing, Kepn ; waw not hanather?

RANKIN. Weve come to it at last. I thought so. Captain Brassbound is a smuggler.

DRINKWATER. Weoll, waw not? Waw not, gavner? Ahrs is a Free Tride nition. It gows agin us as Hinglish-men to see these bloomin furriners settin ap their Castoms

Ahses and spheres o hinfluence and sich lawk hall owver Arfricar. Daownt Harfricar belong as much to huz as to them ? thets wot we sy. Ennywys, there ynt naow awm in ahr business. All we daz is hescort, tourist h o r commercial. Cook's hexcursions to the Hatlas Mahntns : thets hall it is. Waw, its spreadin civlawzytion, it is. Ynt it nah ?

RANKIN. You think Captain Brassbound's crew sufficiently equipped for that, do you ?

DRINKWATER. Hee-quipped ! Haw should think sow. Lawtnin rawfles, twelve shots in the meggezine ! Oo's to storp us ?

RANKIN. The most dangerous chieftain in these parts, the Sheikh Sidi el Assif, has a new American machine pistol which fires ten bullets without loadin ; and his rifle has sixteen shots in the magazine.

DRINKWATER [indignantly] Yuss ; and the people that sells sich things into the ends o them eathen bleck niggers calls theirseolves Christians ! Its a crool shime, sow it is.

RANKIN. If a man has the heart to pull the trigger, it matters little what color his hand is, Mr Drinkwotter. Have ye anything else to say to me this afternoon ?

DRINKWATER [rising] Nathink, gavner, cept to wishyer the bust o yolth, and a many cornverts. Awtenoon, gavner.

As Drinkwater turns to go, a Moorish porter comes from the house with two Krooboys.

THE PORTER [at the door, addressing Rankin] Bikouros [Moroccan for Epicurus, a general Moorish name for the missionaries, who are supposed by the Moors to have chosen their calling through a love of luxurious idleness] : I have brought to your house a Christian dog and his woman.

DRINKWATER. Theres eathen menners fer yer ! Calls Sr Ahrd Ellam an Lidy Winefleet a Christian dorg and is woman ! If ee ed you in the dorck et the Centl Crimnal, youd fawnd aht oo was the dorg and oo was is marster, pretty quick, y o u would.

RANKIN. Have you broat their boxes ?

THE PORTER. By Allah, two camel loads !

RANKIN. Have you been paid ?

THE PORTER. Only one miserable dollar, Bikouros. I have brought them to your house. They will pay you. Give me something for bringing gold to your door.

DRINKWATER. Yah ! You oughter bin bawn a Christian, you ought. You knaow too mach.

RANKIN. You have broat onnly trouble and expense to my door, Hassan ; and you know it. Have I ever charged your wife and children for my medicines ?

HASSAN [*philosophically*] It is always permitted by the Prophet to ask, Bikouros. [*He goes cheerfully into the house with the Krooboys*].

DRINKWATER. Jist thort eed trah it orn, e did. Hooman nitre is the sime everywheres. Them eathens is jast lawk you an' me, gavner.

A lady and gentleman, both English, come into the garden. The gentleman, more than elderly, is facing old age on compulsion, not resignedly. He is clean shaven, and has a brainy rectangular forehead, a resolute nose with strongly governed nostrils, and a tightly fastened down mouth which has evidently shut in much temper and anger in its time. He has a habit of deliberately assumed authority and dignity, but is trying to take life more genially and easily in his character of tourist, which is further borne out by his white hat and summery racecourse attire.

The lady is between thirty and forty, tall, very goodlooking, sympathetic, intelligent, tender and humorous, dressed with cunning simplicity not as a businesslike, tailor made, gaitered tourist, but as if she lived at the next cottage and had dropped in for tea in blouse and flowered straw hat. A woman of great vitality and humanity, who begins a casual acquaintance at the point usually attained by English people after thirty years' acquaintance when they are capable of reaching it at all. She pounces genially on Drinkwater, who is smirking at her, hat in hand, with an air of hearty welcome. The gentleman, on the other hand, comes down the side of the garden next the house, instinctively maintaining a distance between himself and the others.

THE LADY [*to Drinkwater*] How dye do ?   Are you the missionary ?

DRINKWATER [*modestly*] Naow, lidy, aw will not deceive you, thow the mistike his but netral.   Awm wanne of the missionary's good works, lidy—is first cornvert, a umble British seaman—countrymen o yours lidy, and of is lawdship's.   This eah is Mr Renkin, the bust worker in the wust cowst vawnyard.   [*Introducing the judge*] Mr Renkin : is lawdship Sr Ahrd Ellam.   [*He withdraws discreetly into the house*].

SIR HOWARD [*to Rankin*] I am sorry to intrude on you, Mr Rankin ; but in the absence of a hotel there seems to be no alternative.

LADY CICELY [*beaming on him*] Besides, we would so much rather stay with you, if you will have us, Mr Rankin.

SIR HOWARD [*introducing her*] My sister-in-law, Lady Cicely Waynflete, Mr Rankin.

RANKIN. I am glad to be of service to your leddyship. You will be wishing to have some tea after your journey, I'm thinking.

LADY CICELY. Thoughtful man that you are, Mr Rankin. But weve had some already on board the yacht.   And Ive arranged everything with your servants ; so you must go on gardening just as if we were not here.

SIR HOWARD. I am sorry to have to warn you, Mr Rankin, that Lady Cicely, from travelling in Africa, has acquired a habit of walking into people's houses and behaving as if she were in her own.

LADY CICELY. But, my dear Howard, I assure you the natives like it.

RANKIN [*gallantly*] So do I.

LADY CICELY [*delighted*] Oh, that is so nice of you, Mr Rankin.   This is a delicious country !   And the people seem so good !   They have such nice faces !   We had such a handsome Moor to carry our luggage up !   And two perfect pets of Krooboys !   Did you notice their faces, Howard ?

SIR HOWARD. I did ; and I can confidently say, after a

long experience of faces of the worst type looking at me
from the dock, that I have never seen so entirely villainous
a trio as that Moor and the two Krooboys, to whom you
gave five dollars when they would have been perfectly satisfied with one.

RANKIN [*throwing up his hands*] Five dollars ! Tis easy
to see you are not Scotch, my leddy.

LADY CICELY. O, poor things, they must want it more
than we do ; and you know, Howard, that Mahometans
never spend money in drink.

RANKIN. Excuse me a moment, my leddy. I have a
word in season to say to that same Moor. [*He goes into
the house*].

LADY CICELY [*walking about the garden, looking at the
view and at the flowers*] I think this is a perfectly heavenly
place.

Drinkwater returns from the house with a chair.

DRINKWATER [*placing the chair for Sir Howard*] Awskink
yr pawdn for the libbety, Sr Ahrd.

SIR HOWARD [*looking at him*] I have seen you before
somewhere.

DRINKWATER. You ev, Sr Ahrd. But aw do assure yer
it were hall a mistike.

SIR HOWARD. As usual. [*He sits down*]. Wrongfully
convicted, of course.

DRINKWATER [*with sly delight*] Naow, gavner. [*Half
whispering, with an ineffable grin*] Wrorngfully hacquittid !

SIR HOWARD. Indeed ! Thats the first case of the kind I
have ever met.

DRINKWATER. Lawd, Sr Ahrd, wot jagginses them jury-
men was ! You an me knaowed it too, didnt we ?

SIR HOWARD. I daresay we did. I am sorry to say I
forget the exact nature of the difficulty you were in. Can
you refresh my memory ?

DRINKWATER. Owny the aw sperrits o youth, y' lawdship.
Worterleoo Rowd kice. Wot they calls Ooliganism.

SIR HOWARD. Oh ! You were a Hooligan, were you ?

LADY CICELY [*puzzled*] A Hooligan !

DRINKWATER [*deprecatingly*] Nime giv huz pore thortless leds baw a gent on the Dily Chrornicle, lidy. [*Rankin returns. Drinkwater immediately withdraws, stopping the missionary for a moment near the threshold to say, touching his forelock*] Awll eng abaht within ile, gavner, hin kice aw should be wornted. [*He goes into the house with soft steps*].

Lady Cicely sits down on the bench under the tamarisk. Rankin takes his stool from the flowerbed and sits down on her left, Sir Howard being on her right.

LADY CICELY. What a pleasant face your sailor friend has, Mr Rankin ! He has been so frank and truthful with us. You know I dont think anybody can pay me a greater compliment than to be quite sincere with me at first sight. Its the perfection of natural good manners.

SIR HOWARD. You must not suppose, Mr Rankin, that my sister-in-law talks nonsense on purpose. She will continue to believe in your friend until he steals her watch ; and even then she will find excuses for him.

RANKIN [*drily changing the subject*] And how have ye been, Sir Howrrd, since our last meeting that morning nigh forty year ago down at the docks in London ?

SIR HOWARD [*greatly surprised, pulling himself together*] Our last meeting ! Mr Rankin : have I been unfortunate enough to forget an old acquaintance ?

RANKIN. Well, perhaps hardly an acquaintance, Sir Howrrd. But I was a close friend of your brother Miles ; and when he sailed for Brazil I was one of the little party that saw him off. You were one of the party also, if I'm not mistaken. I took particular notice of you because you were Miles's brother and I had never seen ye before. But ye had no call to take notice of me.

SIR HOWARD [*reflecting*] Yes : there was a young friend of my brother's who might well be you. But the name, as I recollect it, was Leslie.

RANKIN. That was me, sir. My name is Leslie Rankin ; and your brother and I were always Miles and Leslie to one another.

SIR HOWARD [*pluming himself a little*] Ah ! that explains

it. I can trust my memory still, Mr Rankin ; though some people do complain that I am growing old.

RANKIN. And where may Miles be now, Sir Howard ?

SIR HOWARD [*abruptly*] Dont you know that he is dead ?

RANKIN [*much shocked*] Never haird of it. Dear, dear : I shall never see him again ; and I can scarcely bring his face to mind after all these years. [*With moistening eyes, which at once touch Lady Cicely's sympathy*] I'm right sorry —right sorry.

SIR HOWARD [*decorously subduing his voice*] Yes : he did not live long : indeed, he never came back to England. It must be nearly thirty years ago now that he died in the West Indies on his property there.

RANKIN [*surprised*] His proaperty ! Miles with a proaperty !

SIR HOWARD. Yes : he became a planter, and did well out there, Mr Rankin. The history of that property is a very curious and interesting one—at least it is so to a lawyer like myself.

RANKIN. I should be glad to hear it for Miles's sake, though I am no lawyer, Sir Howrrd.

LADY CICELY. I never knew you had a brother, Howard ?

SIR HOWARD [*not pleased by this remark*] Perhaps because you never asked me. [*Turning more blandly to Rankin*] I will tell you the story, Mr Rankin. When Miles died, he left an estate in one of the West Indian islands. It was in charge of an agent who was a sharpish fellow, with all his wits about him. Now, sir, that man did a thing which probably could hardly be done with impunity even here in Morocco, under the most barbarous of surviving civilizations. He quite simply took the estate for himself and kept it.

RANKIN. But how about the law ?

SIR HOWARD. The law, sir, in that island, consisted practically of the Attorney General and the Solicitor General ; and these gentlemen were both retained by the agent. Consequently there was no solicitor in the island to take up the case against him.

RANKIN. Is such a thing possible today in the British Empire ?

SIR HOWARD [*calmly*] Oh, quite. Quite.

LADY CICELY. But could not a firstrate solicitor have been sent out from London ?

SIR HOWARD. No doubt, by paying him enough to compensate him for giving up his London practice : that is, rather more than there was any reasonable likelihood of the estate proving worth.

RANKIN. Then the estate was lost ?

SIR HOWARD. Not permanently. It is in my hands at present.

RANKIN. Then how did ye get it back ?

SIR HOWARD [*with crafty enjoyment of his own cunning*] By hoisting the rogue with his own petard. I had to leave matters as they were for many years ; for I had my own position in the world to make. But at last I made it. In the course of a holiday trip to the West Indies, I found that this dishonest agent had left the island, and placed the estate in the hands of an agent of his own, whom he was foolish enough to pay very badly. I put the case before that agent ; and he decided to treat the estate as my property. The robber now found himself in exactly the same position he had formerly forced me into. Nobody in the island would act against me, least of all the Attorney and Solicitor General, who appreciated my influence at the Colonial Office. And so I got the estate back. " The mills of the gods grind slowly," Mr Rankin ; " but they grind exceeding small."

LADY CICELY. Now I suppose if I'd done such a clever thing in England, youd have sent me to prison.

SIR HOWARD. Probably, unless you had taken care to keep outside the law against conspiracy. Whenever you wish to do anything against the law, Cicely, always consult a good solicitor first.

LADY CICELY. So I do. But suppose your agent takes it into his head to give the estate back to his wicked old employer !

SIR HOWARD. I heartily wish he would.

RANKIN [*openeyed*] You wish he would ! !

SIR HOWARD. Yes. A few years ago the collapse of the West Indian sugar industry converted the income of the estate into an annual loss of about £150 a year. If I cant sell it soon, I shall simply abandon it—unless you, Mr Rankin, would like to take it as a present.

RANKIN [*laughing*] I thank your lordship : we have estates enough of that sort in Scotland. Youre setting with your back to the sun, Leddy Ceecily, and losing something worth looking at. See there. [*He rises and points seaward, where the rapid twilight of the latitude has begun*].

LADY CICELY [*getting up to look and uttering a cry of admiration*] Oh, how lovely !

SIR HOWARD [*also rising*] What are those hills over there to the southeast ?

RANKIN. They are the outposts, so to speak, of the Atlas Mountains.

LADY CICELY. The Atlas Mountains ! Where Shelley's witch lived ! We'll make an excursion to them tomorrow, Howard.

RANKIN. Thats impossible, my leddy. The natives are verra dangerous.

LADY CICELY. Why ? Has any explorer been shooting them ?

RANKIN. No. But every man of them believes he will go to Heaven if he kills an unbeliever.

LADY CICELY. Bless you, dear Mr Rankin, the people in England believe that they will go to heaven if they give all their property to the poor. But they dont do it. I'm not a bit afraid of that.

RANKIN. But they are not accustomed to see women going about unveiled.

LADY CICELY. I always get on best with people when they can see my face.

SIR HOWARD. Cicely : you are talking great nonsense ; and you know it. These people have no laws to restrain them, which means, in plain English, that they are habitual thieves and murderers.

RANKIN. Nay, nay : not exactly that, Sir Howrrd.

LADY CICELY [*indignantly*] Of course not. You always think, Howard, that nothing prevents people killing each other but the fear of your hanging them for it. But what nonsense that is ! And how wicked ! If these people werent here for some good purpose, they wouldnt have been made, would they, Mr Rankin ?

RANKIN. That is a point, certainly, Leddy Ceecily.

SIR HOWARD. Oh, if you are going to talk theology—

LADY CICELY. Well, why not ? theology is as respectable as law, I should think. Besides, I'm only talking common-sense. Why do people get killed by savages ? Because instead of being polite to them, and saying How dye do ? like me, people aim pistols at them. Ive been among savages—cannibals and all sorts. Everybody said theyd kill me. But when I met them, I said Howdyedo ? and they were quite nice. The kings always wanted to marry me.

SIR HOWARD. That does not seem to me to make you any safer here, Cicely. You shall certainly not stir a step beyond the protection of the consul, if I can help it, without a strong escort.

LADY CICELY. I dont want an escort.

SIR HOWARD. I do. And I suppose you will expect me to accompany you.

RANKIN. Tis not safe, Leddy Ceecily. Really and truly, tis not safe. The tribes are verra fierce ; and there are cities here that no Christian has ever set foot in. If you go without being well protected, the first chief you meet will seize you and send you back again to prevent his followers murdering you.

LADY CICELY. Oh, how nice of him, Mr Rankin !

RANKIN. He would not do it for your sake, Leddy Ceecily, but for his own. The Sultan would get into trouble with England if you were killed ; and the Sultan would kill the chief to pacify the English government.

LADY CICELY. But I always go everywhere. I know the people here wont touch me. They have such nice faces and such pretty scenery.

SIR HOWARD [*to Rankin, sitting down again resignedly*] You can imagine how much use there is in talking to a woman who admires the faces of the ruffians who infest these ports, Mr Rankin. Can anything be done in the way of an escort?

RANKIN. There is a certain Captain Brassbound here who trades along the coast, and occasionally escorts parties of merchants on journeys into the interior. I understand that he served under Gordon in the Soudan.

SIR HOWARD. That sounds promising. But I should like to know a little more about him before I trust myself in his hands.

RANKIN. I quite agree with you, Sir Howrrd. I'll send Felix Drinkwotter for him. [*He claps his hands. An Arab boy appears at the house door*]. Muley : is sailor man here? [*Muley nods*]. Tell sailor man bring captain. [*Muley nods and goes*].

SIR HOWARD. Who is Drinkwater?

RANKIN. His agent, or mate : I dont rightly know which.

LADY CICELY. Oh, if he has a mate named Felix Drinkwater, it must be quite a respectable crew. It is such a nice name.

RANKIN. You saw him here just now. He is a convert of mine.

LADY CICELY [*delighted*] That nice truthful sailor!

SIR HOWARD [*horrified*] What! The Hooligan!

RANKIN [*puzzled*] Hooligan? No, my lord : he is an Englishman.

SIR HOWARD. My dear Mr Rankin, this man was tried before me on a charge of street ruffianism.

RANKIN. So he told me. He was badly broat up, I am afraid. But he is now a converted man.

LADY CICELY. Of course he is. His telling you so frankly proves it. You know, really, Howard, all those poor people whom you try are more sinned against than sinning. If you would only talk to them in a friendly way instead of passing cruel sentences on them, you would find them quite nice to you. [*Indignantly*] I wont have this poor man trampled on merely because his mother brought him up as a Hooligan. I am sure nobody could be nicer than he was when he spoke to us.

SIR HOWARD. In short, we are to have an escort of Hooligans commanded by a filibuster. Very well, very well. You will most likely admire all their faces ; and I have no doubt at all that they will admire yours.

Drinkwater comes from the house with an Italian dressed in a much worn suit of blue serge, a dilapidated Alpine hat, and boots laced with scraps of twine. He remains near the door, whilst Drinkwater comes forward between Sir Howard and Lady Cicely.

DRINKWATER. Yr honor's servant. [*To the Italian*] Mawtzow : is lawdship Sr Ahrd Ellam [*Marzo touches his hat*]. Er lidyship Lidy Winefleet [*Marzo touches his hat*]. Hawtellian shipmite, lidy. Hahr chef.

LADY CICELY [*nodding affably to Marzo*] Howdyedo ? I love Italy. What part of it were you born in ?

DRINKWATER. Wornt bawn in Hitly at all, lidy. Bawn in Ettn Gawdn [*Hatton Garden*]. Hawce barrer an street pianner Hawtellian, lidy : thets wot e is. Kepn Brarsbahnd's respects to yr honors ; an e awites yr commawnds.

RANKIN. Shall we go indoors to see him ?

SIR HOWARD. I think we had better have a look at him by daylight.

RANKIN. Then we must lose no time : the dark is soon down in this latitude. [*To Drinkwater*] Will ye ask him to step out here to us, Mr Drinkwotter ?

DRINKWATER. Rawt you aw, gavner. [*He goes officiously into the house*].

Lady Cicely and Rankin sit down as before to receive the Captain. The light is by this time waning rapidly, the darkness creeping west into the orange crimson.

LADY CICELY [*whispering*] Dont you feel rather creepy,

Mr Rankin ? I wonder what he'll be like.

RANKIN. I misdoubt me he will not answer, your leddy-ship.

There is a scuffling noise in the house; and Drinkwater shoots out through the doorway across the garden with every appearance of having been violently kicked. Marzo immediately hurries down the garden on Sir Howard's right out of the neighborhood of the doorway.

DRINKWATER [*trying to put a cheerful air on much mortification and bodily anguish*] Narsty step to thet ere door—tripped me hap, it did. [*Raising his voice and narrowly escaping a squeak of pain*] Kepn Brarsbahnd. [*He gets as far from the house as possible, on Rankin's left. Rankin rises to receive his guest*].

An olive complexioned man with dark southern eyes and hair comes from the house. Age about 36. Handsome features, but joyless; dark eyebrows drawn towards one another; mouth set grimly; nostrils large and strained; a face set to one tragic purpose. A man of few words, fewer gestures, and much significance. On the whole, interesting, and even attractive, but not friendly. He stands for a moment, saturnine in the ruddy light, to see who is present, looking in a singular and rather deadly way at Sir Howard; then with some surprise and uneasiness at Lady Cicely. Finally he comes down into the middle of the garden, and confronts Rankin, who has been staring at him in consternation from the moment of his entrance, and continues to do so in so marked a way that the glow in Brassbound's eyes deepens as he begins to take offence.

BRASSBOUND. Well, sir, have you stared your fill at me ?

RANKIN [*recovering himself with a start*] I ask your pardon for my bad manners, Captain Brassbound. Ye are extraordinair lek an auld college friend of mine, whose face I said not ten minutes gone that I could no longer bring to mind. It was as if he had come from the grave to remind me of it.

BRASSBOUND. Why have you sent for me ?

RANKIN. We have a matter of business with ye, Captain.

BRASSBOUND. Who are " we " ?

RANKIN. This is Sir Howard Hallam, who will be well known to ye as one of Her Majesty's judges.

BRASSBOUND [*turning the singular look again on Sir Howard*] The friend of the widow ! the protector of the fatherless !

SIR HOWARD [*startled*] I did not know I was so favorably spoken of in these parts, Captain Brassbound. We want an escort for a trip into the mountains.

BRASSBOUND [*ignoring this announcement*] Who is the lady ?

RANKIN. Lady Ceecily Waynflete, his lordship's sister-in-law.

LADY CICELY. Howdyedo, Captain Brassbound ? [*He bows gravely*].

SIR HOWARD [*a little impatient of these questions, which strike him as somewhat impertinent*] Let us come to business, if you please. We are thinking of making a short excursion to see the country about here. Can you provide us with an escort of respectable, trustworthy men ?

BRASSBOUND. No.

DRINKWATER [*in strong remonstrance*] Nah, nah, nah ! Nah look eah, Kepn, y' knaow—

BRASSBOUND [*between his teeth*] Hold your tongue.

DRINKWATER [*abjectly*] Yuss, Kepn.

RANKIN. I understood it was your business to provide escorts, Captain Brassbound.

BRASSBOUND. You were rightly informed. That is my business.

LADY CICELY. Then why wont you do it for us ?

BRASSBOUND. You are not content with an escort. You want respectable, trustworthy men. You should have brought a division of London policemen with you. My men are neither respectable nor trustworthy.

DRINKWATER [*unable to contain himself*] Nah, nah, look eah, Kepn. If you want to be moddist, be moddist on your aown accahnt, nort on mawn.

BRASSBOUND. You see what my men are like. That

rascal [*indicating Marzo*] would cut a throat for a dollar if he had courage enough.

MARZO. I not understand. I no spik Englis.

BRASSBOUND. This thing [*pointing to Drinkwater*] is the greatest liar, thief, drunkard, and rapscallion on the west coast.

DRINKWATER [*affecting an ironic indifference*] Gow orn, gow orn. Sr Ahrd ez erd witnesses to maw kerrickter afoah. E knaows ah mech to blieve of em.

LADY CICELY. Captain Brassbound : I have heard all that before about the blacks ; and I found them very nice people when they were properly treated.

DRINKWATER [*chuckling : the Italian is also grinning*] Nah, Kepn, nah ! Owp yr prahd o y'seolf nah.

BRASSBOUND. I quite understand the proper treatment for him, madam. If he opens his mouth again without my leave, I will break every bone in his skin.

LADY CICELY [*in her most sunnily matter-of-fact way*] Does Captain Brassbound always treat you like this, Mr Drinkwater ?

Drinkwater hesitates, and looks apprehensively at the Captain.

BRASSBOUND. Answer, you dog, when the lady orders you. [*To Lady Cicely*] Do not address him as Mr Drinkwater, madam : he is accustomed to be called Brandyfaced Jack.

DRINKWATER [*indignantly*] Eah, aw sy ! nah look eah, Kepn : maw nime is Drinkworter. You awsk em et Sin Jorn's in the Worterleoo Rowd. Orn maw grenfawther's tombstown, it is.

BRASSBOUND. It will be on your own tombstone, presently, if you cannot hold your tongue. [*Turning to the others*] Let us understand one another, if you please. An escort here, or anywhere where there are no regular disciplined forces, is what its captain makes it. If I undertake this business, *I* shall be your escort. I may require a dozen men, just as I may require a dozen horses. Some of the horses will be vicious ; so will all the men. If either horse

or man tries any of his viciousness on me, so much the
worse for him ; but it will make no difference to you. I
will order my men to behave themselves before the lady ;
and they shall obey their orders. But the lady will please
understand that I take my own way with them and suffer no
interference.

LADY CICELY. Captain Brassbound : I dont want an
escort at all. It will simply get us all into danger ; and I
shall have the trouble of getting it out again. Thats what
escorts always do. But since Sir Howard prefers an escort,
I think you had better stay at home and let me take charge
of it. I know your men will get on perfectly well if theyre
properly treated.

DRINKWATER [with enthusiasm] Feed aht o yr and, lidy,
we would.

BRASSBOUND [with sardonic assent] Good. I agree. [To
Drinkwater] You shall go without me.

DRINKWATER [terrified] Eah ! Wot are you a syin orn ?
We cawnt gow withaht yer. [To Lady Cicely] Naow, lidy :
it wouldnt be for yr hown good. Yer cawnt hexpect a lot
o poor honeddikited men lawk huz to ran ahrseolvs into
dineger withaht naow Kepn to teoll us wot to do. Naow,
lidy : hoonawted we stend : deevawdid we fall.

LADY CICELY. Oh, if you prefer your captain, have him
by all means. Do you like to be treated as he treats
you ?

DRINKWATER [with a smile of vanity] Weoll, lidy : y'
cawnt deenaw that e's a Paffick Genlmn. Bit hawbitrairy,
preps ; but hin a genlmn you looks for sich. It tikes a
hawbitrairy wanne to knock aht them eathen Shikes, aw
teoll yer.

BRASSBOUND. Thats enough. Go.

DRINKWATER. Weoll, aw was hownly a teolln the lidy
thet—[A threatening movement from Brassbound cuts him
short. He flies for his life into the house, followed by the
Italian].

BRASSBOUND. Your ladyship sees. These men serve me
by their own free choice. If they are dissatisfied, they go.

If *I* am dissatisfied, they go. They take care that I am not dissatisfied.

SIR HOWARD [*who has listened with approval and growing confidence*] Captain Brassbound : you are the man I want. If your terms are at all reasonable, I will accept your services if we decide to make an excursion. You do not object, Cicely, I hope.

LADY CICELY. Oh no. After all, those men must really like you, Captain Brassbound. I feel sure you have a kind heart. You have such nice eyes.

SIR HOWARD [*scandalized*] My dear Cicely : you really must restrain your expressions of confidence in people's eyes and faces. [*To Brassbound*] Now, about terms, Captain ?

BRASSBOUND. Where do you propose to go ?

SIR HOWARD. I hardly know. Where can we go, Mr Rankin ?

RANKIN. Take my advice, Sir Howard. Dont go far.

BRASSBOUND. I can take you to Meskala, from which you can see the Atlas Mountains. From Meskala I can take you to an ancient castle in the hills, where you can put up as long as you please. The customary charge is half a dollar a man per day and his food. *I* charge double.

SIR HOWARD. I suppose you answer for your men being sturdy fellows, who will stand to their guns if necessary.

BRASSBOUND. I can answer for their being more afraid of me than of the Moors.

LADY CICELY. That doesnt matter in the least, Howard. The important thing, Captain Brassbound, is : first, that we should have as few men as possible, because men give such a lot of trouble travelling. And then, they must have good lungs and not be always catching cold. Above all, their clothes must be of good wearing material. Otherwise I shall be nursing and stitching and mending all the way ; and it will be trouble enough, I assure you, to keep them washed and fed without that.

BRASSBOUND [*haughtily*] My men, madam, are not children in the nursery.

LADY CICELY [*with unanswerable conviction*] Captain Brassbound : all men are children in the nursery. I see that you dont notice things. That poor Italian had only one proper bootlace : the other was a bit of string. And I am sure from Mr Drinkwater's complexion that he ought to have some medicine.

BRASSBOUND [*outwardly determined not to be trifled with: inwardly puzzled and rather daunted*] Madam : if you want an escort, I can provide you with an escort. If you want a Sunday School treat, I can not provide it.

LADY CICELY [*with sweet melancholy*] Ah, dont you wish you could, Captain? Oh, if I could only shew you my children from Waynflete Sunday School ! The darlings would love this place, with all the camels and black men. I'm sure you would enjoy having them here, Captain Brassbound ; and it would be such an education for your men ! [*Brassbound stares at her with drying lips*].

SIR HOWARD. Cicely : when you have quite done talking nonsense to Captain Brassbound, we can proceed to make some definite arrangement with him.

LADY CICELY. But it's arranged already. We'll start at eight o'clock tomorrow morning, if you please, Captain. Never mind about the Italian : I have a big box of clothes with me for my brother in Rome ; and there are some bootlaces in it. Now go home to bed and dont fuss yourself. All you have to do is to bring your men round ; and I'll see to the rest. Men are always so nervous about moving. Goodnight. [*She offers him her hand. Surprised he pulls off his cap for the first time. Some scruple prevents him from taking her hand at once. He hesitates; then turns to Sir Howard and addresses him with warning earnestness*].

BRASSBOUND. Sir Howard Hallam : I advise you not to attempt this expedition.

SIR HOWARD. Indeed ! Why ?

BRASSBOUND. You are safe here. I warn you, in those hills there is a justice that is not the justice of your courts in England. If you have wronged a man, you may meet that man there. If you have wronged a woman, you may meet her son there. The justice of those hills is the justice of vengeance.

SIR HOWARD [*faintly amused*] You are superstitious, Captain. Most sailors are, I notice. However, I have complete confidence in your escort.

BRASSBOUND [*almost threateningly*] Take care. The avenger may be one of the escort.

SIR HOWARD. I have already met the only member of your escort who might have borne a grudge against me, Captain ; and he was acquitted.

BRASSBOUND. You are fated to come, then ?

SIR HOWARD [*smiling*] It seems so.

BRASSBOUND. On your head be it ! [*To Lady Cicely, accepting her hand at last*] Goodnight.

He goes. It is by this time starry night.

ACT II

Midday. A room in a Moorish castle. A divan seat runs round the dilapidated adobe walls, which are partly painted, partly faced with white tiles patterned in green and yellow. The ceiling is made up of little squares, painted in bright colors, with gilded edges, and ornamented with gilt knobs. On the cement floor are mattings, sheepskins, and leathern cushions with geometrical patterns on them. There is a tiny Moorish table in the middle; and at it a huge saddle, with saddle cloths of various colors, shewing that the room is used by foreigners accustomed to chairs. Anyone sitting at the table in this seat would have the chief entrance, a large horse-shoe arch, on his left, and another saddle seat between him and the arch; whilst, if susceptible to draughts, he would probably catch cold from a little Moorish door in the wall behind him to his right.

Two or three of Brassbound's men, overcome by the mid-day heat, sprawl supine on the floor, with their reefer coats under their heads, their knees uplifted, and their calves laid comfortably on the divan. Those who wear shirts have them open at the throat for greater coolness. Some have jerseys. All wear boots and belts, and have guns ready to their hands. One of them, lying with his head against the second saddle seat, wears what was once a fashionable white English yachting suit. He is evidently a pleasantly worthless young English gentle-man gone to the bad, but retaining sufficient self-respect to shave carefully and brush his hair, which is wearing thin, and does not seem to have been luxuriant even in its best days.

The silence is broken only by the snores of the young gentleman, whose mouth has fallen open, until a few distant shots half waken him. He shuts his mouth convulsively, and opens his eyes sleepily. A door is violently kicked outside; and the voice of Drinkwater is heard raising urgent alarm.

DRINKWATER. Wot ow ! Wike ap there, will yr. Wike ap. [*He rushes in through the horseshoe arch, hot and*

excited, and runs round, kicking the sleepers]. Nah then.
Git ap. Git ap, will yr, Kiddy Redbrook. [*He gives the
young gentleman a rude shove*].

REDBROOK [*sitting up*] Stow that, will you. Whats amiss?

DRINKWATER [*disgusted*] Wots amiss ! Didnt eah naow
fawrin, I spowse.

REDBROOK. No.

DRINKWATER [*sneering*] Naow. Thort it sifer nort, didnt
yr ?

REDBROOK [*with crisp intelligence*] What ! Youre run-
ning away, are you ? [*He springs up, crying*] Look alive,
Johnnies : theres danger. Brandyfaced Jack's on the run.
[*They spring up hastily, grasping their guns*].

DRINKWATER. Dineger ! Yuss : should think there wors
dineger. It's howver, thow, as it mowstly his baw the tawm
youre awike. [*They relapse into lassitude*]. Waw wasnt
you on the look-aht to give us a end ? Bin hattecked baw
the Benny Seeras [*Beni Siras*], we ev, an ed to rawd for it
pretty strite, too, aw teoll yr. Mawtzow is it : the bullet
glawnst all rahnd is bloomin brisket. Brarsbahnd e dropt
the Shike's oss at six unnern fifty yawds. [*Bustling them
about*] Nah then : git the plice ready for the British herristorcracy, Lawd Ellam an Lidy Wineflete.

REDBROOK. Lady faint, eh ?

DRINKWATER. Fynt ! Not lawkly. Wornted to gow an
talk to the Benny Seeras : blaow me if she didnt ! Harskt
huz wot we was frahtnd of. Tyin ap Mawtzow's wound,
she is, like a bloomin orspittle nass. [*Sir Howard, with a
copious pagri on his white hat, enters through the horseshoe
arch, followed by a couple of men supporting the wounded
Marzo, who, weeping and terrorstricken by the prospect of
death and of subsequent torments for which he is conscious
of having eminently qualified himself, has his coat off and a
bandage round his chest. One of his supporters is a black-
bearded, thickset, slow, middle-aged man with an air of
damaged respectability named—as it afterwards appears—
Johnson. Lady Cicely walks beside Marzo. Redbrook, a
little shamefaced, crosses the room to the opposite wall as far*

away as possible from the visitors. Drinkwater turns and receives them with jocular ceremony]. Weolcome to Brarsbahnd Cawstl, Sr Ahrd an lidy. This eah is the corfee and commercial room.

Sir Howard goes to the table and sits on the saddle, rather exhausted. Lady Cicely comes to Drinkwater.

LADY CICELY. Where is Marzo's bed?

DRINKWATER. Is bed, lidy? Weoll: e ynt petickler, lidy. E ez is chawce of henny flegstown agin thet wall.

They deposit Marzo on the flags against the wall close to the little door. He groans. Johnson phlegmatically leaves him and joins Redbrook.

LADY CICELY. But you cant leave him there in that state.

DRINKWATER. Ow: e's hall rawt. [*Strolling up callously to Marzo*] Youre hall rawt, ynt yer, Mawtzow? [*Marzo whimpers*]. Corse y'aw.

LADY CICELY [*to Sir Howard*] Did you ever see such a helpless lot of poor creatures? [*She makes for the little door*].

DRINKWATER. Eah! [*He runs to the door and places himself before it*]. Where mawt yr lidyship be gowin?

LADY CICELY. I'm going through every room in this castle to find a proper place to put that man. And now I'll tell you where youre going. Youre going to get some water for Marzo, who is very thirsty. And then, when Ive chosen a room for him, youre going to make a bed for him there.

DRINKWATER [*sarcastically*] Ow! Henny ather little suvvice? Mike yrseolf at owm, y' knaow, lidy.

LADY CICELY [*considerately*] Dont go if youd rather not, Mr Drinkwater. Perhaps youre too tired. [*Turning to the archway*] I'll ask Captain Brassbound: he wont mind.

DRINKWATER [*terrified, running after her and getting between her and the arch*] Naow, naow! Naow, lidy: downt you gow disturbin the kepn. Awll see to it.

LADY CICELY [*gravely*] I was sure you would, Mr Drinkwater. You have such a kind face. [*She turns back and goes out through the small door*].

DRINKWATER [*looking after her*] Garn !

SIR HOWARD [*to Drinkwater*] Will you ask one of your friends to shew me to my room whilst you are getting the water ?

DRINKWATER [*insolently*] Yr room ! Ow : this ynt good enaf fr yr, ynt it ? [*Ferociously*] Oo a you orderin abaht, ih ?

SIR HOWARD [*rising quietly, and taking refuge between Redbrook and Johnson, whom he addresses*] Can you find me a more private room than this ?

JOHNSON [*shaking his head*] Ive no orders. You must wait til the capn comes, sir.

DRINKWATER [*following Sir Howard*] Yuss; an whawl youre witin, yll tike your horders from me : see ?

JOHNSON [*with slow severity, to Drinkwater*] Look here : do you see three genlmen talkin to one another here, civil and private, eh ?

DRINKWATER [*chapfallen*] No offence, Miste Jornsn—

JOHNSON [*ominously*] Ay ; but there is offence. Wheres your manners, you guttersnipe ? [*Turning to Sir Howard*] Thats the curse o this kind o life, sir : you got to associate with all sorts. My father, sir, was Capn Johnson o Hull —owned his own schooner, sir. We're mostly gentlemen here, sir, as youll find, except the poor ignorant foreigner and that there scum of the submerged tenth. [*Contemptuously talking at Drinkwater*] He aint nobody's son : he's only a offspring o coster folk or such.

DRINKWATER [*bursting into tears*] Clawss feelin ! thets wot it is ; clawss feelin ! Wot are yer, arter all, bat a bloomin gang o wust cowst cazhls [*casual ward paupers*] ? [*Johnson is scandalized; and there is a general thrill of indignation*]. Better ev naow fembly, an rawse aht of it, lawk me, than ev a specble one and disgrice it, lawk you.

JOHNSON. Brandyfaced Jack : I name you for conduct and language unbecoming to a gentleman. Those who agree will signify the same in the usual manner.

ALL [*vehemently*] Aye.

DRINKWATER [*wildly*] Naow.

JOHNSON. Felix Drinkwater : are you goin out, or are you goin to wait til youre chucked out ? You can cry in the passage. If you give any trouble, youll have something to cry for.

They make a threatening movement towards Drinkwater.

DRINKWATER [*whimpering*] You lee me alown : awm gowin. Theres n'maw true demmecrettick feelin eah than there is in the owl bloomin M division of Noontn Corzwy coppers [*Newington Causeway policemen*].

As he slinks away in tears towards the arch, Brassbound enters. Drinkwater promptly shelters himself on the captain's left hand, the others retreating to the opposite side as Brassbound advances to the middle of the room. Sir Howard retires behind them and seats himself on the divan, much fatigued.

BRASSBOUND [*to Drinkwater*] What are you snivelling at ?

DRINKWATER. You awsk the wust cowst herristorcracy. They fawnds maw cornduck hanbecammin to a genlmn.

Brassbound is about to ask Johnson for an explanation, when Lady Cicely returns through the little door, and comes between Brassbound and Drinkwater.

LADY CICELY [*to Drinkwater*] Have you fetched the water ?

DRINKWATER. Yuss : nah you begin orn me. [*He weeps afresh*].

LADY CICELY [*surprised*] Oh ! This wont do, Mr Drinkwater. If you cry, I cant let you nurse your friend.

DRINKWATER [*frantic*] Thetll brike maw awt, wownt it nah ? [*With a lamentable sob, he throws himself down on the divan, raging like an angry child*].

LADY CICELY [*after contemplating him in astonishment for a moment*] Captain Brassbound : are there any charwomen in the Atlas Mountains ?

BRASSBOUND. There are people here who will work if you pay them, as there are elsewhere.

LADY CICELY. This castle is very romantic, Captain ; but it hasnt had a spring cleaning since the Prophet lived in it. Theres only one room I can put the wounded man into. Its the only one that has a bed in it : the second room on the right out of that passage.

BRASSBOUND [*haughtily*] That is my room, madam.

LADY CICELY [*relieved*] Oh, thats all right. It would have been so awkward if I had had to ask one of your men to turn out. You wont mind, I know. [*All the men stare at her. Even Drinkwater forgets his sorrows in his stupefaction*].

BRASSBOUND. Pray, madam, have you made any arrangements for my accommodation ?

LADY CICELY [*reassuringly*] Yes : you can have my room instead, wherever it may be : I'm sure you chose me a nice one. I must be near my patient ; and I dont mind roughing it. Now I must have Marzo moved very carefully. Where is that truly gentlemanly Mr Johnson ?—oh, there you are, Mr Johnson. [*She runs to Johnson, past Brassbound, who has to step back hastily out of her way with every expression frozen out of his face except one of extreme and indignant dumbfoundedness*]. Will you ask your strong friend to help you with Marzo : strong people are always so gentle.

JOHNSON. Let me introdooce Mr Redbrook. Your ladyship may know his father, the very Rev. Dean Redbrook. [*He goes to Marzo*].

REDBROOK. Happy to oblige you, Lady Cicely.

LADY CICELY [*shaking hands*] Howdyedo ? Of course I knew your father—Dunham wasnt it ? Were you ever called—

REDBROOK. The kid ? Yes.

LADY CICELY. But why—

REDBROOK [*anticipating the rest of the question*] Cards and drink, Lady Sis. [*He follows Johnson to the patient. Lady Cicely goes too*]. Now, Count Marzo. [*Marzo groans as Johnson and Redbrook raise him*].

LADY CICELY. Now theyre not hurting you, Marzo. They couldnt be more gentle.

MARZO. Drink.

LADY CICELY. I'll get you some water myself. Your friend Mr Drinkwater was too overcome—take care of the corner—thats it—the second door on the right. [*She goes out with Marzo and his bearers through the little door*].

BRASSBOUND [*still staring*] Well, I a m damned !

DRINKWATER [*getting up*] Weoll, blimey !

BRASSBOUND [*turning irritably on him*] What did you say ?

DRINKWATER. Weoll, wot did yer sy yrseolf, kepn ? Fust tawm aw vever see y' afride of ennybody. [*The others laugh*].

BRASSBOUND. Afraid !

DRINKWATER [*maliciously*] She's took y'bed from hander yr for a bloomin penny hawcemen. If y' ynt afride, let eah yer speak ap to er wen she cams bawck agin.

BRASSBOUND [*to Sir Howard*] I wish you to understand, Sir Howard, that in this castle, it is *I* who give orders, and no one else. Will you be good enough to let Lady Cicely Waynflete know that.

SIR HOWARD [*sitting up on the divan and pulling himself together*] You will have ample opportunity for speaking to Lady Cicely yourself when she returns. [*Drinkwater chuckles; and the rest grin*].

BRASSBOUND. My manners are rough, Sir Howard. I have no wish to frighten the lady.

SIR HOWARD. Captain Brassbound : if you can frighten Lady Cicely, you will confer a great obligation on her family. If she had any sense of danger, perhaps she would keep out of it.

BRASSBOUND. Well, sir, if she were ten Lady Cicelys, she must consult me while she is here.

DRINKWATER. Thets rawt, kepn. Lets eah you steblish yr hawthority. [*Brassbound turns impatiently on him: he retreats remonstrating*] Nah, nah, nah !

SIR HOWARD. If you feel at all nervous, Captain Brassbound, I will mention the matter with pleasure.

BRASSBOUND. Nervous, sir ! no. Nervousness is not in my line. You will find me perfectly capable of saying what I want to say—with considerable emphasis, if necessary. [*Sir Howard assents with a polite but incredulous nod*].

DRINKWATER. Eah, eah !

Lady Cicely returns with Johnson and Redbrook. She carries a jar.

LADY CICELY [*stopping between the door and the arch*]
Now for the water. Where is it ?

REDBROOK. Theres a well in the courtyard. I'll come
and work the bucket.

LADY CICELY. So good of you, Mr Kidbrook. [*She
makes for the horseshoe arch, followed by Redbrook*].

DRINKWATER. Nah, Kepn Brarsbahnd : you got sathink
to sy to the lidy, ynt yr ?

LADY CICELY [*stopping*] I'll come back to hear it presently,
Captain. And oh, while I remember it, [*coming forward
between Brassbound and Drinkwater*] do please tell me,
Captain, if I interfere with your arrangements in any way.
If I disturb you the least bit in the world, stop me at once.
You have all the responsibility ; and your comfort and
your authority must be the first thing. Youll tell me,
wont you ?

BRASSBOUND [*awkwardly, quite beaten*] Pray do as you
please, madam.

LADY CICELY. Thank you. Thats so like you, Captain.
Thank you. Now, Mr Redbrook ! Show me the way to
the well. [*She follows Redbrook out through the arch*].

DRINKWATER. Yah !   Yah !   Shime !   Beat baw a
woman !

JOHNSON [*coming forward on Brassbound's right*] Whats
wrong, now ?

DRINKWATER [*with an air of disappointment and disillusion*]
Downt awsk me, Miste Jornsn. The kepn's naow clawss
arter all.

BRASSBOUND [*a little shamefacedly*] What has she been
fixing up in there, Johnson ?

JOHNSON. Well : Marzo's in your bed. Lady wants to
make a kitchen of the Sheik's audience chamber, and to
put me and the Kid handy in his bedroom in case Marzo
gets erysipelas and breaks out violent. From what I can
make out, she means to make herself matron of this institution. I spose its all right, isnt it ?

DRINKWATER. Yuss, an horder huz abaht as if we was
keb tahts ! An the kepn afride to talk bawck at er !

Lady Cicely returns with Redbrook. She carries the jar full of water.

LADY CICELY [*putting down the jar, and coming between Brassbound and Drinkwater as before*] And now, Captain, before I go to poor Marzo, what have you to say to me ?

BRASSBOUND. I ! Nothing.

DRINKWATER. Downt fank it, gavner. Be a men !

LADY CICELY [*looking at Drinkwater, puzzled*] Mr Drinkwater said you had.

BRASSBOUND [*recovering himself*] It was only this. That fellow there [*pointing to Drinkwater*] is subject to fits of insolence. If he is impertinent to your ladyship, or disobedient, you have my authority to order him as many kicks as you think good for him ; and I will see that he gets them.

DRINKWATER [*lifting up his voice in protest*] Nah, nah—

LADY CICELY. Oh, I couldnt think of such a thing, Captain Brassbound. I am sure it would hurt Mr Drinkwater.

DRINKWATER [*lachrymosely*] Lidy's hinkyp'ble o sich bawbrous usage.

LADY CICELY. But theres one thing I should like, if Mr Drinkwater wont mind my mentioning it. It's so important if he's to attend on Marzo.

BRASSBOUND. What is that ?

LADY CICELY. Well—you wont mind, Mr Drinkwater, will you ?

DRINKWATER [*suspiciously*] Wot is it ?

LADY CICELY. There would be so much less danger of erysipelas if you would be so good as to take a bath.

DRINKWATER [*aghast*] A bawth !

BRASSBOUND [*in tones of command*] Stand by, all hands. [*They stand by*]. Take that man and wash him. [*With a roar of laughter they seize him*].

DRINKWATER [*in an agony of protest*] Naow, naow. Look eah—

BRASSBOUND [*ruthlessly*] In cold water.

DRINKWATER [*shrieking*] Na-a-a-a-ow. Aw cawnt, aw

teol yer. Naow. Aw sy, look eah. Naow, naow, naow, naow, naow, NAOW ! ! !

He is dragged away through the arch in a whirlwind of laughter, protests, and tears.

LADY CICELY. I'm afraid he isnt used to it, poor fellow ; but really it will do him good, Captain Brassbound. Now I must be off to my patient. [*She takes up her jar and goes out by the little door, leaving Brassbound and Sir Howard alone together*].

SIR HOWARD [*rising*] And now, Captain Brass—

BRASSBOUND [*cutting him short with a fierce contempt that astonishes him*] I will attend to you presently. [*Calling*] Johnson. Send me Johnson there. And Osman. [*He pulls off his coat and throws it on the table, standing at his ease in his blue jersey*].

SIR HOWARD [*after a momentary flush of anger, with a controlled force that compels Brassbound's attention in spite of himself*] You seem to be in a strong position with reference to these men of yours.

BRASSBOUND. I am in a strong position with reference to everyone in this castle.

SIR HOWARD [*politely but threateningly*] I have just been noticing that you think so. I do not agree with you. Her Majesty's Government, Captain Brassbound, has a strong arm and a long arm. If anything disagreeable happens to me or to my sister-in-law, that arm will be stretched out. If that happens you will not be in a strong position. Excuse my reminding you of it.

BRASSBOUND [*grimly*] Much good may it do you ! [*Johnson comes in through the arch*]. Where is Osman, the Sheikh's messenger ? I want him too.

JOHNSON. Coming, Captain. He had a prayer to finish.

Osman, a tall, skinny, whiteclad, elderly Moor, appears in the archway.

BRASSBOUND. Osman Ali [*Osman comes forward between Brassbound and Johnson*] : you have seen this unbeliever [*indicating Sir Howard*] come in with us ?

OSMAN. Yea, and the shameless one with the naked face,

who flattered my countenance and offered me her hand.

JOHNSON. Yes ; and you took it too, Johnny, didnt you ?

BRASSBOUND. Take horse, then ; and ride fast to your master the Sheikh Sidi el Assif—

OSMAN [*proudly*] Kinsman to the Prophet.

BRASSBOUND. Tell him what you have seen here. That is all. Johnson : give him a dollar ; and note the hour of his going, that his master may know how fast he rides.

OSMAN. The believer's word shall prevail with Allah and his servant Sidi el Assif.

BRASSBOUND. Off with you.

OSMAN. Make good thy master's word ere I go out from his presence, O Johnson el Hull.

JOHNSON. He wants the dollar.

Brassbound gives Osman a coin.

OSMAN [*bowing*] Allah will make hell easy for the friend of Sidi el Assif and his servant. [*He goes out through the arch*].

BRASSBOUND [*to Johnson*] Keep the men out of this until the Sheikh comes. I have business to talk over. When he does come, we must keep together all : Sidi el Assif's natural instinct will be to cut every Christian throat here.

JOHNSON. We look to you, Captain, to square him, since you invited him over.

BRASSBOUND. You can depend on me ; and you know it, I think.

JOHNSON [*phlegmatically*] Yes : we know it. [*He is going out when Sir Howard speaks*].

SIR HOWARD. You know also, Mr Johnson, I hope, that you can depend on me.

JOHNSON [*turning*] On you, sir ?

SIR HOWARD. Yes : on me. If my throat is cut, the Sultan of Morocco may send Sidi's head with a hundred thousand dollars blood-money to the Colonial Office ; but it will not be enough to save his kingdom—any more than it would save your life, if your Captain here did the same thing.

JOHNSON [*struck*] Is that so, Captain ?

BRASSBOUND. I know the gentleman's value—better perhaps than he knows it himself. I shall not lose sight of it.

Johnson nods gravely, and is going out when Lady Cicely returns softly by the little door and calls to him in a whisper. She has taken off her travelling things and put on an apron. At her chatelaine is a case of sewing materials.

LADY CICELY. Mr Johnson. [*He turns*]. Ive got Marzo to sleep. Would you mind asking the gentlemen not to make a noise under his window in the courtyard.

JOHNSON. Right, maam. [*He goes out*].

Lady Cicely sits down at the tiny table, and begins stitching at a sling bandage for Marzo's arm. Brassbound walks up and down on her right, muttering to himself so ominously that Sir Howard quietly gets out of his way by crossing to the other side and sitting down on the second saddle seat.

SIR HOWARD. Are you yet able to attend to me for a moment, Captain Brassbound?

BRASSBOUND [*still walking about*] What do you want?

SIR HOWARD. Well, I am afraid I want a little privacy, and, if you will allow me to say so, a little civility. I am greatly obliged to you for bringing us safely off today when we were attacked. So far, you have carried out your contract. But since we have been your guests here, your tone and that of the worst of your men has changed—intentionally changed, I think.

BRASSBOUND [*stopping abruptly and flinging the announcement at him*] You are not my guest : you are my prisoner.

SIR HOWARD. Prisoner !

Lady Cicely, after a single glance up, continues stitching, apparently quite unconcerned.

BRASSBOUND. I warned you. You should have taken my warning.

SIR HOWARD [*immediately taking the tone of cold disgust for moral delinquency*] Am I to understand, then, that you are a brigand? Is this a matter of ransom?

BRASSBOUND [*with unaccountable intensity*] All the wealth of England shall not ransom you.

SIR HOWARD. Then what do you expect to gain by this ?

BRASSBOUND. Justice on a thief and a murderer.

Lady Cicely lays down her work and looks up anxiously.

SIR HOWARD [*deeply outraged, rising with venerable dignity*] Sir : do you apply those terms to me ?

BRASSBOUND. I do. [*He turns to Lady Cicely, and adds, pointing contemptuously to Sir Howard*] Look at him. You would not take this virtuously indignant gentleman for the uncle of a brigand, would you ?

Sir Howard starts. The shock is too much for him: he sits down again, looking very old; and his hands tremble; but his eyes and mouth are intrepid, resolute, and angry.

LADY CICELY. Uncle ! What do you mean ?

BRASSBOUND. Has he never told you about my mother ? this fellow who puts on ermine and scarlet and calls himself Justice.

SIR HOWARD [*almost voiceless*] You are the son of that woman !

BRASSBOUND [*fiercely*] " That woman ! " [*He makes a movement as if to rush at Sir Howard*].

LADY CICELY [*rising quickly and putting her hand on his arm*] Take care. You mustnt strike an old man.

BRASSBOUND [*raging*] He did not spare my mother— " that woman," he calls her—because of her sex. I will not spare him because of his age. [*Lowering his tone to one of sullen vindictiveness*] But I am not going to strike him. [*Lady Cicely releases him, and sits down, much perplexed. Brassbound continues, with an evil glance at Sir Howard*] I shall do no more than justice.

SIR HOWARD [*recovering his voice and vigor*] Justice ! I think you mean vengeance, disguised as justice by your passions.

BRASSBOUND. To many and many a poor wretch in the dock you have brought vengeance in that disguise—the vengeance of society, disguised as justice by its passions. Now the justice you have outraged meets you disguised as vengeance. How do you like it ?

SIR HOWARD. I shall meet it, I trust, as becomes an

innocent man and an upright judge. What do you charge against me?

BRASSBOUND. I charge you with the death of my mother and the theft of my inheritance.

SIR HOWARD. As to your inheritance, sir, it was yours whenever you came forward to claim it. Three minutes ago I did not know of your existence. I affirm that most solemnly. I never knew—never dreamt—that my brother Miles left a son. As to your mother, her case was a hard one—perhaps the hardest that has come within even my experience. I mentioned it, as such, to Mr Rankin, the missionary, the evening we met you. As to her death, you know—you must know—that she died in her native country, years after our last meeting. Perhaps you were too young to know that she could hardly have expected to live long.

BRASSBOUND. You mean that she drank.

SIR HOWARD. I did not say so. I do not think she was always accountable for what she did.

BRASSBOUND. Yes : she was mad too ; and whether drink drove her to madness or madness drove her to drink matters little. The question is, who drove her to both ?

SIR HOWARD. I presume the dishonest agent who seized her estate did. I repeat, it was a hard case—a frightful injustice. But it could not be remedied.

BRASSBOUND. You told her so. When she would not take that false answer you drove her from your doors. When she exposed you in the street and threatened to take with her own hands the redress the law denied her, you had her imprisoned, and forced her to write you an apology and leave the country to regain her liberty and save herself from a lunatic asylum. And when she was gone, and dead, and forgotten, you found for yourself the remedy you could not find for her. You recovered the estate easily enough then, robber and rascal that you are. Did he tell the missionary that, Lady Cicely, eh ?

LADY CICELY [sympathetically] Poor woman ! [To Sir Howard] Couldnt you have helped her, Howard ?

SIR HOWARD. No. This man may be ignorant enough to suppose that when I was a struggling barrister I could do everything I did when I was Attorney-General. You know better. There is some excuse for his mother. She was an uneducated Brazilian, knowing nothing of English society, and driven mad by injustice.

BRASSBOUND. Your defence—

SIR HOWARD [interrupting him determinedly] I do not defend myself. I call on you to obey the law.

BRASSBOUND. I intend to do so. The law of the Atlas Mountains is administered by the Sheikh Sidi el Assif. He will be here within an hour. He is a judge, like yourself. You can talk law to him. He will give you both the law and the prophets.

SIR HOWARD. Does he know what the power of England is?

BRASSBOUND. He knows that the Mahdi killed my master Gordon, and that the Mahdi died in his bed and went to paradise.

SIR HOWARD. Then he knows also that England's vengeance was on the Mahdi's track.

BRASSBOUND. Ay, on the track of the railway from the Cape to Cairo? Who are you, that a nation should go to war for you? If you are missing, what will your newspapers say? A foolhardy tourist! What will your learned friends at the bar say? That it was time for you to make room for younger and better men. You a national hero! You had better find a goldfield in the Atlas Mountains. Then all the governments of Europe will rush to your rescue. Until then, take care of yourself; for you are going to see at last the hypocrisy in the sanctimonious speech of the judge who is sentencing you, instead of the despair in the white face of the wretch you are recommending to the mercy of your god.

SIR HOWARD [deeply and personally offended by this slight to his profession, and for the first time throwing away his assumed dignity and rising to approach Brassbound with his fists clenched; so that Lady Cicely lifts one eye from her work to assure herself that the table is between them] I have no more to say to you, sir. I am not afraid of you, nor of any bandit with whom you may be in league. As to your property, it is ready for you as soon as you come to your senses and claim it as your father's heir. Commit a crime, and you will become an outlaw, and not only lose the property, but shut the doors of civilization against yourself for ever.

BRASSBOUND. I will not sell my mother's revenge for ten properties.

LADY CICELY [*placidly*] Besides, really, Howard, as the property now costs £150 a year to keep up instead of bringing in anything, I am afraid it would not be of much use to him. [*Brassbound stands amazed at this revelation*].

SIR HOWARD [*taken aback*] I must say, Cicely, I think you might have chosen a more suitable moment to mention that fact.

BRASSBOUND [*with disgust*] Agh! Trickster! Lawyer! Even the price you offer for your life is to be paid in false coin. [*Calling*] Hallo there! Johnson! Redbrook! Some of you there! [*To Sir Howard*] You ask for a little privacy : you shall have it. I will not endure the company of such a fellow.

SIR HOWARD [*very angry, and full of the crustiest pluck*] You insult me, sir. You are a rascal. You are a rascal.

Johnson, Redbrook, and a few others come in through the arch.

BRASSBOUND. Take this man away.

JOHNSON. Where are we to put him?

BRASSBOUND. Put him where you please so long as you can find him when he is wanted.

SIR HOWARD. You will be laid by the heels yet, my friend.

REDBROOK [*with cheerful tact*] Tut tut, Sir Howard : whats the use of talking back? Come along : we'll make you comfortable.

Sir Howard goes out through the arch between Johnson and Redbrook, muttering wrathfully. The rest, except Brassbound and Lady Cicely, follow.

Brassbound walks up and down the room, nursing his indignation. In doing so he unconsciously enters upon an unequal contest with Lady Cicely, who sits quietly stitching. It soon becomes clear that a tranquil woman can go on sewing longer than an angry man can go on fuming. Further, it begins to dawn on Brassbound's wrath-blurred perception that Lady Cicely has at some unnoticed stage in the proceedings finished Marzo's bandage, and is now stitching a coat. He stops; glances at his shirt-sleeves; finally realizes the situation.

BRASSBOUND. What are you doing there, madam?

LADY CICELY. Mending your coat, Captain Brassbound.

BRASSBOUND. I have no recollection of asking you to take that trouble.

LADY CICELY. No : I dont suppose you even knew it was torn. Some men are born untidy. You cannot very well receive Sidi el—whats his name ?—with your sleeve half out.

BRASSBOUND [*disconcerted*] I—I dont know how it got torn.

LADY CICELY. You should not get virtuously indignant with people. It bursts clothes more than anything else, Mr Hallam.

BRASSBOUND [*flushing quickly*] I beg you will not call me Mr Hallam. I hate the name.

LADY CICELY. Black Paquito is your pet name, isnt it ?

BRASSBOUND [*huffily*] I am not usually called so to my face.

LADY CICELY [*turning the coat a little*] I'm so sorry. [*She takes another piece of thread and puts it into her needle, looking placidly and reflectively upward meanwhile*]. Do you know, you are wonderfully like your uncle.

BRASSBOUND. Damnation !

LADY CICELY. Eh ?

BRASSBOUND. If I thought my veins contained a drop of his black blood, I would drain them empty with my knife. I have no relations. I had a mother : that was all.

LADY CICELY [*unconvinced*] I daresay you have your mother's complexion. But didnt you notice Sir Howard's

temper, his doggedness, his high spirit : above all, his belief
in ruling people by force, as you rule your men ; and in
revenge and punishment, just as you want to revenge your
mother ? Didnt you recognize yourself in that ?

BRASSBOUND [*startled*] Myself !—in that !

LADY CICELY [*returning to the tailoring question as if her
last remark were of no consequence whatever*] Did this sleeve
catch you at all under the arm ? Perhaps I had better make
it a little easier for you.

BRASSBOUND [*irritably*] Let my coat alone. It will do
very well as it is. Put it down.

LADY CICELY. Oh, dont ask me to sit doing nothing. It
bores me so.

BRASSBOUND. In Heaven's name, then do what you like !
Only dont worry me with it.

LADY CICELY. I'm so sorry. All the Hallams are irritable.

BRASSBOUND [*penning up his fury with difficulty*] As I have
already said, that remark has no application to me.

LADY CICELY [*resuming her stitching*] Thats so funny !
They all hate to be told that they are like one another.

BRASSBOUND [*with the beginnings of despair in his voice*]
Why did you come here ? My trap was laid for him, not
for you. Do you know the danger you are in ?

LADY CICELY. Theres always a danger of something or
other. Do you think it's worth bothering about.

BRASSBOUND [*scolding her*] Do I think ! Do you think
my coat's worth mending ?

LADY CICELY [*prosaically*] Oh yes : it's not so far gone
as that.

BRASSBOUND. Have you any feeling ? Or are you a fool ?

LADY CICELY. I'm afraid I'm a dreadful fool. But I cant
help it. I was made so, I suppose.

BRASSBOUND. Perhaps you dont realize that your friend
my good uncle will be pretty fortunate if he is allowed to
live out his life as a slave with a set of chains on him ?

LADY CICELY. Oh, I dont know about that, Mr H—I
mean Captain Brassbound. Men are always thinking that
they are going to do something grandly wicked to their

enemies ; but when it comes to the point, really bad men are just as rare as really good ones.

BRASSBOUND. You forget that I am like my uncle, according to you. Have you any doubt as to the reality of his badness ?

LADY CICELY. Bless me ! your uncle Howard is one of the most harmless of men—much nicer than most professional people. Of course he does dreadful things as a judge ; but then if you take a man and pay him £5,000 a year to be wicked, and praise him for it, and have policemen and courts and laws and juries to drive him into it so that he cant help doing it, what can you expect ? Sir Howard's all right when he's left to himself. We caught a burglar one night at Waynflete when he was staying with us ; and I insisted on his locking the poor man up, until the police came, in a room with a window opening on the lawn. The man came back next day and said he must return to a life of crime unless I gave him a job in the garden ; and I did. It was much more sensible than giving him ten years penal servitude : Howard admitted it. So you see he's not a bit bad really.

BRASSBOUND. He had a fellow feeling for the thief, knowing he was a thief himself. Do you forget that he sent my mother to prison ?

LADY CICELY [softly] Were you very fond of your poor mother, and always very good to her ?

BRASSBOUND [rather taken aback] I was not worse than other sons, I suppose.

LADY CICELY [opening her eyes very widely] Oh ! Was that all ?

BRASSBOUND [exculpating himself, full of gloomy remembrances] You dont understand. It was not always possible to be very tender with my mother. She had unfortunately a very violent temper ; and she—she—

LADY CICELY. Yes : so you told Howard. [With genuine pity for him] You must have had a very unhappy childhood.

BRASSBOUND [grimly] Hell. That was what my childhood was. Hell.

LADY CICELY. Do you think she would really have killed Howard, as she threatened, if he hadnt sent her to prison?

BRASSBOUND [*breaking out again, with a growing sense of being morally trapped*] What if she did? Why did he rob her? Why did he not help her to get the estate, as he got it for himself afterwards?

LADY CICELY. He says he couldnt, you know. But perhaps the real reason was that he didnt like her. You know, dont you, that if you dont like people you think of all the reasons for not helping them, and if you like them you think of all the opposite reasons.

BRASSBOUND. But his duty as a brother!

LADY CICELY. Are you going to do your duty as a nephew!

BRASSBOUND. Dont quibble with me. I am going to do my duty as a son; and you know it.

LADY CICELY. But I should have thought that the time for that was in your mother's lifetime, when you could have been kind and forbearing with her. Hurting your uncle wont do her any good, you know.

BRASSBOUND. It will teach other scoundrels to respect widows and orphans. Do you forget that there is such a thing as justice?

LADY CICELY [*gaily shaking out the finished coat*] Oh, if you are going to dress yourself in ermine and call yourself Justice, I give you up. You are just your uncle over again; only he gets £5,000 a year for it, and you do it for nothing. [*She holds the coat up to see whether any further repairs are needed*].

BRASSBOUND [*sulkily*] You twist my words very cleverly. But no man or woman has ever changed me.

LADY CICELY. Dear me! That must be very nice for the people you deal with, because they can always depend on you; but isnt it rather inconvenient for yourself when you change your mind?

BRASSBOUND. I never change my mind.

LADY CICELY [*rising with the coat in her hands*] Oh!

Oh ! ! Nothing will ever persuade me that you are as pig-headed as that.

BRASSBOUND [*offended*] Pigheaded !

LADY CICELY [*with quick, caressing apology*] No, no, no. I didnt mean that. Firm ! unalterable ! Resolute ! Iron-willed ! Stonewall Jackson ! Thats the idea, isnt it ?

BRASSBOUND [*hopelessly*] You are laughing at me.

LADY CICELY. No : trembling, I assure you. Now will you try this on for me : I'm so afraid I have made it too tight under the arm. [*She holds it behind him*].

BRASSBOUND [*obeying mechanically*] You take me for a fool, I think. [*He misses the sleeve*].

LADY CICELY. No : all men look foolish when they are feeling for their sleeves—

BRASSBOUND. Agh ! [*He turns and snatches the coat from her; then puts it on himself and buttons the lowest button*].

LADY CICELY [*horrified*] Stop. No. You must never pull a coat at the skirts, Captain Brassbound : it spoils the sit of it. Allow me. [*She pulls the lapels of his coat vigorously forward*] Put back your shoulders. [*He frowns, but obeys*]. Thats better. [*She buttons the top button*]. Now button the rest from the top down. Does it catch you at all under the arm ?

BRASSBOUND [*miserably—all resistance beaten out of him*] No.

LADY CICELY. Thats right. Now before I go back to poor Marzo, say thank you to me for mending your jacket, like a nice polite sailor.

BRASSBOUND [*sitting down at the table in great agitation*] Damn you ! you have belittled my whole life to me. [*He bows his head on his hands, convulsed*].

LADY CICELY [*quite understanding, and putting her hand kindly on his shoulder*] Oh no. I am sure you have done lots of kind things and brave things, if you could only recollect them. With Gordon for instance ? Nobody can belittle that.

He looks up at her for a moment; then kisses her hand. She presses his and turns away with her eyes so wet that she

*sees Drinkwater, coming in through the arch just then, with a
prismatic halo round him. Even when she sees him clearly,
she hardly recognizes him; for he is ludicrously clean and
smoothly brushed; and his hair, formerly mud color, is now
lively red.*

DRINKWATER. Look eah, kepn. [*Brassbound springs up
and recovers himself quickly*]. Eahs the bloomin Shike jest
appeahd on the orawzn wiv abaht fifty men. Thyll be eah
insaw o ten minnits, they will.

LADY CICELY. The Sheikh !

BRASSBOUND. Sidi el Assif and fifty men ! [*To Lady
Cicely*] You were too late : I gave you up my vengeance
when it was no longer in my hand. [*To Drinkwater*] Call
all hands to stand by and shut the gates. Then all here to
me for orders ; and bring the prisoner.

DRINKWATER. Rawt, kepn. [*He runs out*].

LADY CICELY. Is there really any danger for Howard ?

BRASSBOUND. Yes. Danger for all of us unless I keep to
my bargain with this fanatic.

LADY CICELY. What bargain ?

BRASSBOUND. I pay him so much a head for every party
I escort through to the interior. In return he protects me
and lets my caravans alone. But I have sworn an oath to
him to take only Jews and true believers—no Christians,
you understand.

LADY CICELY. Then why did you take us ?

BRASSBOUND. I took my uncle on purpose—and sent
word to Sidi that he was here.

LADY CICELY. Well, thats a pretty kettle of fish, isnt it ?

BRASSBOUND. I will do what I can to save him—and
you. But I fear my repentance has come too late, as
repentance usually does.

LADY CICELY [*cheerfully*] Well, I must go and look after
Marzo, at all events. [*She goes out through the little door.
Johnson, Redbrook, and the rest come in through the arch,
with Sir Howard, still very crusty and determined. He keeps
close to Johnson, who comes to Brassbound's right, Redbrook
taking the other side*].

BRASSBOUND. Wheres Drinkwater ?

JOHNSON. On the lookout. Look here, Capn : we dont half like this job. The gentleman has been talking to us a bit ; and we think that he is a gentleman, and talks straight sense.

REDBROOK. Righto, Brother Johnson. [*To Brassbound*] Wont do, governor. Not good enough.

BRASSBOUND [*fiercely*] Mutiny, eh ?

REDBROOK. Not at all, governor. Dont talk Tommy rot with Brother Sidi only five minutes gallop off. Cant hand over an Englishman to a nigger to have his throat cut.

BRASSBOUND [*unexpectedly acquiescing*] Very good. You know, I suppose, that if you break my bargain with Sidi, youll have to defend this place and fight for your lives in five minutes. That cant be done without discipline : you know that too. I'll take my part with the rest under whatever leader you are willing to obey. So choose your captain and look sharp about it. [*Murmurs of surprise and discontent*].

VOICES. No, no. Brassbound must command.

BRASSBOUND. Youre wasting your five minutes. Try Johnson.

JOHNSON. No. I havnt the head for it.

BRASSBOUND. Well, Redbrook.

REDBROOK. Not this Johnny, thank you. Havnt character enough.

BRASSBOUND. Well, theres Sir Howard Hallam for you ! He has character enough.

A VOICE. He's too old.

ALL. No, no. Brassbound, Brassbound.

JOHNSON. Theres nobody but you, Captain.

REDBROOK. The mutiny's over, governor. You win, hands down.

BRASSBOUND [*turning on them*] Now listen, you, all of you. If I am to command here, I am going to do what I like, not what you like. I'll give this gentleman here to Sidi or to the devil if I choose. I'll not be intimidated or talked back to. Is that understood ?

REDBROOK [*diplomatically*] He's offered a present of five hundred quid if he gets safe back to Mogador, governor. Excuse my mentioning it.

SIR HOWARD. Myself and Lady Cicely.

BRASSBOUND. What ! A judge compound a felony ! You greenhorns, he is more likely to send you all to penal servitude if you are fools enough to give him the chance.

VOICES. So he would. Whew ! [*Murmurs of conviction*].

REDBROOK. Righto, governor. Thats the ace of trumps.

BRASSBOUND [*to Sir Howard*] Now, have you any other card to play ? Any other bribe ? Any other threat ? Quick. Time presses.

SIR HOWARD. My life is in the hands of Providence. Do your worst.

BRASSBOUND. Or my best. I still have that choice.

DRINKWATER [*running in*] Look eah, kepn. Eahs anather lot cammin from the sahth heast. Hunnerds of em, this tawm. The owl dezzit is lawk a bloomin Awd Pawk demonstration. Aw blieve it's the Kidy from Kintorfy. [*General alarm. All look to Brassbound*].

BRASSBOUND [*eagerly*] The Cadi ! How far off ?

DRINKWATER. Matter o two mawl.

BRASSBOUND. We're saved. Open the gates to the Sheikh. [*They stare at him*]. Look alive there.

DRINKWATER [*appalled, almost in tears*] Naow, naow. Lissen, kepn [*pointing to Sir Howard*] : e'll give huz fawv unnerd red uns. [*To the others*] Ynt yer spowk to im, Miste Jornsn—Miste Redbrook—

BRASSBOUND [*cutting him short*] Now then, do you understand plain English ? Johnson and Redbrook : take what men you want and open the gates to the Sheikh. Let him come straight to me. Look alive, will you.

JOHNSON. Ay ay, sir.

REDBROOK. Righto, governor.

They hurry out, with a few others. Drinkwater stares after them, dumbfounded by their obedience.

BRASSBOUND [*taking out a pistol*] You wanted to sell me to my prisoner, did you, you dog.

DRINKWATER [*falling on his knees with a yell*] Naow ! [*Brassbound turns on him as if to kick him. He scrambles away and takes refuge behind Sir Howard*].

BRASSBOUND. Sir Howard Hallam : you have one chance left. The Cadi of Kintafi stands superior to the Sheikh as the responsible governor of the whole province. It is the Cadi who will be sacrificed by the Sultan if England demands satisfaction for any injury to you. If we can hold the Sheikh in parley until the Cadi arrives, you may frighten the Cadi into forcing the Sheikh to release you. The Cadi's coming is a lucky chance for you.

SIR HOWARD. If it were a real chance, you would not tell me of it. Dont try to play cat and mouse with me, man.

DRINKWATER [*aside to Sir Howard, as Brassbound turns contemptuously away to the other side of the room*] It ynt mach of a chawnst, Sir Ahrd. But if there was a ganbowt in Mogador Awbr, awd put a bit on it, aw would.

Johnson, Redbrook, and the others return, rather mistrustfully ushering in Sidi el Assif, attended by Osman and a troop of Arabs. Brassbound's men keep together on the archway side, backing their captain. Sidi's followers cross the room behind the table and assemble near Sir Howard, who stands his ground. Drinkwater runs across to Brassbound and stands at his elbow as he turns to face Sidi.

Sidi el Assif, clad in spotless white, is a nobly handsome Arab, hardly thirty, with fine eyes, bronzed complexion, and instinctively dignified carriage. He places himself between the two groups, with Osman in attendance at his right hand.

OSMAN [*pointing out Sir Howard*] This is the infidel Cadi. [*Sir Howard bows to Sidi, but, being an infidel, receives only the haughtiest stare in acknowledgment*]. This [*pointing to Brassbound*] is Brassbound the Franguestani captain, the servant of Sidi.

DRINKWATER [*not to be outdone, points out the Sheikh and Osman to Brassbound*] This eah is the Commawnder of the Fythful an' is Vizzeer Hosman.

SIDI. Where is the woman ?

OSMAN. The shameless one is not here.

BRASSBOUND. Sidi el Assif, kinsman of the Prophet : you are welcome.

REDBROOK [*with much aplomb*] There is no majesty and no might save in Allah, the Glorious, the Great !

DRINKWATER. Eah, eah !

OSMAN [*to Sidi*] The servant of the captain makes his profession of faith as a true believer.

SIDI. It is well.

BRASSBOUND [*aside to Redbrook*] Where did you pick that up ?

REDBROOK [*aside to Brassbound*] Captain Burton's Arabian Nights—copy in the library of the National Liberal Club.

LADY CICELY [*calling without*] Mr Drinkwater. Come and help me with Marzo. [*The Sheikh pricks up his ears. His nostrils and eyes expand*].

OSMAN. The shameless one !

BRASSBOUND [*to Drinkwater, seizing him by the collar and slinging him towards the door*] Off with you.

Drinkwater goes out through the little door.

OSMAN. Shall we hide her face before she enters ?

SIDI. No.

Lady Cicely, who has resumed her travelling equipment, and has her hat slung across her arm, comes through the little door supporting Marzo, who is very white, but able to get about. Drinkwater has his other arm. Redbrook hastens to relieve Lady Cicely of Marzo, taking him into the group behind Brassbound. Lady Cicely comes forward between Brassbound and the Sheikh, to whom she turns affably.

LADY CICELY [*proffering her hand*] Sidi el Assif, isnt it ? How dye do ? [*He recoils, blushing somewhat*].

OSMAN [*scandalized*] Woman : touch not the kinsman of the Prophet.

LADY CICELY. Oh, I see. I'm being presented at court. Very good. [*She makes a presentation curtsey*].

REDBROOK. Sidi el Assif : this is one of the mighty women Sheikhs of Franguestan. She goes unveiled among Kings ; and only princes may touch her hand.

LADY CICELY. Allah upon thee, Sidi el Assif ! Be a good little Sheikh, and shake hands.

SIDI [*timidly touching her hand*] Now this is a wonderful thing, and worthy to be chronicled with the story of Solomon and the Queen of Sheba. Is it not so, Osman Ali ?

OSMAN. Allah upon thee, master ! it is so.

SIDI. Brassbound Ali : the oath of a just man fulfils itself without many words. The infidel Cadi, thy captive, falls to my share.

BRASSBOUND [*firmly*] It cannot be, Sidi el Assif. [*Sidi's brows contract gravely*]. The price of his blood will be required of our lord the Sultan. I will take him to Morocco and deliver him up there.

SIDI [*impressively*] Brassbound : I am in mine own house and amid mine own people. *I* am the Sultan here. Consider what you say ; for when my word goes forth for life or death, it may not be recalled.

BRASSBOUND. Sidi el Assif : I will buy the man from you at what price you choose to name ; and if I do not pay faithfully, you shall take my head for his.

SIDI. It is well. You shall keep the man, and give me the woman in payment.

SIR HOWARD AND BRASSBOUND [*with the same impulse*] No, no.

LADY CICELY [*eagerly*] Yes, yes. Certainly, Mr Sidi. Certainly.

Sidi smiles gravely.

SIR HOWARD. Impossible.

BRASSBOUND. You dont know what youre doing.

LADY CICELY. Oh, dont I ? Ive not crossed Africa and stayed with six cannibal chiefs for nothing. [*To the Sheikh*] It's all right, Mr Sidi : I shall be delighted.

SIR HOWARD. You are mad. Do you suppose this man will treat you as a European gentleman would ?

LADY CICELY. No : he'll treat me like one of Nature's gentlemen : look at his perfectly splendid face ! [*Addressing Osman as if he was her oldest and most attached retainer*]

Osman : be sure you choose me a good horse ; and get a nice strong camel for my luggage.

Osman, after a moment of stupefaction, hurries out. Lady Cicely puts on her hat and pins it to her hair, the Sheikh gazing at her during the process with timid admiration.

DRINKWATER [*chuckling*] She'll mawch em all to church next Sunder lawk a bloomin lot o cherrity kids : you see if she downt.

LADY CICELY [*busily*] Goodbye, Howard : dont be anxious about me ; and above all, dont bring a parcel of men with guns to rescue me. I shall be all right now that I am getting away from the escort. Captain Brassbound : I rely on you to see that Sir Howard gets safe to Mogador. [*Whispering*] Take your hand off that pistol. [*He takes his hand out of his pocket, reluctantly*]. Goodbye.

A tumult without. They all turn apprehensively to the arch. Osman rushes in.

OSMAN. The Cadi, the Cadi. He is in anger. His men are upon us. Defend—

The Cadi, a vigorous, fatfeatured, choleric, whitehaired and bearded elder, rushes in, cudgel in hand, with an overwhelming retinue, and silences Osman with a sounding thwack. In a moment the back of the room is crowded with his followers. The Sheikh retreats a little towards his men ; and the Cadi comes impetuously forward between him and Lady Cicely.

THE CADI. Now woe upon thee, Sidi el Assif, thou child of mischief !

SIDI [*sternly*] Am I a dog, Muley Othman, that thou speakest thus to me ?

THE CADI. Wilt thou destroy thy country, and give us all into the hands of them that set the sea on fire but yesterday with their ships of war ? Where are the Franguestani captives ?

LADY CICELY. Here we are, Cadi. How dye do ?

THE CADI. Allah upon thee, thou moon at the full ! Where is thy kinsman, the Cadi of Franguestan ? I am his friend, his servant. I come on behalf of my master the Sultan to do him honor, and to cast down his enemies.

SIR HOWARD. You are very good, I am sure.

SIDI [*graver than ever*] Muley Othman—

THE CADI [*fumbling in his breast*] Peace, peace, thou inconsiderate one. [*He takes out a letter*].

BRASSBOUND. Cadi—

THE CADI. Oh thou dog, thou, thou accursed Brassbound, son of a wanton : it is thou hast led Sidi el Assif into this wrongdoing. Read this writing that thou hast brought upon me from the commander of the warship.

BRASSBOUND. Warship ! [*He takes the letter and opens it, his men whispering to one another very low-spiritedly meanwhile*].

REDBROOK. Warship ! Whew !

JOHNSON. Gunboat, praps.

DRINKWATER. Lawk bloomin Worterleoo buses, they are, on this cowst.

Brassbound folds up the letter, looking glum.

SIR HOWARD [*sharply*] Well, sir, are we not to have the benefit of that letter ? Your men are waiting to hear it, I think.

BRASSBOUND. It is not a British ship. [*Sir Howard's face falls*].

LADY CICELY. What is it, then ?

BRASSBOUND. An American cruiser. The Santiago.

THE CADI [*tearing his beard*] Woe ! alas ! it is where they set the sea on fire.

SIDI. Peace, Muley Othman : Allah is still above us.

JOHNSON. Would you mind readin it to us, capn ?

BRASSBOUND [*grimly*] Oh, I'll read it to you. " Mogador Harbor. 26 Sept 1899. Captain Hamlin Kearney, of the cruiser Santiago, presents the compliments of the United States to the Cadi Muley Othman el Kintafi, and announces that he is coming to look for the two British travellers Sir Howard Hallam and Lady Cicely Waynflete, in the Cadi's jurisdiction. As the search will be conducted with machine guns, the prompt return of the travellers to Mogador Harbor will save much trouble to all parties."

THE CADI. As I live, O Cadi, and thou, moon of loveliness, ye shall be led back to Mogador with honor. And thou, accursed Brassbound, shalt go thither a prisoner in chains, thou and thy people. [*Brassbound and his men make a movement to defend themselves*]. Seize them.

LADY CICELY. Oh, please dont fight. [*Brassbound, seeing that his men are hopelessly outnumbered, makes no resistance. They are made prisoners by the Cadi's followers*].

SIDI [*attempting to draw his scimitar*] The woman is mine : I will not forgo her. [*He is seized and overpowered after a Homeric struggle*].

SIR HOWARD [*drily*] I told you you were not in a strong position, Captain Brassbound. [*Looking implacably at him*] You are laid by the heels, my friend, as I said you would be.

LADY CICELY. But I assure you—

BRASSBOUND [*interrupting her*] What have you to assure him of ? You persuaded me to spare him. Look at his face. Will you be able to persuade him to spare me ?

ACT III

Torrid forenoon filtered through small Moorish windows high up in the adobe walls of the largest room in Leslie Rankin's house. A clean cool room, with the table (a Christian article) set in the middle, a presidentially elbowed chair behind it, and an inkstand and paper ready for the sitter. A couple of cheap American chairs right and left of the table, facing the same way as the presidential chair, give a judicial aspect to the arrangement. Rankin is placing a little tray with a jug and some glasses near the inkstand when Lady Cicely's voice is heard at the door, which is behind him in the corner to his right.

LADY CICELY. Good morning. May I come in ?

RANKIN. Certainly. [*She comes in to the nearest end of the table. She has discarded all travelling equipment, and is dressed exactly as she might be in Surrey on a very hot day*]. Sit ye doon, Leddy Ceecily.

LADY CICELY [*sitting down*] How nice youve made the room for the inquiry !

RANKIN [*doubtfully*] I could wish there were more chairs. Yon American captain will preside in this ; and that leaves but one for Sir Howrrd and one for your leddyship. I could almost be tempted to call it a maircy that your friend that owns the yacht has sprained his ankle and cannot come. I misdoubt me it will not look judeecial to have Captain Kearney's officers squatting on the floor.

LADY CICELY. Oh, they wont mind. What about the prisoners ?

RANKIN. They are to be broat here from the town gaol presently.

LADY CICELY. And where is that silly old Cadi, and my handsome Sheikh Sidi ? I must see them before the inquiry, or theyll give Captain Kearney quite a false impression of what happened.

RANKIN. But ye cannot see them. They decamped last

312

night, back to their castles in the Atlas.

LADY CICELY [*delighted*] No !

RANKIN. Indeed and they did. The poor Cadi is so
tarrified by all he has haird of the destruction of the Spanish
fleet, that he darent trust himself in the captain's hands.
[*Looking reproachfully at her*] On our journey back here, ye
seem to have frightened the poor man yourself, Leddy
Ceecily, by talking to him about the fanatical Chreestianity
of the Americans. Ye have largely yourself to thank if he's
gone.

LADY CICELY. Allah be praised ! What a weight off our
minds, Mr Rankin !

RANKIN [*puzzled*] And why ? Do ye not understand how
necessary their evidence is ?

LADY CICELY. Their evidence ! It would spoil everything. They would perjure themselves out of pure spite
against poor Captain Brassbound.

RANKIN [*amazed*] Do ye call him poor Captain Brassbound ! Does not your leddyship know that this Brassbound is—Heaven forgive me for judging him !—a precious
scoundrel ? Did ye not hear what Sir Howrrd told me on
the yacht last night ?

LADY CICELY. All a mistake, Mr Rankin : all a mistake,
I assure you. You said just now, Heaven forgive you for
judging him ! Well, thats just what the whole quarrel is
about. Captain Brassbound is just like you : he thinks
we have no right to judge one another ; and as Sir Howard
gets £5,000 a year for doing nothing else but judging people,
he thinks poor Captain Brassbound a regular Anarchist.
They quarrelled dreadfully at the castle. You mustnt mind
what Sir Howard says about him : you really mustnt.

RANKIN. But his conduct—

LADY CICELY. Perfectly saintly, Mr Rankin. Worthy of
yourself in your best moments. He forgave Sir Howard,
and did all he could to save him.

RANKIN. Ye astoanish me, Leddy Ceecily.

LADY CICELY. And think of the temptation to behave
badly when he had us all there helpless !

RANKIN. The temptation ! ay : thats true. Yere ower bonny to be cast away among a parcel o lone, lawless men, my leddy.

LADY CICELY [*naïvely*] Bless me, thats quite true ; and I never thought of it ! Oh, after that you really must do all you can to help Captain Brassbound.

RANKIN [*reservedly*] No : I cannot say that, Leddy Ceecily. I doubt he has imposed on your good nature and sweet disposeetion. I had a crack with the Cadi as well as with Sir Howrrd ; and there is little question in my mind but that Captain Brassbound is no better than a breegand.

LADY CICELY [*apparently deeply impressed*] I wonder whether he can be, Mr Rankin. If you think so, thats heavily against him in my opinion, because you have more knowledge of men than anyone else here. Perhaps I'm mistaken. I only thought you might like to help him as the son of your old friend.

RANKIN [*startled*] The son of my old friend ! What dye mean ?

LADY CICELY. Oh ! Didnt Sir Howard tell you that ? Why, Captain Brassbound turns out to be Sir Howard's nephew, the son of the brother you knew.

RANKIN [*overwhelmed*] I saw the likeness the night he came here ! It's true : it's true. Uncle and nephew !

LADY CICELY. Yes : thats why they quarrelled so.

RANKIN [*with a momentary sense of ill usage*] I think Sir Howrrd might have told me that.

LADY CICELY. Of course he ought to have told you. You see he only tells one side of the story. That comes from his training as a barrister. You mustnt think he's naturally deceitful : if he'd been brought up as a clergyman, he'd have told you the whole truth as a matter of course.

RANKIN [*too much perturbed to dwell on his grievance*] Leddy Ceecily : I must go to the prison and see the lad. He may have been a bit wild ; but I cant leave poor Miles's son unbefriended in a foreign gaol.

LADY CICELY [*rising, radiant*] Oh, how good of you ! You have a real kind heart of gold, Mr Rankin. Now, before you go, shall we just put our heads together, and consider how to give Miles's son every chance—I mean of course every chance that he ought to have.

RANKIN [*rather addled*] I am so confused by this astoanishing news—

LADY CICELY. Yes, yes : of course you are. But dont you think he would make a better impression on the American captain if he were a little more respectably dressed ?

RANKIN. Mebbe. But how can that be remedied here in Mogador ?

LADY CICELY. Oh, Ive thought of that. You know I'm going back to England by way of Rome, Mr Rankin ; and I'm bringing a portmanteau full of clothes for my brother there : he's ambassador, you know, and has to be very particular as to what he wears. I had the portmanteau brought here this morning. Now would you mind taking it to the prison, and smartening up Captain Brassbound a little. Tell him he ought to do it to shew his respect for me ; and he will. It will be quite easy : there are two Krooboys waiting to carry the portmanteau. You will : I know you will. [*She edges him to the door*]. And do you think there is time to get him shaved ?

RANKIN [*succumbing, half bewildered*] I'll do my best.

LADY CICELY. I know you will. [*As he is going out*] Oh ! one word, Mr Rankin. [*He comes back*]. The Cadi didnt know that Captain Brassbound was Sir Howard's nephew, did he ?

RANKIN. No.

LADY CICELY. Then he must have misunderstood everything quite dreadfully. I'm afraid, Mr Rankin—though you know best, of course—that we are bound not to repeat anything at the inquiry that the Cadi said. He didnt know, you see.

RANKIN [*cannily*] I take your point, Leddy Ceecily. It alters the case. I shall certainly make no allusion to it.

LADY CICELY [*magnanimously*] Well, then, I wont either. There !

They shake hands on it. Sir Howard comes in.

SIR HOWARD. Good morning, Mr Rankin. I hope you got home safely from the yacht last night.

RANKIN. Quite safe, thank ye, Sir Howrrd.

LADY CICELY. Howard : he's in a hurry. Dont make him stop to talk.

SIR HOWARD. Very good, very good. [*He comes to the table and takes Lady Cicely's chair*].

RANKIN. Oo revoir, Leddy Ceecily.

LADY CICELY. Bless you, Mr Rankin. [*Rankin goes out. She comes to the other end of the table, looking at Sir Howard with a troubled, sorrowfully sympathetic air, but unconsciously making her right hand stalk about the table on the tips of its fingers in a tentative stealthy way which would put Sir Howard on his guard if he were in a suspicious frame of mind, which, as it happens, he is not*]. I'm so sorry for you, Howard, about this unfortunate inquiry.

SIR HOWARD [*swinging round on his chair, astonished*] Sorry for me ! Why ?

LADY CICELY. It will look so dreadful. Your own nephew, you know.

SIR HOWARD. Cicely : an English judge has no nephews, no sons even, when he has to carry out the law.

LADY CICELY. But then he oughtnt to have any property either. People will never understand about the West Indian Estate. Theyll think youre the wicked uncle out of the Babes in the Wood. [*With a fresh gush of compassion*] I'm so so sorry for you.

SIR HOWARD [*rather stiffly*] I really do not see how I need your commiseration, Cicely. The woman was an impossible person, half mad, half drunk. Do you understand what such a creature is when she has a grievance, and imagines some innocent person to be the author of it ?

LADY CICELY [*with a touch of impatience*] Oh, quite. Thatll be made clear enough. I can see it all in the papers already : our half mad, half drunk sister-in-law, making scenes with you in the street, with the police called in, and prison and all the rest of it. The family will be furious.

[*Sir Howard quails. She instantly follows up her advantage with*] Think of papa !

SIR HOWARD. I shall expect Lord Waynflete to look at the matter as a reasonable man.

LADY CICELY. Do you think he's so greatly changed as that, Howard ?

SIR HOWARD [*falling back on the fatalism of the depersonalized public man*] My dear Cicely : there is no use discussing the matter. It cannot be helped, however disagreeable it may be.

LADY CICELY. Of course not. Thats whats so dreadful. Do you think people will understand ?

SIR HOWARD. I really cannot say. Whether they do or no, *I* cannot help it.

LADY CICELY. If you were anybody but a judge, it wouldnt matter so much. But a judge mustnt even be misunderstood. [*Despairingly*] Oh, it's dreadful, Howard : it's terrible ! What would poor Mary say if she were alive now ?

SIR HOWARD [*with emotion*] I dont think, Cicely, that my dear wife would misunderstand me.

LADY CICELY. No : she'd know you mean well. And when you came home and said, " Mary : Ive just told all the world that your sister-in-law was a police court criminal, and that I sent her to prison ; and your nephew is a brigand, and I'm sending him to prison," she'd have thought it must be all right because you did it. But you dont think she would have liked it, any more than papa and the rest of us, do you ?

SIR HOWARD [*appalled*] But what am I to do ? Do you ask me to compound a felony ?

LADY CICELY [*sternly*] Certainly not. I would not allow such a thing, even if you were wicked enough to attempt it. No. What I say is, that you ought not to tell the story yourself.

SIR HOWARD. Why ?

LADY CICELY. Because everybody would say you are such a clever lawyer you could make a poor simple sailor like Captain Kearney believe anything. The proper thing for you to do, Howard, is to let me tell the exact truth. Then you can simply say that you are bound to confirm me. Nobody can blame you for that.

SIR HOWARD [*looking suspiciously at her*] Cicely : you are up to some devilment.

LADY CICELY [*promptly washing her hands of his interests*] Oh, very well. Tell the story yourself, in your own clever way. I only proposed to tell the exact truth. You call that devilment. So it is, I daresay, from a lawyer's point of view.

SIR HOWARD. I hope youre not offended.

LADY CICELY [*with the utmost goodhumor*] My dear Howard, not a bit. Of course youre right : you know how these things ought to be done. I'll do exactly what you tell me, and confirm everything you say.

SIR HOWARD [*alarmed by the completeness of his victory*] Oh, my dear, you mustnt act in my interest. You must give your evidence with absolute impartiality. [*She nods, as if thorough impressed and reproved, and gazes at him with the steadfast candor peculiar to liars who read novels. His eyes turn to the ground; and his brow clouds perplexedly. He rises; rubs his chin nervously with his forefinger; and adds*] I think, perhaps, on reflection, that there is something to be said for your proposal to relieve me of the very painful duty of telling what has occurred.

LADY CICELY [*holding off*] But youd do it so very much better.

SIR HOWARD. For that very reason, perhaps, it had better come from you.

LADY CICELY [*reluctantly*] Well, if youd rather.

SIR HOWARD. But mind, Cicely, the exact truth.

LADY CICELY [*with conviction*] The exact truth. [*They shake hands on it*].

SIR HOWARD [*holding her hand*] Fiat justitia : ruat cœlum!

LADY CICELY. Let Justice be done, though the ceiling fall !

An American bluejacket appears at the door.

BLUEJACKET. Captain Kearney's cawmpliments to Lady Waynflete ; and may he come in ?

LADY CICELY. Yes. By all means. Where are the prisoners ?

BLUEJACKET. Party gawn to the jail to fetch em, marm.

LADY CICELY. Thank you. I should like to be told when they are coming, if I might.

BLUEJACKET. You shall so, marm. [*He stands aside, saluting, to admit his captain, and goes out*].

Captain Hamlin Kearney is a robustly built western American, with the keen, squeezed, wind beaten eyes and obstinately enduring mouth of his profession. A curious ethnological specimen, with all the nations of the old world at war in his veins, he is developing artificially in the direction of sleekness and culture under the restraints of an over-whelming dread of European criticism, and climatically in the direction of the indigenous North American, who is already in possession of his hair, his cheek-bones, and the manlier instincts in him which the sea has rescued from civilization. The world, pondering on the great part of its own future which is in his hands, contemplates him with wonder as to what the devil he will evolve into in another century or two. Meanwhile he presents himself to Lady Cicely as a blunt sailor who has something to say to her concerning her conduct which he wishes to put politely, as becomes an officer address-ing a lady, but also with an emphatically implied rebuke, as an American addressing an English person who has taken a liberty.

LADY CICELY [*as he enters*] So glad youve come, Captain Kearney.

KEARNEY [*coming between Sir Howard and Lady Cicely*] When we parted yesterday ahfternoon, Lady Waynflete, I was unaware that in the course of your visit to my ship you had entirely altered the sleeping arrangements of my stokers. I thahnk you. As captain of the ship, I am customairily cawnsulted before the orders of English visitors are carried out ; but as your alterations appear to cawndooce to the comfort of the men, I have not interfered with them.

LADY CICELY. How clever of you to find out ! I believe you know every bolt in that ship.

Kearney softens perceptibly.

SIR HOWARD. I am really very sorry that my sister-in-law has taken so serious a liberty, Captain Kearney. It is a mania of hers—simply a mania. Why did your men pay any attention to her ?

KEARNEY [*with gravely dissembled humor*] Well, I ahsked that question too. I said, Why did you obey that lady's orders instead of waiting for mine ? They said they didnt see exactly how they could refuse. I ahsked whether they cawnsidered that discipline. They said, Well, sir, will you talk to the lady yourself next time ?

LADY CICELY. I'm so sorry. But you know, Captain, the one thing that one misses on board a man-of-war is a woman.

KEARNEY. We often feel that deprivation verry keenly, Lady Waynflete.

LADY CICELY. My uncle is first Lord of the Admiralty ; and I am always telling him what a scandal it is that an English captain should be forbidden to take his wife on board to look after the ship.

KEARNEY. Stranger still, Lady Waynflete, he is not forbidden to take any other lady. Yours is an extraordinairy country—to an Americann.

LADY CICELY. But it's most serious, Captain. The poor men go melancholy mad, and ram each other's ships and do all sorts of things.

SIR HOWARD. Cicely : I beg you will not talk nonsense to Captain Kearney. Your ideas on some subjects are really hardly decorous.

LADY CICELY [*to Kearney*] Thats what English people are like, Captain Kearney. They wont hear of anything concerning your poor sailors except Nelson and Trafalgar. You understand me, dont you ?

KEARNEY [*gallantly*] I cawnsider that you have more sense in your wedding ring finger than the British Ahdmiralty has in its whole cawnstitootion, Lady Waynflete.

LADY CICELY. Of course I have. Sailors always understand things.

The bluejacket reappears.

BLUEJACKET [*to Lady Cicely*] Prisoners coming up the hill, marm.

KEARNEY [*turning sharply on him*] Who sent you in to say that?

BLUEJACKET [*calmly*] British lady's orders, sir. [*He goes out, unruffled, leaving Kearney dumbfounded*].

SIR HOWARD [*contemplating Kearney's expression with dismay*] I am really very sorry, Captain Kearney. I am quite aware that Lady Cicely has no right whatever to give orders to your men.

LADY CICELY. I didnt give orders : I just asked him. He has such a nice face ! Dont you think so, Captain Kearney ? [*He gasps, speechless*]. And now will you excuse me a moment. I want to speak to somebody before the inquiry begins. [*She hurries out*].

KEARNEY. There is sertnly a wonderful chahm about the British aristocracy, Sir Howard Hallam. Are they all like that ? [*He takes the presidential chair*].

SIR HOWARD [*resuming his seat on Kearney's right*] Fortunately not, Captain Kearney. Half a dozen such women would make an end of law in England in six months.

The bluejacket comes to the door again.

BLUEJACKET. All ready, sir.

KEARNEY. Verry good. I'm waiting.

The bluejacket turns and intimates this to those without. The officers of the Santiago enter.

SIR HOWARD [*rising and bobbing to them in a judicial manner*] Good morning, gentlemen.

They acknowledge the greeting rather shyly, bowing or touching their caps, and stand in a group behind Kearney.

KEARNEY [*to Sir Howard*] You will be glahd to hear that I have a verry good account of one of our prisoners from our chahplain, who visited them in the gaol. He has expressed a wish to be cawnverted to Episcopalianism.

SIR HOWARD [*drily*] Yes, I think I know him.

T.P.—11

KEARNEY. Bring in the prisoners.

BLUEJACKET [*at the door*] They are engaged with the British lady, sir. Shall I ask her—

KEARNEY [*jumping up and exploding in storm piercing tones*] Bring in the prisoners. Tell the lady those are my orders. Do you hear? Tell her so. [*The bluejacket goes out dubiously. The officers look at one another in mute comment on the unaccountable pepperiness of their commander*].

SIR HOWARD [*suavely*] Mr Rankin will be present, I presume.

KEARNEY [*angrily*] Rahnkin! Who is Rahnkin?

SIR HOWARD. Our host the missionary.

KEARNEY [*subsiding unwillingly*] Oh! Rahnkin, is he? He'd better look sharp or he'll be late. [*Again exploding*] What are they doing with those prisoners?

Rankin hurries in, and takes his place near Sir Howard.

SIR HOWARD. This is Mr Rankin, Captain Kearney.

RANKIN. Excuse my delay, Captain Kearney. The leddy sent me on an errand. [*Kearney grunts*]. I thoaght I should be late. But the first thing I heard when I arrived was your officer giving your compliments to Leddy Ceecily, and would she kindly allow the prisoners to come in, as you were anxious to see her again. Then I knew I was in time.

KEARNEY. Oh, that was it, was it? May I ask, sir, did you notice any sign on Lady Waynflete's part of cawmplying with that verry moderate request.

LADY CICELY [*outside*] Coming, coming.

The prisoners are brought in by a guard of armed bluejackets. Drinkwater first, again elaborately clean, and conveying by a virtuous and steadfast smirk a cheerful confidence in his innocence. Johnson solid and inexpressive, Redbrook unconcerned and debonair, Marzo uneasy. These four form a little group together on the captain's left. The rest wait unintelligently on Providence in a row against the wall on the same side, shepherded by the bluejackets. The first bluejacket, a petty officer, posts himself on the captain's right, behind Rankin and Sir Howard. Finally Brassbound appears

*with Lady Cicely on his arm. He is in fashionable frock coat
and trousers, spotless collar and cuffs, and elegant boots. He
carries a glossy tall hat in his hand. To an unsophisticated
eye, the change is monstrous and appalling; and its effect
on himself is so unmanning that he is quite out of countenance
—a shaven Samson. Lady Cicely, however, is greatly pleased
with it; and the rest regard it as an unquestionable improvement. The officers fall back gallantly to allow her to pass.
Kearney rises to receive her, and stares with some surprise at
Brassbound as she stops at the table on his left. Sir Howard
rises punctiliously when Kearney rises and sits when he
sits.*

KEARNEY. Is this another gentleman of your party,
Lady Waynflete? I presume I met you lahst night, sir, on
board the yacht.

BRASSBOUND. No. I am your prisoner. My name is
Brassbound.

DRINKWATER [*officiously*] Kepn Brarsbahnd, of the
schooner Thenksgiv—

REDBROOK [*hastily*] Shut up, you fool. [*He elbows
Drinkwater into the background*].

KEARNEY [*surprised and rather suspicious*] Well, I hardly
understahnd this. However, if you are Captain Brassbound, you can take your place with the rest. [*Brassbound
joins Redbrook and Johnson. Kearney sits down again, after
inviting Lady Cicely, with a solemn gesture, to take the vacant
chair*]. Now let me see. You are a man of experience in
these matters, Sir Howard Hallam. If you had to conduct
this business, how would you start?

LADY CICELY. He'd call on the counsel for the prosecution, wouldnt you, Howard?

SIR HOWARD. But there is no counsel for the prosecution,
Cicely.

LADY CICELY. Oh yes there is. I'm counsel for the
prosecution. You mustnt let Sir Howard make a speech,
Captain Kearney: his doctors have positively forbidden
anything of that sort. Will you begin with me?

KEARNEY. By your leave, Lady Waynflete, I think I will

just begin with myself.   Sailor fashion will do as well here as lawyer fashion.

LADY CICELY. Ever so much better, dear Captain Kearney.   [*Silence. Kearney composes himself to speak. She breaks out again*].   You look so nice as a judge !

A general smile.   Drinkwater splutters into a half suppressed laugh.

REDBROOK [*in a fierce whisper*] Shut up, you fool, will you ?   [*Again he pushes him back with a furtive kick*].

SIR HOWARD [*remonstrating*] Cicely !

KEARNEY [*grimly keeping his countenance*] Your ladyship's cawmpliments will be in order at a later stage. Captain Brassbound : the position is this.   My ship, the United States cruiser Santiago, was spoken off Mogador lahst Thursday by the yacht Redgauntlet.   The owner of the aforesaid yacht, who is not present through having sprained his ahnkle, gave me sertn information.   In cawnsequence of that information the Santiago made the twenty knots to Mogador Harbor inside of fifty-seven minutes. Before noon next day a messenger of mine gave the Cadi of the district sertn information.   In cawnsequence of that information the Cadi stimulated himself to some ten knots an hour, and lodged you and your men in Mogador jail at my disposal.   The Cadi then went back to his mountain fahstnesses ;   so we shall not have the pleasure of his company here today.   Do you follow me so far ?

BRASSBOUND. Yes.   I know what you did and what the Cadi did.   The point is, why did you do it ?

KEARNEY. With doo patience we shall come to that presently.   Mr Rahnkin : will you kindly take up the parable ?

RANKIN. On the very day that Sir Howrrd and Lady Cicely started on their excursion I was applied to for medicine by a follower of the Sheikh Sidi el Assif.   He told me I should never see Sir Howrrd again, because his master knew he was a Christian and would take him out of the hands of Captain Brassbound.   I hurried on board the yacht and told the owner to scour the coast for a gunboat or cruiser to come into the harbor and put persuasion on the authorities. [*Sir Howard turns and looks at Rankin with a sudden doubt of his integrity as a witness*].

KEARNEY. But I understood from our chahplain that you reported Captain Brassbound as in league with the Sheikh to deliver Sir Howard up to him.

RANKIN. That was my first hasty conclusion, Captain Kearney. But it appears that the compact between them was that Captain Brassbound should escort travellers under the Sheikh's protection at a certain payment per head, provided none of them were Christians. As I understand it, he tried to smuggle Sir Howrrd through under this compact, and the Sheikh found him out.

DRINKWATER. Rawt, gavner. Thets jest ah it wors. The Kepn—

REDBROOK [*again suppressing him*] Shut up, you fool, I tell you.

SIR HOWARD [*to Rankin*] May I ask have you had any conversation with Lady Cicely on this subject?

RANKIN [*naïvely*] Yes. [*Sir Howard grunts emphatically, as who should say " I thought so." Rankin continues, addressing the court*] May I say how sorry I am that there are so few chairs, Captain and gentlemen.

KEARNEY [*with genial American courtesy*] Oh, thats all right, Mr Rahnkin. Well, I see no harm so far : its human fawlly, but not human crime. Now the counsel for the prosecution can proceed to prosecute. The floor is yours, Lady Waynflete.

LADY CICELY [*rising*] I can only tell you the exact truth—

DRINKWATER [*involuntarily*] Naow, downt do thet, lidy—

REDBROOK [*as before*] Shut up, you fool, will you.

LADY CICELY. We had a most delightful trip in the hills ; and Captain Brassbound's men could not have been nicer —I must say that for them—until we saw a tribe of Arabs —such nice looking men !—and then the poor things were frightened.

KEARNEY. The Arabs?

LADY CICELY. No : Arabs are never frightened. The

escort, of course : escorts are always frightened. I wanted to speak to the Arab chief ; but Captain Brassbound cruelly shot his horse ; and the chief shot the Count ; and then—

KEARNEY. The Count ! What Count ?

LADY CICELY. Marzo. Thats Marzo [*pointing to Marzo, who grins and touches his forehead*].

KEARNEY [*slightly overwhelmed by the unexpected profusion of incident and character in her story*] Well, what happened then ?

LADY CICELY. Then the escort ran away—all escorts do—and dragged me into the castle, which you really ought to make them clean and whitewash thoroughly, Captain Kearney. Then Captain Brassbound and Sir Howard turned out to be related to one another [*Sensation*] ; and then of course there was a quarrel. The Hallams always quarrel.

SIR HOWARD [*rising to protest*] Cicely ! Captain Kearney : this man told me—

LADY CICELY [*swiftly interrupting him*] You mustnt say what people told you : it's not evidence. [*Sir Howard chokes with indignation*].

KEARNEY [*calmly*] Allow the lady to pro-ceed, Sir Howard Hallam.

SIR HOWARD [*recovering his self-control with a gulp, and resuming his seat*] I beg your pardon, Captain Kearney.

LADY CICELY. Then Sidi came.

KEARNEY. Sidney ! Who was Sidney ?

LADY CICELY. No, Sidi. The Sheikh. Sidi el Assif. A noble creature, with such a fine face ! He fell in love with me at first sight—

SIR HOWARD [*remonstrating*] Cicely !

LADY CICELY. He did : you know he did. You told me to tell the exact truth.

KEARNEY. I can readily believe it, madam. Proceed.

LADY CICELY. Well, that put the poor fellow into a most cruel dilemma. You see, he could claim to carry off Sir Howard, because Sir Howard is a Christian. But as I am only a woman, he had no claim to me.

KEARNEY [*somewhat sternly, suspecting Lady Cicely of aristocratic atheism*] But you are a Christian woman.

LADY CICELY. No : the Arabs dont count women. They dont believe we have any souls.

RANKIN. That is true, Captain : the poor benighted creatures !

LADY CICELY. Well, what was he to do ? He wasnt in love with Sir Howard ; and he was in love with me. So he naturally offered to swop Sir Howard for me. Dont you think that was nice of him, Captain Kearney ?

KEARNEY. I should have done the same myself, Lady Waynflete. Proceed.

LADY CICELY. Captain Brassbound, I must say, was nobleness itself, in spite of the quarrel between himself and Sir Howard. He refused to give up either of us, and was on the point of fighting for us when in came the Cadi with your most amusing and delightful letter, captain, and bundled us all back to Mogador after calling my poor Sidi the most dreadful names, and putting all the blame on Captain Brassbound. So here we are. Now, Howard, isnt that the exact truth, every word of it ?

SIR HOWARD. It is the truth, Cicely, and nothing but the truth. But the English law requires a witness to tell the whole truth.

LADY CICELY. What nonsense ! As if anybody ever knew the whole truth about anything ! [*Sitting down, much hurt and discouraged*] I'm sorry you wish Captain Kearney to understand that I am an untruthful witness.

SIR HOWARD. No : but—

LADY CICELY. Very well, then : please dont say things that convey that impression.

KEARNEY. But Sir Howard told me yesterday that Captain Brassbound threatened to sell him into slavery.

LADY CICELY [*springing up again*] Did Sir Howard tell you the things he said about Captain Brassbound's mother ? [*Renewed sensation*]. I told you they quarrelled, Captain Kearney. I said so, didnt I ?

REDBROOK [*crisply*] Distinctly. [*Drinkwater opens his*

mouth to corroborate].   Shut up, you fool.

LADY CICELY. Of course I did.   Now, Captain Kearney, do you want me—does Sir Howard want me—does anybody want me to go into the details of that shocking family quarrel?   Am I to stand here in the absence of any individual of my own sex and repeat the language of two angry men?

KEARNEY [*rising impressively*] The United States navy will have no hahnd in offering any violence to the pure instincts of womanhood.   Lady Waynflete : I thahnk you for the delicacy with which you have given your evidence.   [*Lady Cicely beams on him gratefully and sits down triumphant*]. Captain Brassbound : I shall not hold you respawnsible for what you may have said when the English bench addressed you in the language of the English forecastle— [*Sir Howard is about to protest*] No, Sir Howard Hallam ; excuse me.   In moments of pahssion I have called a man that myself.   We are all glahd to find real flesh and blood beneath the ermine of the judge.   We will now drop a subject that should never have been broached in a lady's presence.   [*He resumes his seat, and adds, in a businesslike tone*] Is there anything further before we release these men?

BLUEJACKET. There are some dawcuments handed over by the Cadi, sir.   He reckoned they were sort of magic spells.   The chahplain ordered them to be reported to you and burnt, with your leave, sir.

KEARNEY. What are they?

BLUEJACKET [*reading from a list*] Four books, torn and dirty, made up of separate numbers, value each wawn penny, and entitled Sweeny Todd, the Demon Barber of London ; The Skeleton Horseman—

DRINKWATER [*rushing forward in painful alarm and anxiety*] It's maw lawbrary, gavner.   Downt burn em.

KEARNEY. Youll be better without that sort of reading, my man.

DRINKWATER [*in intense distress, appealing to Lady Cicely*] Downt let em burn em, lidy.   They dassent if you horder em not to.   [*With desperate eloquence*] Yer dunno wot them books is to me. They took me aht of the sawdid reeyellities of the Worterleoo Rowd. They formed maw mawnd : they shaowed me sathink awgher than the squalor of a corster's lawf—

REDBROOK [*collaring him*] Oh shut up, you fool. Get out. Hold your ton—

DRINKWATER [*frantically breaking from him*] Lidy, lidy : sy a word for me. Ev a feelin awt. [*His tears choke him: he clasps his hands in dumb entreaty*].

LADY CICELY [*touched*] Dont burn his books, Captain. Let me give them back to him.

KEARNEY. The books will be handed over to the lady.

DRINKWATER [*in a small voice*] Thenkyer, lidy. [*He retires among his comrades, snivelling subduedly*].

REDBROOK [*aside to him as he passes*] You silly ass, you. [*Drinkwater sniffs and does not reply*].

KEARNEY. I suppose you and your men accept this lady's account of what passed, Captain Brassbound.

BRASSBOUND [*gloomily*] Yes. It is true—as far as it goes.

KEARNEY [*impatiently*] Do you wawnt it to go any further?

MARZO. She leave out something. Arab shoot me. She nurse me. She cure me.

KEARNEY. And who are you, pray ?

MARZO [*seized with a sanctimonious desire to demonstrate his higher nature*] Only dam thief. Dam liar. Dam rascal. She no lady.

JOHNSON [*revolted by the seeming insult to the English peerage from a low Italian*] What ? Whats that you say ?

MARZO. No lady nurse dam rascal. Only saint. She saint. She get me to heaven—get us all to heaven. We do what we like now.

LADY CICELY. Indeed you will do nothing of the sort, Marzo, unless you like to behave yourself very nicely indeed. What hour did you say we were to lunch at, Captain Kearney ?

KEARNEY. You recall me to my dooty, Lady Waynflete. My barge will be ready to take off you and Sir Howard to the Santiago at one o'clawk. [*He rises*]. Captain Brassbound : this innquery has elicited no reason why I should detain you or your men. I advise you to ahct as escort in future to heathens exclusively. Mr Rahnkin : I thanhk you in the name of the United States for the hospitahlity you have extended to us today ; and I invite you to accompany me bahck to my ship with a view to lunch at half-past-one. Gentlemen : we will wait on the governor of the gaol on our way to the harbor. [*He goes out, following his officers, and followed by the bluejackets and the petty officer*].

SIR HOWARD [*to Lady Cicely*] Cicely : in the course of my professional career I have met with unscrupulous witnesses, and, I am sorry to say, unscrupulous counsel also. But the combination of unscrupulous witness and unscrupulous counsel I have met today has taken away my breath. You have made me your accomplice in defeating justice.

LADY CICELY. Yes : arnt you glad it's been defeated for once ? [*She takes his arm to go out with him*]. Captain Brassbound : I will come back to say goodbye before I go. [*He nods gloomily. She goes out with Sir Howard, following the Captain and his staff*].

RANKIN [*running to Brassbound and taking both his hands*] I'm right glad yere cleared. I'll come back and have a crack with ye when yon lunch is over. God bless ye. [*He goes out quickly*].

Brassbound and his men, left by themselves in the room, free and unobserved, go straight out of their senses. They laugh; they dance; they embrace one another; they set to partners and waltz clumsily; they shake hands repeatedly and maudlinly. Three only retain some sort of self-possession. Marzo, proud of having successfully thrust himself into a leading part in the recent proceedings and made a dramatic speech, inflates his chest, curls his scanty moustache, and throws himself into a swaggering pose, chin up and right foot forward, despising the emotional English barbarians around him. Brassbound's eyes and the working of his mouth shew that he is infected with the general excitement ; but he bridles himself savagely. Redbrook, trained to affect indifference, grins cynically; winks at Brassbound; and finally relieves himself by assuming the character of a circus ringmaster, flourishing an imaginary whip and egging on the rest to wilder exertions. A climax is reached when Drinkwater, let loose without a stain on his character for the second time, is rapt by belief in his star into an ecstasy in which, scorning all partnership, he becomes as it were a whirling dervish, and executes so miraculous a clog dance that the others gradually cease their slower antics to stare at him.

BRASSBOUND [*tearing off his hat and striding forward as Drinkwater collapses, exhausted, and is picked up by Redbrook*] Now to get rid of this respectable clobber and feel like a man again. Stand by, all hands, to jump on the captain's tall hat. [*He puts the hat down and prepares to jump on it. The effect is startling, and takes him completely aback. His followers, far from appreciating his iconoclasm, are shocked into scandalized sobriety, except Redbrook, who is intensely tickled by their prudery*].

DRINKWATER. Naow, look eah, kepn : that ynt rawt. Dror a lawn somewhere.

JOHNSON. I say nothin agen a bit of fun, Capn ; but lets be gentlemen.

REDBROOK. I suggest to you, Brassbound, that the clobber belongs to Lady Sis. Aint you going to give it back to her ?

BRASSBOUND [*picking up the hat and brushing the dust off it anxiously*] Thats true. I'm a fool. All the same, she shall not see me again like this. [*He pulls off the coat and waistcoat together*]. Does any man here know how to fold up this sort of thing properly ?

REDBROOK. Allow me, governor. [*He takes the coat and waistcoat to the table, and folds them up*].

BRASSBOUND [*loosening his collar and the front of his shirt*] Brandyfaced Jack : youre looking at these studs. I know whats in your mind.

DRINKWATER [*indignantly*] Naow yer downt : nort a bit on it. Wots in maw mawnd is secrifawce, seolf-secrifawce.

BRASSBOUND. If one brass pin of that lady's property is missing, I'll hang you with my own hands at the gaff of the

Thanksgiving—and would, if she were lying under the guns of all the fleets in Europe. [*He pulls off the shirt and stands in his blue jersey, with his hair ruffled. He passes his hand through it and exclaims*] Now I am half a man, at any rate.

REDBROOK. A horrible combination, governor : church-warden from the waist down, and the rest pirate. Lady Sis wont speak to you in it.

BRASSBOUND. I'll change altogether. [*He leaves the room to get his own trousers*].

REDBROOK [*softly*] Look here, Johnson, and gents gener-ally. [*They gather about him*]. Spose she takes him back to England !

MARZO [*trying to repeat his success*] Im ! Im only dam pirate. She saint, I tell you—no take any man nowhere.

JOHNSON [*severely*] Dont you be a ignorant and immoral foreigner. [*The rebuke is well received; and Marzo is hustled into the background and extinguished*]. She wont take him for harm ; but she might take him for good. And then where should we be ?

DRINKWATER. Brarsbahnd ynt the ownly kepn in the world. Wot mikes a kepn is brines an knollidge o lawf. It ynt thet thers naow sitch pusson : it's thet you dunno where to look fr im. [*The implication that he is such a person is so intolerable that they receive it with a prolonged burst of booing*].

BRASSBOUND [*returning in his own clothes, getting into his jacket as he comes*] Stand by, all. [*They start asunder guiltily, and wait for orders*]. Redbrook : you pack that clobber in the lady's portmanteau, and put it aboard the yacht for her. Johnson : you take all hands aboard the Thanksgiving ; look through the stores ; weigh anchor ; and make all ready for sea. Then send Jack to wait for me at the slip with a boat ; and give me a gunfire for a signal. Lose no time.

JOHNSON. Ay, ay, sir. All aboard, mates.

ALL. Ay, ay. [*They rush out tumultuously*].

When they are gone, Brassbound sits down at the end of the table, with his elbows on it and his head on his fists, gloomily thinking. Then he takes from the breast pocket of his jacket a leather case, from which he extracts a scrappy packet of dirty letters and newspaper cuttings. These he throws on the table. Next comes a photograph in a cheap frame. He throws it down untenderly beside the papers; then folds his arms, and is looking at it with grim distaste when Lady Cicely enters. His back is towards her; and he does not hear her. Perceiving this, she shuts the door loudly enough to attract attention. He starts up.

LADY CICELY [*coming to the opposite end of the table*] So youve taken off all my beautiful clothes !

BRASSBOUND. Your brother's, you mean. A man should wear his own clothes ; and a man should tell his own lies. I'm sorry you had to tell mine for me today.

LADY CICELY. Oh, women spend half their lives telling little lies for men, and sometimes big ones. We're used to it. But mind ! I dont admit that I told any today.

BRASSBOUND. How did you square my uncle ?

LADY CICELY. I dont understand the expression.

BRASSBOUND. I mean—

LADY CICELY. I'm afraid we havnt time to go into what you mean before lunch. I want to speak to you about your future. May I ?

BRASSBOUND [*darkening a little, but politely*] Sit down. [*She sits down. So does he*].

LADY CICELY. What are your plans ?

BRASSBOUND. I have no plans. You will hear a gun fired in the harbor presently. That will mean that the Thanksgiving's anchor's weighed and that she is waiting for her captain to put out to sea. And her captain doesnt know now whether to turn her head north or south.

LADY CICELY. Why not north for England ?

BRASSBOUND. Why not south for the Pole ?

LADY CICELY. But you must do something with yourself ?

BRASSBOUND [*settling himself with his fists and elbows weightily on the table and looking straight and powerfully at her*] Look you : when you and I first met, I was a man with a purpose. I stood alone : I saddled no friend, woman or man, with that purpose, because it was against law, against religion, against my own credit and safety. But I believed in it ; and I stood alone for it, as a man should stand for his belief, against law and religion as much as against wickedness and selfishness. Whatever I may be, I am none of your fairweather sailors thatll do nothing for their creed but go to Heaven for it. I was ready to go to hell for mine. Perhaps you dont understand that.

LADY CICELY. Oh bless you, yes. It's so very like a certain sort of man.

BRASSBOUND. I daresay ; but Ive not met many of that sort. Anyhow, that was what I was like. I dont say I was happy in it ; but I wasnt unhappy, because I wasnt drifting. I was steering a course and had work in hand. Give a man health and a course to steer ; and he'll never stop to trouble about whether he's happy or not.

LADY CICELY. Sometimes he wont even stop to trouble about whether other people are happy or not.

BRASSBOUND. I dont deny that : nothing makes a man so selfish as work. But I was not self-seeking : it seemed to me that I had put justice above self. I tell you life meant something to me then. Do you see that dirty little bundle of scraps of paper ?

LADY CICELY. What are they ?

BRASSBOUND. Accounts cut out of newspapers. Speeches made by my uncle at charitable dinners, or sentencing men to death—pious, highminded speeches by a man who was to me a thief and a murderer ! To my mind they were more weighty, more momentous, better revelations of the wickedness of law and respectability than the book of the prophet Amos. What are they now ? [*He quietly tears the newspaper cuttings into little fragments and throws them away, looking fixedly at her meanwhile*].

LADY CICELY. Well, thats a comfort, at all events.

BRASSBOUND. Yes ; but it's a part of my life gone : your doing, remember. What have I left ? See here ! [*he takes up the letters*] the letters my uncle wrote to my mother, with her comments on their cold drawn insolence, their treachery and cruelty. And the piteous letters she wrote to him later on, returned unopened. Must they go too ?

LADY CICELY [*uneasily*] I cant ask you to destroy your mother's letters.

BRASSBOUND. Why not, now that you have taken the meaning out of them ? [*He tears them*]. Is that a comfort too ?

LADY CICELY. It's a little sad ; but perhaps it is best so.

BRASSBOUND. That leaves one relic : her portait. [*He plucks the photograph out of its cheap case*].

LADY CICELY [*with vivid curiosity*] Oh, let me see. [*He hands it to her. Before she can control herself, her expression changes to one of unmistakeable disappointment and repulsion*].

BRASSBOUND [*with a single sardonic cachinnation*] Ha ! You expected something better than that. Well, youre right. Her face does not look well opposite yours.

LADY CICELY [*distressed*] I said nothing.

BRASSBOUND. What could you say ? [*He takes back the portrait: she relinquishes it without a word. He looks at it ; shakes his head; and takes it quietly between his finger and thumb to tear it*].

LADY CICELY [*staying his hand*] Oh, not your mother's picture !

BRASSBOUND. If that were your pic⸱ ⸱ꞈ, would you like your son to keep it for younger and better women to see ?

LADY CICELY [*releasing his hand*] Oh, you are dreadful ! Tear it, tear it. [*She covers her eyes for a moment to shut out the sight*].

BRASSBOUND [*tearing it quietly*] You killed her for me that day in the castle ; and I am better without her. [*He throws away the fragments*]. Now everything is gone. You have taken the old meaning out of my life ; but you have put no new meaning into it. I can see that you have some clue to the world that makes all its difficulties easy for you ; but I'm not clever enough to seize it. Youve lamed me by shewing me that I take life the wrong way when I'm left to myself.

LADY CICELY. Oh no. Why do you say that ?

BRASSBOUND. What else can I say ? See what Ive done ! My uncle is no worse a man than myself—better, most likely ; for he has a better head and a higher place. Well, I took him for a villain out of a storybook. My mother would have opened anybody else's eyes : she shut mine. I'm a stupider man than Brandyfaced Jack even ; for he got his romantic nonsense out of his penny numbers and such like trash ; but I got just the same nonsense out of life and experience. [*Shaking his head*] It was vulgar— vulgar. I see that now ; for youve opened my eyes to the past ; but what good is that for the future ? What am I to do ? Where am I to go ?

LADY CICELY. It's quite simple. Do whatever you like. Thats what I always do.

BRASSBOUND. That answer is no good to me. What I like is to have something to do ; and I have nothing. You might as well talk like the missionary and tell me to do my duty.

LADY CICELY [*quickly*] Oh no thank you. Ive had quite enough of your duty, and Howard's duty. Where would you both be now if I'd let you do it ?

BRASSBOUND. We'd have been somewhere, at all events. It seems to me that now I am nowhere.

LADY CICELY. But arnt you coming back to England with us ?

BRASSBOUND. What for ?

LADY CICELY. Why, to make the most of your opportunities.

BRASSBOUND. What opportunities ?

LADY CICELY. Dont you understand that when you are the nephew of a great bigwig, and have influential connections, and good friends among them, lots of things can be done for you that are never done for ordinary ship captains.

BRASSBOUND. Ah : but I'm not an aristocrat, you see.

And like most poor men, I'm proud. I dont like being patronized.

LADY CICELY. What is the use of saying that? In my world, which is now your world—our world—getting patronage is the whole art of life. A man cant have a career without it.

BRASSBOUND. In my world a man can navigate a ship and get his living by it.

LADY CICELY. Oh, I see youre one of the Idealists—the Impossibilists! We have them, too, occasionally, in our world. Theres only one thing to be done with them.

BRASSBOUND. Whats that?

LADY CICELY. Marry them straight off to some girl with enough money for them, and plenty of sentiment. Thats their fate.

BRASSBOUND. Youve spoiled even that chance for me. Do you think I could look at any ordinary woman after you? You seem to be able to make me do pretty well what you like; but you cant make me marry anybody but yourself.

LADY CICELY. Do you know, Captain Paquito, that Ive married no less than seventeen men [*Brassbound stares*] to other women. And they all opened the subject by saying that they would never marry anybody but me.

BRASSBOUND. Then I shall be the first man you ever found to stand to his word.

LADY CICELY [*part pleased, part amused, part sympathetic*] Do you really want a wife?

BRASSBOUND. I want a commander. Dont undervalue me: I am a good man when I have a good leader. I have courage: I have determination: I'm not a drinker: I can command a schooner and a shore party if I cant command a ship or an army. When work is put upon me, I turn neither to save my life nor to fill my pocket. Gordon trusted me; and he never regretted it. If you trust me, you shant regret it. All the same, theres something wanting in me: I suppose I'm stupid.

LADY CICELY. Oh, youre not stupid.

BRASSBOUND. Yes I am. Since you saw me for the first time in that garden, youve heard me say nothing clever. And Ive heard you say nothing that didnt make me laugh, or make me feel friendly, as well as telling me what to think and what to do. Thats what I mean by real cleverness. Well, I havnt got it. I can give an order when I know what order to give. I can make men obey it, willing or unwilling. But I'm stupid, I tell you : stupid. When theres no Gordon to command me, I cant think of what to do. Left to myself, Ive become half a brigand. I can kick that little gutterscrub Drinkwater ; but I find myself doing what he puts into my head because I cant think of anything else. When you came, I took your orders as naturally as I took Gordon's, though I little thought my next commander would be a woman. I want to take service under you. And theres no way in which that can be done except marrying you. Will you let me do it ?

LADY CICELY. I'm afraid you dont quite know how odd a match it would be for me according to the ideas of English society.

BRASSBOUND. I care nothing about English society : let it mind its own business.

LADY CICELY [rising, a little alarmed] Captain Paquito : I a m not in love with you.

BRASSBOUND [also rising, with his gaze still steadfastly on her] I didnt suppose you were : the commander is not usually in love with his subordinate.

LADY CICELY. Nor the subordinate with the commander.

BRASSBOUND [assenting firmly] Nor the subordinate with the commander.

LADY CICELY [learning for the first time in her life what terror is, as she finds that he is unconsciously mesmerizing her] Oh, you are dangerous !

BRASSBOUND. Come : are you in love with anybody else ? Thats the question.

LADY CICELY [shaking her head] I have never been in love with any real person ; and I never shall. How could

I manage people if I had that mad little bit of self left in me ? Thats my secret.

BRASSBOUND. Then throw away the last bit of self. Marry me.

LADY CICELY [*vainly struggling to recall her wandering will*] Must I ?

BRASSBOUND. There is no must. You c a n. I ask you to. My fate depends on it.

LADY CICELY. It's frightful ; for I dont mean to—dont wish to.

BRASSBOUND. But you will.

LADY CICELY [*quite lost, slowly stretches out her hand to give it to him*] I— [*Gunfire from the Thanksgiving. His eyes dilate. It wakes her from her trance*] What is that ?

BRASSBOUND. It is farewell. Rescue for you—safety, freedom ! You were made to be something better than the wife of Black Paquito. [*He kneels and takes her hands*] You can do no more for me now : I have blundered somehow on the secret of command at last [*he kisses her hands*] : thanks for that, and for a man's power and purpose restored and righted. And farewell, farewell, farewell.

LADY CICELY [*in a strange ecstasy, holding his hands as he rises*] Oh, farewell. With my heart's deepest feeling, farewell, farewell.

BRASSBOUND. With my heart's noblest honor and triumph, farewell. [*He turns and flies*].

LADY CICELY. How glorious ! how glorious ! And what an escape !

NOTES TO CAPTAIN BRASSBOUND'S CONVERSION

SOURCES OF THE PLAY

I CLAIM as a notable merit in the authorship of this play that I have been intelligent enough to steal its scenery, its surroundings, its atmosphere, its geography, its knowledge of the east, its fascinating Cadis and Krooboys and Sheikhs and mud castles from an excellent book of philosophic travel and vivid adventure entitled Mogreb-el-Acksa (Morocco the Most Holy) by Cunninghame Graham. My own first hand knowledge of Morocco is based on a morning's walk through Tangier, and a cursory observation of the coast through a binocular from the deck of an Orient steamer, both later in date than the writing of the play.

Cunninghame Graham is the hero of his own book ; but I have not made him the hero of my play, because so incredible a personage must have destroyed its likelihood —such as it is. There are moments when I do not myself believe in his existence. And yet he must be real ; for I have seen him with these eyes ; and I am one of the few men living who can decipher the curious alphabet in which he writes his private letters. The man is on public record too. The battle of Trafalgar Square, in which he personally and bodily assailed civilization as represented by the concentrated military and constabular forces of the capital of the world, can scarcely be forgotten by the more discreet spectators, of whom I was one. On that occasion civilization, qualitatively his inferior, was quantitatively so hugely in excess of him that it put him in prison, but had not sense enough to keep him there. Yet his getting out of prison was as nothing compared to his getting into the House of Commons. How he did it I know not ; but the thing certainly happened, somehow. That he made pregnant utterances as a legislator may be taken as proved by the keen philosophy of the travels and tales he has since tossed

to us ; but the House, strong in stupidity, did not understand him until in an inspired moment he voiced a universal
impulse by bluntly damning its hypocrisy. Of all the
eloquence of that silly parliament, there remains only one
single damn. It has survived the front bench speeches of
the eighties as the word of Cervantes survives the oracula-
tions of the Dons and Deys who put him, too, in prison.
The shocked house demanded that he should withdraw his
cruel word. " I never withdraw," said he ; and I promptly
stole the potent phrase for the sake of its perfect style, and
used it as a cockade for the Bulgarian hero of Arms and the
Man. The theft prospered ; and I naturally take the first
opportunity of repeating it. In what other Lepantos
besides Trafalgar Square Cunninghame Graham has fought,
I cannot tell. He is a fascinating mystery to a sedentary
person like myself. The horse, a dangerous animal whom,
when I cannot avoid, I propitiate with apples and sugar, he
bestrides and dominates fearlessly, yet with a true republican
sense of the rights of the fourlegged fellow-creature whose
martyrdom, and man's shame therein, he has told most
powerfully in his Cavalry, a tale with an edge that will cut
the soft cruel hearts and strike fire from the hard kind ones.
He handles the other lethal weapons as familiarly as the
pen : medieval sword and modern Mauser are to him as
umbrellas and kodaks are to me. His tales of adventure
have the true Cervantes touch of the man who has been
there—so refreshingly different from the scenes imagined
by bloodyminded clerks who escape from their servitude
into literature to tell us how men and cities are conceived
in the counting house and the volunteer corps. He is, I
understand, a Spanish hidalgo : hence the superbity of his
portrait by Lavery (Velasquez being no longer available).
He is, I know, a Scotch laird. How he contrives to be
authentically the two things at the same time is no more
intelligible to me than the fact that everything that has ever
happened to him seems to have happened in Paraguay or
Texas instead of in Spain or Scotland. He is, I regret to
add, an impenitent and unashamed dandy : such boots,

such a hat, would have dazzled D'Orsay himself. With that hat he once saluted me in Regent St. when I was walking with my mother. Her interest was instantly kindled; and the following conversation ensued. " Who is that ? " " Cunninghame Graham." " Nonsense ! Cunninghame Graham is one of your Socialists : that man is a gentleman." This is the punishment of vanity, a fault I have myself always avoided, as I find conceit less troublesome and much less expensive. Later on somebody told him of Tarudant, a city in Morocco in which no Christian had ever set foot. Concluding at once that it must be an exceptionally desirable place to live in, he took ship and horse ; changed the hat for a turban ; and made straight for the sacred city, via Mogador. How he fared, and how he fell into the hands of the Cadi of Kintafi, who rightly held that there was more danger to Islam in one Cunninghame Graham than in a thousand Christians, may be learnt from his account of it in Mogreb-el-Acksa, without which Captain Brassbound's Conversion would never have been written.

I am equally guiltless of any exercise of invention concerning the story of the West Indian estate which so very nearly serves as a peg to hang Captain Brassbound. To Mr Frederick Jackson of Hindhead, who, against all his principles, encourages and abets me in my career as a dramatist, I owe my knowledge of those main facts of the case which became public through an attempt to make the House of Commons act on them. This being so, I must add that the character of Captain Brassbound's mother, like the recovery of the estate by the next heir, is an interpolation of my own. It is not, however, an invention. One of the evils of the pretence that our institutions represent abstract principles of justice instead of being mere social scaffolding is that persons of a certain temperament take the pretence seriously, and, when the law is on the side of injustice, will not accept the situation, and are driven mad by their vain struggle against it. Dickens has drawn the type in his Man from Shropshire in Bleak House. Most public men and all lawyers have been appealed to by victims of this sense of injustice—the most unhelpable of afflictions in a society like ours.

ENGLISH AND AMERICAN DIALECTS

The fact that English is spelt conventionally and not phonetically makes the art of recording speech almost impossible. What is more, it places the modern dramatist, who writes for America as well as England, in a most trying position. Take for example my American captain and my English lady. I have spelt the word conduce, as uttered by the American captain, as cawndooce, to suggest (very roughly) the American pronunciation to English readers. Then why not spell the same word, when uttered by Lady Cicely, as kerndewce, to suggest the English pronunciation to American readers ? To this I have absolutely no defence : I can only plead that an author who lives in England necessarily loses his consciousness of the peculiarities of English speech, and sharpens his consciousness of the points in which American speech differs from it ; so that it is more convenient to leave English peculiarities to be recorded by American authors. I must, however, most vehemently disclaim any intention of suggesting that English pronunciation is authoritative and correct. My own tongue is neither American English nor English English, but Irish English ; so I am as nearly impartial in the matter as it is in human nature to be. Besides, there is no standard English pronunciation any more than there is an American one : in England every county has its catchwords, just as no doubt every State in the Union has. I cannot believe that the pioneer American, for example, can spare time to learn that last refinement of modern speech, the exquisite diphthong, a farfetched combination of the French eu and the English e, with which a New Yorker pronounces such words as world, bird, &c. I have spent months without success in trying to achieve glibness with it.

To Felix Drinkwater also I owe some apology for

implying that all his vowel pronunciations are unfashionable. They are very far from being so. As far as my social experience goes (and I have kept very mixed company) there is no class in English society in which a good deal of Drinkwater pronunciation does not pass unchallenged save by the expert phonetician. This is no mere rash and ignorant jibe of my own at the expense of my English neighbors. Academic authority in the matter of English speech is represented at present by Mr Henry Sweet, of the University of Oxford, whose *Elementarbuch des gesprochenen Englisch*, translated into his native language for the use of British islanders as a Primer of Spoken English, is the most accessible standard work on the subject. In such words as plum, come, humbug, up, gun, etc., Mr Sweet's evidence is conclusive. Ladies and gentlemen in Southern England pronounce them as plam, kam, hambag, ap, gan, etc., exactly as Felix Drinkwater does. I could not claim Mr Sweet's authority if I dared to whisper that such coster English as the rather pretty dahn tahn for down town, or the decidedly ugly cowcow for cocoa is current in very polite circles. The entire nation, costers and all, would undoubtedly repudiate any such pronunciation as vulgar. All the same, if I were to attempt to represent current " smart " Cockney speech as I have attempted to represent Drinkwater's, without the niceties of Mr Sweet's Romic alphabets, I am afraid I should often have to write dahn tahn and cowcow as being at least nearer to the actual sound than down town and cocoa. And this would give such offence that I should have to leave the country ; for nothing annoys a native speaker of English more than a faithful setting down in phonetic spelling of the sounds he utters. He imagines that a departure from conventional spelling indicates a departure from the correct standard English of good society. Alas ! this correct standard English of good society is unknown to phoneticians. It is only one of the many figments that bewilder our poor snobbish brains. No such thing exists ; but what does that matter to people trained from infancy to make a point of honor of belief in abstractions and incredibilities ? And so I am compelled to hide Lady Cicely's speech under the veil of conventional orthography.

I need not shield Drinkwater, because he will never read my book. So I have taken the liberty of making a special example of him, as far as that can be done without a phonetic alphabet, for the benefit of the mass of readers outside London who still form their notions of cockney dialect on Sam Weller. When I came to London in 1876, the Sam Weller dialect had passed away so completely that I should have given it up as a literary fiction if I had not discovered it surviving in a Middlesex village, and heard of it from an Essex one. Some time in the eighties the late Andrew Tuer called attention in the Pall Mall Gazette to several peculiarities of modern cockney, and to the obsolescence of the Dickens dialect that was still being copied from book to book by authors who never dreamt of using their ears, much less of training them to listen. Then came Mr Anstey's cockney dialogues in Punch, a great advance, and Mr Chevalier's coster songs and patter. The Tompkins verses contributed by Mr Barry Pain to the London Daily Chronicle also did something to bring the literary convention for cockney English up to date. But Tompkins sometimes perpetrated horrible solecisms. He would pronounce face as fice, accurately enough ; but he would rhyme it quite impossibly to nice, which Tompkins would have pronounced as nawce : for example Mawl Enn Rowd for Mile End Road. This aw for i, which I have made Drinkwater use, is the latest stage of the old diphthongal oi, which Mr Chevalier still uses. Irish, Scotch, and north country readers must remember that Drinkwater's rs are absolutely unpronounced when they follow a vowel, though they modify the vowel very considerably. Thus, though luggage is pronounced by him as laggige, turn is not pronounced as tarn, but as teun with the eu sounded as in French. The London r seems thoroughly understood in America, with the result, however, that the use of the r by Artemus Ward and other American dialect writers causes

Irish people to misread them grotesquely. I once saw the pronunciation of *malheureux* represented in a cockney handbook by mal-err-err : not at all a bad makeshift to instruct a Londoner, but out of the question elsewhere in the British Isles. In America, representations of English speech dwell too derisively on the dropped or interpolated h. American writers have apparently not noticed the fact that the south English h is not the same as the never-dropped Irish and American h, and that to ridicule an Englishman for dropping it is as absurd as to ridicule the whole French and Italian nation for doing the same. The American h, helped out by a general agreement to pronounce wh as hw, is tempestuously audible, and cannot be dropped without being immediately missed. The London h is so comparatively quiet at all times, and so completely inaudible in wh, that it probably fell out of use simply by escaping the ears of children learning to speak. However that may be it is kept alive only by the literate classes who are reminded constantly of its existence by seeing it on paper. Roughly speaking, I should say that in England he who bothers about his hs is a fool, and he who ridicules a dropped h a snob. As to the interpolated h, my experience as a London vestryman has convinced me that it is often effective as a means of emphasis, and that the London language would be poorer without it. The objection to it is no more respectable than the objection of a street boy to a black man or to a lady in knickerbockers.

I have made only the most perfunctory attempt to represent the dialect of the missionary. There is no literary notation for the grave music of good Scotch.

BLACKDOWN
  August 1900

THE END

THE DEVIL'S DISCIPLE

was first revived at the Savoy Theatre, London, October 14th, 1907, with the following cast:

DICK DUDGEON	Matheson Lang
CHRISTY DUDGEON	James Annand
REV. A. ANDERSON	C. Rann Kennedy
GENERAL BURGOYNE	H. Granville Barker
MAJOR SWINDON	Arnold Lucy
SERGEANT	Kenyon Musgrave
LAWYER HAWKINS	Arthur Chesney
UNCLE WILLIAM DUDGEON	H. Williams
UNCLE TITUS DUDGEON	Jules Shaw
CHAPLAIN MR BRUDENELL	Lewis Casson
MRS DUDGEON	Miss Bateman
JUDITH ANDERSON	E. Wynne Matthison
AUNT WILLIAM DUDGEON	Mrs Maltby
AUNT TITUS DUDGEON	Ethel Harper

CÆSAR AND CLEOPATRA

was first produced in London at the Savoy Theatre,
November 25th, 1907, with the following cast :

PERSIAN GUARDSMAN	S. A. Cookson
BELZANOR	A. W. Tyrer
NUBIAN SENTINEL	Frank Bickley
BEL AFFRIS	C. B. Vaughan
FTATATEETA	Elizabeth Watson
JULIUS CÆSAR	Sir J. Forbes Robertson
CLEOPATRA	Gertrude Elliott
POTHINUS	Charles Langley
THEODOTUS	Sam T. Pearce
PTOLEMY XIV	Philip Tonge
ACHILLAS	John M. Troughton
RUFIO	Percy Rhodes
BRITANNUS	Ian Robertson
LUCIUS SEPTIMIUS	Walter Ringham
WOUNDED SOLDIER	William Pilling
PROFESSOR OF MUSIC	Frank Ridley
CHARMIAN	Dorothy Paget
IRAS	Dora Harker
MAJOR-DOMO	A. Wheatman
APOLLODORUS	Lewis Willoughby

CAPTAIN BRASSBOUND'S CONVERSION

was first performed publicly in London at the Court Theatre, March 20th, 1906, with the following cast :

LADY CICELY WAYNFLETE	Ellen Terry
SIR HOWARD HALLAM	J. H. Barnes
CAPTAIN BRASSBOUND	Frederick Kerr
RANKIN	F. Cremlin
DRINKWATER	Edmund Gwenn
REDBROOK	C. L. Delph
JOHNSON	Edmund Gurney
MARZO	Michael Sherbrooke
SIDI EL ASSIF	Lewis Casson
THE CADI	Trevor Lowe
OSMAN	Gordon Bailey
HASSAN	Jules Shaw
CAPTAIN HAMLIN KEARNEY, U.S.N.	James Carew
AMERICAN BLUEJACKET	Frederick Lloyd

PRINCIPAL WORKS OF BERNARD SHAW

An Unsocial Socialist, 1884
Cashel Byron's Profession, 1885-6
The Irrational Knot, 1885-7
Love Among the Artists, 1887-8
Fabian Essays in Socialism (edited), 1889
The Quintessence of Ibsenism, 1891
Widowers' Houses, 1893
The Perfect Wagnerite, 1898
Plays Pleasant and Unpleasant, 1898
The Man of Destiny, 1898
Fabianism and the Empire, 1900
Three Plays for Puritans, 1901
The Admirable Bashville, 1901
Man and Superman, 1903
Is Free Trade alive or dead?, 1906
How he Lied to her Husband, 1907
John Bull's Other Island, 1907
Major Barbara, 1907
The Sanity of Art, 1908
The Doctor's Dilemma, 1911
Getting Married, 1911
The Shewing-Up of Blanco Posnet, 1911
Commonsense about the War, 1914
Misalliance, 1914
The Dark Lady of the Sonnets, 1914
Fanny's First Play, 1914
Androcles and the Lion, Overruled, and Pygmalion, 1916
Preface to the W.E.A. Education Year Book, 1918
Great Catherine, 1919
Heartbreak House, 1919
Back to Methuselah, 1921
Saint Joan, 1924
Translations and Tomfooleries, 1926
The Intelligent Woman's Guide to Socialism, 1928
Immaturity, 1930
The Apple Cart, 1930
Doctors' Delusion, Crude Criminology, Sham Education, 1931
The Adventures of the Black Girl in her Search for God, 1932
Short Stories, Scraps, and Shavings, 1932
Too True to be Good, 1934
Village Wooing and On the Rocks, 1934
The Simpleton of the Unexpected Isles, 1936
The Six of Calais, 1936
The Millionairess, 1936
Geneva, 1939
In Good King Charles's Golden Days, 1939
Everybody's Political What's What?, 1944